Meeting the Information Challenge

In 1998, Nelson Mandela spoke of the huge, untapped market which Africa represents and of the need to create a dedicated African Telecommunications Development Fund. 'Such a fund,' he said, 'would finance the infrastructure projects needed to extend technology to every village in Africa, and would certainly put the continent on the map of the global information society.'

This volume is dedicated to the realisation of Mandela's vision and to those who provide practical partnership in this process.

Meeting the Information Challenge
The Experience of Africa

Edited by

Margaret Grieco, Royal Colle and Muna Ndulo

CAMBRIDGE SCHOLARS PRESS

Meeting the Information Challenge: The Experience of Africa, edited by Margaret Grieco, Royal Colle and Muna Ndulo

This book first published 2006 by

Cambridge Scholars Press

15 Angerton Gardens, Newcastle, NE5 2JA, UK

British Library Cataloguing in Publication Data
A catalogue record for this book is available from the British Library

ISBN 1-84718-010-8

Contents

List of Boxes vii
List of Figures viii
List of Tables ix

Introduction: Meeting the Information Challenge –The Experience of Africa vii
Margaret Grieco, Royal Colle and Muna Ndulo

One Potential of ICTs for Rural Development 1
S. Janakiram

Two Towards a Knowledge-, Science- and Technology-based African Self-development Strategy 15
Joseph Okpaku Sr

Three What it's Like Out There: Profiles of Connectivity at African Universities 25
Nancy J. Hafkin

Four Why E-Readiness Matters: The TEEAL and AGORA Resources 39
Mary Ochs

Five The Millennium Development Goals and ICT 49
Egondu Onyejekwe

Six ICTs, Universities, and Development: Toward eQuality 73
Maria A. Beebe

Seven Universities as Alternate Incubators of Information Communication Centers for Ghana's Development 91
Benjamin K. Addom

Eight World Computer Exchange: An Inventory of Activities 115
Timothy Anderson

Nine The Challenge: Universities and ICT Incubation 127
Royal D. Colle

Ten Meeting the Information Challenge: Exploring Partnership Models with Africa 137
Stephen E. Little

Eleven	Sharing Information on the Best Practices in Sustainable Development in Kenya *Paul K. Mwanzilo*	155
Twelve	ICTs in African Education: The dot-EDU Project *William W. Wright Jr*	173
Thirteen	Gender Dimensions of E-Government and E-Democracy in Developing Countries *Eva M. Rathgeber*	185
Epilogue	Economic Frameworks for IT Development: An Epilogue on Bridging the Digital Divide Sheila Robinson	199
Contributors		211

List of Boxes

One	Framework—the four M modular approach for rural information and knowledge system	9
Two	Implementation steps for the four M modular approach	10
Three	Distance education in Africa	80
Four	**Transnational collaboration and Africa**	**81**

List of Figures

One	Evolution of ICT	4
Two	Emerging trends in ICT—single to integrated, complex systems	8
Three	Rural information and knowledge system	11
Four	Work towards more wisdom than data	12
Five	AGORA workshop in Harare, Zimbabwe, April 2004	41
Six	General satisfaction with TEEAL	43
Seven	How useful is TEEAL?	44
Eight	Has TEEAL literature influenced your research?	45
Nine	Has TEEAL influenced how you search for information?	45
Ten	How useful is TEEAL in your teaching?	45
Eleven	Has access to TEEAL improved your teaching quality?	46
Twelve	Extreme poverty	52
Thirteen	Long-term growth in GDP per capita, in 1990 US$	53
Fourteen	The giving gap: additional foreign aid needed to reach 0.5% of GDP in billions of dollars	55
Fifteen	The growing importance of trade	58
Sixteen	Sixteen oneRoam World Cell Subscription zones	60
Seventeen	Closing the digital divide is essential for being competitive	62
Eighteen	Millenium Development Goal	74
Nineteen	Convergence of ICTs	78
Twenty	International Internet bandwidth	86
Twenty-one	African connectivity to the rest of the world	87
Twenty-two	Template for the action plan	105
Twenty-three	Economic framework for ICT	200

List of Tables

One	ICT applications in MDG	2
Two	Changing information needs	6
Three	Connectivity source	28
Four	Type of Internet service provider	28
Five	Bandwidth leaders	29
Six	Bandwidth per Internet-accessed computer	28
Seven	Bandwidth per Internet-accessed computer: highest ratings	30
Eight	Bandwidth per Internet-accessed computer: lowest ratings	30
Nine	Bandwidth costs/mo. (US$)	31
Ten	Costs per KBPS/mo.: highest (US$)	31
Eleven	Costs per KBPS/mo: lowest (US$)	32
Twelve	Bandwidth costs per month and year (US$)	32
Thirteen	Institutional changes that had to happen within institutions to make NetTel@Africa possible—these changes may be transformative in scope	83
Fourteen	General profile of the respondents	97
Fifteen	Summary of ICT human resource level at the universities	97
Sixteen	Summary of ICT infrastructure level at the universities	98
Seventeen	Some academic programs in the universities	99
Eighteen	Student internship programs	100
Nineteen	Position of Faculty on Outreach Work	101
Twenty	Position of the Universities on Outreach Work by Faculty	101
Twenty-one	Summary of ICT posture by the university faculties	102
Twenty-two	Interlibrary loans 2002	163
Twenty-three	Interlibrary loans 2003	164
Twenty-four	Interlibrary loans 2003—2005	165
Twenty-five	dot-EDU associate awards, worldwide	176
Twenty-six	dot-EDU core-funded activities worldwide (October 2005)	182
Twenty-seven	Newly implemented dot-EDU activities	183

Introduction: Meeting the Information Challenge – The Experience of Africa

Margaret Grieco, Royal Colle and Muna Ndulo

New information technologies contain both opportunities and threats for Africa. The major threat is that Africa will not be well integrated into the new information structures early enough: the major opportunity lies in the capabilities and capacities of the new information communication technology to better connect African universities both to resources within their own continent and elsewhere. Africa's universities have a major role to play in development and Africa's new leadership must itself meet the information challenge. Within this volume, we will see that this is no easy matter. The barriers to Africa's meeting of the information challenge are many but, as we shall see, they are not insurmountable. A first step to overcoming these barriers and meeting the information challenge is the charting of the existing state of play of new information communication technology within African universities, and around activities connected with the universities such as agricultural outreach. This volume takes that step.

Charting the existing state of play is of little consequence if there is no willingness to create and produce change but within this volume we shall see that there are institutions and agencies engaged in making a difference to Africa's currently impoverished state of communications. Amongst the contributors to this volume are inspirational business people who are focused, in their investment, on the need to ensure not only that Africa has access but also to ensure that Africa produces content within the new world of communications. Also amongst the contributors to the volume are educators who talk to their own experience of operating within African universities, the tele-communication barriers and difficulties they experienced and who identify the forms of partnership with wealthier and better resourced agencies that can be used to begin to bridge the digital divide. Some of the contributors focus on the importance of the link between the university and agricultural outreach and identify the current connectivity constraints. Other contributors focus on paths that can be taken to overcome connectivity difficulties whilst providing high quality information channels – here the development of CD-Rom libraries for education and training purposes, most particularly in respect of agriculture, is shown to have great practical utility and potential. And yet other contributors focus upon the provision of affordable information technology equipment to Africa's education sector with a clear commitment to organisation for sustainability.

Each of the chapters in this volume has an optimistic outlook but all of the chapters recognize the many barriers which are faced in meeting the information challenge. The information technology experience of Africa's universities and education sectors can be improved and there are many models available for undertaking this improvement but whichever model is adopted at whichever location, it is critical that African institutions fully participate in the design and strategy for improvement.

Cornell University,
March 2006

Chapter One

Potential of ICTs for Rural Development

S. Janakiram*[1]

Introduction

Provision of locally relevant information and knowledge services are increasing in importance and are being recognized as essential components of the development process to: (i) empower the poor communities; (ii) enhance job-creating skills, (iii) bring about institutional changes; (iv) improve participatory decision-making processes (from grassroots to international level); (v) coordinate development efforts; and (vi) promote understanding and tolerance among diverse populations. These processes can now be accelerated with recent advances in information and communication technologies (ICTs). However, realization of the full potential of ICTs for rural development needs to be viewed in a broader framework comprising both the institutional and information technology infrastructure aspects and take into consideration the main emerging trends in ICTs and the needs of the rural population. This chapter makes an attempt to provide such a framework, identify areas needing attention by development practitioners and what we hope to see in the years ahead in the use of ICT for rural development.

Role of ICTs in the Development Process

Global level—ICTs and Millennium Development Goals (MDGs)

The Millennium Development Goals adopted by the member states of the United Nations in 2000 range from reducing extreme poverty by half to putting all children in primary school and limiting the spread of infectious diseases such as HIV/AIDS by 2015. Achievement of these globally-accepted benchmarks could only be made possible and met by 2015 if, in the words of the UN Secretary General, Mr Kofi Annan (United Nations, 2005) "all break with business as usual and dramatically accelerate and scale up action now". This is especially applicable if ICT applications in each of the eight MDGs (a few examples are provided in Table One) are to reach the untouched population, especially in the rural and remote parts of the developing world.

---

* Champion, ICT for rural development, sustainable agricultural systems, Knowledge and Institutions Thematic Group, and board member, E-development thematic group, World Bank.

Table One **ICT applications in MDGs**

Millennium Development Goals	ICT Applications—some examples
• Sustainable poverty reduction – Eradicate extreme poverty and hunger (Goal 1) – Ensure environmental sustainability (Goal 7)	• Use of information technologies to provide market information to increase negotiating power of farmers and access new markets • Information system for flood protection system, GIS to systems combat illegal logging
• Education – Achieve universal primary education (Goal 2)	• Use of television and radio for promoting literacy, electronic libraries, school networks to promote information and knowledge sharing and learning
• Empowerment – Promote gender equality and empower women (Goal 3)	• Radio and TV programs by and for rural people, building new forms of virtual community networks and alliances
• Health – Improve maternal health (Goal 5) – Combat HIV/AIDS, malaria, and other diseases (Goal 6) – Reduce child mortality (Goal 4)	• Bringing the latest medical advances to rural population in remote areas through tele-medicine, use of PDAs to improve management and monitoring of health care
• Partnership – Develop a global partnership for development (Goal 8)	• Global communications, Internet have helped increase trade in the services sector between developed and developing countries and created new partnerships and jobs

Country Level—ICT in Poverty Reduction Strategy Papers (PRSPs)

Poverty Reduction Strategy Papers (PRSP) describe a country's macroeconomic, structural and social policies and programs over a three year or longer horizon to promote broad-based growth and reduce poverty, as well as associated external financing needs and major sources of financing.[2] They are prepared by the member countries of the World Bank and the International Monetary Fund through a participatory process involving domestic stakeholders as well as external development partners. They are updated every three years with annual progress reports. The role which ICT can play in the reduction of poverty is being realized only recently in the PRSPs—and some countries take a narrow view—as the following main findings from analysis of 28 PRSPs by OECD indicates (OECD, 2003):

- ICT were defined as strategic elements in PRSP in 12 countries, viz. Albania, Azerbaijan, Cambodia, Cameroon, Chad, Gambia, Ghana, Mali, Mozambique, Niger, Rwanda and Sri Lanka; and
- ICT was not included as an independent strategic component, but telecommunication was mentioned as an important factor for rural/agricultural development in rest of the 16 countries, viz. Bolivia, Burkina Faso, Ethiopia, Guinea, Guyana, Honduras, Malawi, Mauritania, Nicaragua, Senegal, Tajikistan, Tanzania, Uganda, Vietnam, Yemen, and Zambia.

Ground Level: ICT Applications in Agriculture Projects

The dissemination of relevant information and advice to farmers has a long and chequered history (see Garforth and Jones, n.d.) prior to the emergence of modem forms of ICTs. The first known example of disseminating agricultural information was in Mesopotamia (roughly present-day Iraq) around 1800 BC. Archaeologists have unearthed clay tablets from this period which had inscriptions of advice on watering crops and getting rid of rats—important for mitigating any potential loss of taxation revenue from farmers (Ahmed, 1982, as quoted in Bne Saad, 1990). Some hieroglyphs on Egyptian columns also gave advice on avoiding crop damage and loss of life from Nile's floods. Modern forms of ICTs began with the invention of the telegraph in 1837, followed by photography, motion picture in 1861, magnetic recordings in 1899, television camera in 1923, sound movies in 1926, television in 1939, digital computers in 1946, the Intel microprocessor chip in 1971, and on to newer integrated technologies, wireless communications, etc. (see Figure One).

Some of the main findings of a review of agricultural projects financed by development institutions were:

- almost all the development projects used a combination of ICT tools developed over the past 2,500 plus years to provide information and knowledge to rural people in 50 plus years of Bank operations;
- inadequate value was given to content development, making them user-friendly and needs-based, finding simple ways to disseminate them using available communication mechanisms;
- there was inadequate capacity-building in universities to develop easy to understand locally relevant content for the rural population;

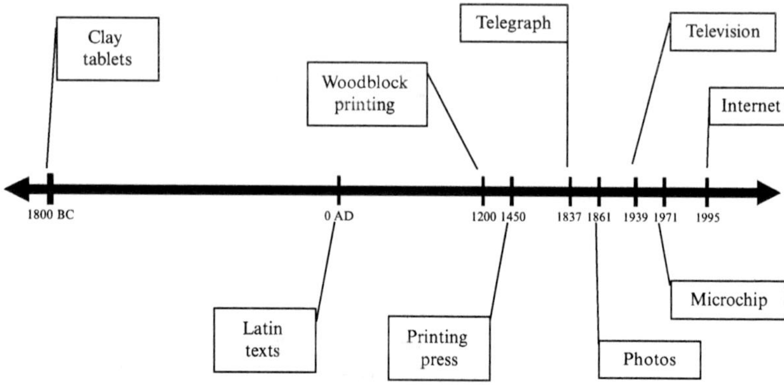

Figure One **Evolution of ICT**

- linkages between communication infrastructure projects financed by bilateral and multilateral development institutions, public and private sectors were weak;
- detailed cost breakdown of ICT in each project is combined with other categories of project expenditures making it hard to determine costs of ICT in operations; and
- there was a lack of systematic and robust impact analysis of the use of ICT in projects.

Trends in ICT for Rural Development

The advances in ICT tools are rapidly changing the traditional ways of providing extension to the rural poor, the majority of whom depend on farm and non-farm activities for their livelihood and survival. There are two main trends which are shaping the way ICTs will be applied to meet their needs, improve their farm and non-farm productivity and increase their income levels:

- the first trend is the rapidly changing and increasing demand for multidisciplinary and multi-sectoral information and knowledge by the rural households—a move from addressing the needs of the primary income earner, e.g. the farmer in most developing countries to the "rural household unit"; and
- the second trend is the convergence of various technologies of traditional and modern technologies into integrated complex systems

Changing Information and Knowledge Needs of the Rural Farm Population

Information and knowledge needs by the rural population are rapidly changing from single disciplines to multiple disciplines and multiple sectors. The type of information traditionally demanded by the landless poor, subsistence farmers, small farmers and medium to large farmers in many developing countries is provided in Table Two, which indicates the varied nature of the types of information needs, but is usually focused on a single sector or discipline. However, the information needs are shifting towards meeting those demanded by the rural household as an unit which is more holistic in nature and covers a variety of subsectors—from A to Z, depending on what each of the rural household members is interested and engaged in to earn a living or pursue their interest or increase income-earning opportunities. Demand for information and knowledge is therefore increasing, becoming complex, is a factor of production and is becoming a basic need.

But it must be:

- timely;
- relevant;
- easily accessible;
- understandable; and
- affordable.

Convergence of Traditional and Modern Technologies

In many parts of the developing world, radio continues to be the predominant mode for the delivery of information and knowledge to the rural population and is often the only medium for obtaining information. Telephone is becoming increasingly popular as a means of communication—both fixed and mobile, but especially the latter. Rapid advances in ICT have brought about an integration of these "stand-alone" communication technologies, which have been made possible through the computer and Internet. However, benefits from ICT investments have been unevenly distributed between and within countries resulting in what has become to be widely known as the "digital divide", and "information poverty". Most of the beneficiaries of the ICT revolution are those with resources and skills—who can get ready and affordable access—which leaves out majority of the world's rural poor. While it is widely acknowledged by those working to reduce poverty and promoting rural development that appropriate ICT interventions are absolutely essential to bridge the information and knowledge gaps, there is little systematic research carried out to arrive at an evidence-based conclusion that ICTs do matter most and must be an integral part of any rural development strategy.

Reaching this high level of integration requires a combination of an enabling policy environment to promote access in both urban and rural areas, a legal

Table Two Changing information needs

From … the information needs of the primary income earner—the farmer

Landless poor	Subsistence farmer	Small farmer	Medium to large farmer
Entitlements – Laws and regulations – Employment opportunities – Social benefits – Education and training – Health – Other	• Technologies to maintain at least subsistence levels of agricultural production • Minimizing risk • Cultural practices • Prices • Weather • Inputs – Water – Seeds – Fertilizer, pesticides, etc • Credit • Other	– Same as those for subsistence farmers Plus – Market opportunities – Where to market – What to market – When to market – Developing market niches – Farm – Management – Other	• Same as those for small farmers Plus •Shaping policies •Management and administration •Technologies •Environmental rules and regulations •Other

To … Information needs of the rural household range from A—Z

- Agriculture—AIDS
- Business—Biology—Banking
- Culture—Credit—Correspondence
- Debt—Data
- Education—Entitlements—Entertainment—Environment—Extension
- Foods—Forestry—Finance
- Government services—Genetics—GMOs
- Health—Horoscope
- Industry—Information
- Job opportunities
- Land titles—Laws—Licenses—Learning
- Market—Microfinance—Manufacturing—Matrimony
- Nutrition
- Permits—Procurement
- Recreation—Registration
- Social benefits—Skills
- Technology—Trade—Tourism—Tax—Tickets
- Weather
- Zoology

environment which permits a fair and competitive market in telecommunications and provision of relevant content to the rural population, since most of the Internet content available at present is in English. The speed at which the developing countries can create an integrated ICT system—or "a wired society"—would greatly depend on how rapidly the essential elements (policies, infrastructure, content, institutions and skills) develop and analysis of costs and benefits. However, there is a word of caution here as the experience of the West indicates that it takes many years before one can, with any reasonable degree of confidence attribute one of the most significant impact indicators—viz. productivity gains—to ICT investments. Studies (by Ahituv and Giladi 1993, Dos Santos, Peffers and Manor 1993, Markus and Soh 1993, Strassman 1985, 1990) have indicated little direct correlation or relationship between what firms have spent on information technologies and the firm's profitability. If this were the case in developed economies, where data availability and tools to analyze them are readily available, then the situation in less developed countries would make the exercise tedious, time-consuming, resource intensive and perhaps inconclusive. Additional complicating factors such as the need for a long lag time between when investments are made, the time it takes to realize full benefits and the fact that ICTs targeted at poverty alleviation are innovations at early stages add to the difficulties in developing a more robust impact evaluation methodology. On the other hand, several authors (Heeks 1999; Hitt and Brynjolfsson 1996, Parsons 2000, Richardson 1996, Sirimanne 1996, Wresch 1996, Zijp 1994) have pointed out that there is a "gap" in answering the question of where precisely has the impact of ICT been in improving rural livelihoods and consumer welfare. This would require the development of innovative evaluation methodologies and approaches.

ICT for rural development strategies, therefore, should build upon existing communication technologies, while making provision towards the creation of integrated complex ICT systems. The trend is towards convergence of various ICT tools and their integration, e.g. what were stand-alone ICT tools such as radio, telephone, audio, video, print and computers, could all be obtained as one integrated unit, if the necessary supporting telecommunications and enabling policy environment existed.

Information and communication systems play a critical role in reducing poverty, promoting economic growth and sustainable development and integrating developing and transition economies into the world economy.

Framework for ICT for rural development

The basic principles of the proposed framework places emphasis on:

- **I**: Information—needs assessment, **I**ndigenous knowledge, **I**ntellectual property rights, freedom of **I**nformation, developing relevant **I**nstitutions and making it another BASIC NEED;

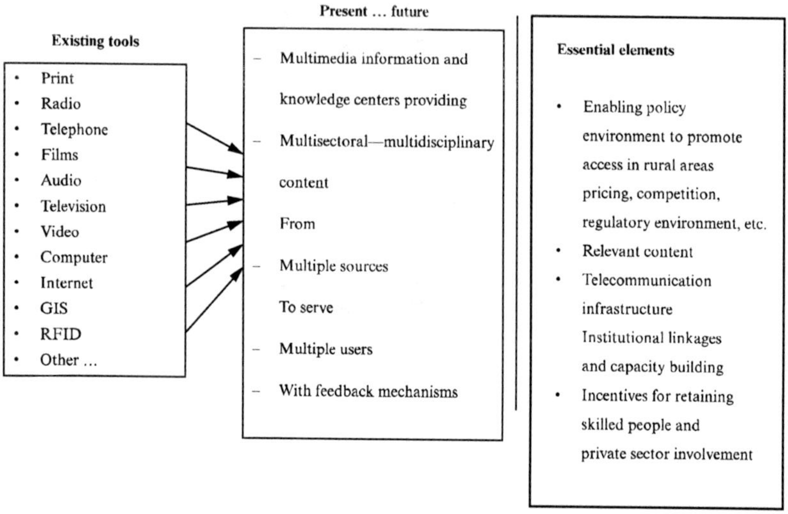

Figure Two **Emerging trends in ICT—single to integrated, complex systems**

- **C**: Improving **C**ommunication, **C**ontent, **C**onnectivity, **C**apacity building, promoting a **C**ulture of sharing information – to bring about **C**hange in attitudes, behavior and more efficient ways of doing business and delivery of services, and; and
- **T**: Build on existing "**T**raditional" technologies along with "modern" technologies – with emphasis on income generating **T**ransaction service applications and to bring increased **T**ransparency and gain public **T**rust.

The framework uses a broader definition of ICT, viz. ICT consists of a range of tools that build human network, increase public awareness and provide access to information and knowledge for the use of the people. It consists of a range of communication media and devices such as print, telephone, fax, radio, television, video, audio, computer, Internet, remote sensing, GIS and RFID as well as technologies that are still on the drawing board.[3] Simply stated, ICTs therefore, are merely the means to transmit, disseminate and exchange information and knowledge from one location to another, from one person to another, from one community to another, from one village to another, from one city to another and from one nation to another—all made possible by advances of various communication devices—especially the world wide web created by the Internet.

The main elements of the framework is provided in Box One and the implementation steps are described in Box Two.

Box One: Framework– the four M modular approach for rural information and knowledge system[4]

Objective: To enable the free flow of information and knowledge to improve decision making and participation of rural households, communities, enterprises, institutions, etc for economic growth and poverty reduction. The approach taken to achieve this broad objective was a modular concept using **M**ulti-media to develop and disseminate **M**ulti-disciplinary information and knowledge from **M**ultiple sources to **M**ultiple users with built in user needs assessment and feedback mechanisms—in short the Four **M** modular approach for rural information and knowledge system (see Figure Three).

Multimedia: which consisted of print, radio, television, telephone, video, computer network, exhibitions and fairs to disseminate rural information and knowledge.

Multiple-disciplines: consisted of legal—. laws and regulations, reforms, business- accounting, finance, business plan, market prices, credit, management, appropriate agricultural technologies, environment—soils, water, weather, etc

Multiple sources: obtaining and adapting, as needed, information and knowledge from local and international agricultural research institutions, universities and academies, input suppliers, producer organizations, agricultural departments, foreign and local data banks, etc.

Multiple users: were rural households, entrepreneurs, communities, various types of public and private institutions, agro-industries, departments of agriculture, etc.,

and institutional mechanisms to carry out needs assessment, develop locally relevant content in easy to understand local language and feedback mechanisms involving both specialists (in extension, agriculture, media, communications, technology, economics and social sciences) and end-users to implement the Four M modular concept for rural information and knowledge system.

Areas needing attention by development practitioners

The following is a proposed agenda for action.

- *Development of locally relevant content in local languages*—the development and dissemination of locally relevant content in local languages which meets the information and knowledge needs of the rural population—a major role for universities.

Box Two: Implementation steps for the four M modular approach

- Step One: End user information, knowledge, business, capacity needs assessment of target users in the rural areas
  - farm and non-farm population
  - local government
  - rural enterprises
  - hospitals
  - schools, universities and training institutions
  - others

- Step Two: Development of appropriate content and partnerships
  - content and partnerships to meet user needs
    - public, private, academic, non-governmental institutions
    - publicly available content from the World Wide Web and adapted to meet the needs of the rural population
    - other

- Step Three: Dissemination of content and partnership linkages through a variety of information communication technologies
  - such as TV, radio, telephone, video, CD-Rom, print, e-mail, Internet, teleconferencing, etc.

- Step Four: Ongoing feedback for monitoring and evaluation
  - for content improvement, selection of appropriate media, cost recovery mechanisms, assessing changing demands for new types of information, knowledge and business opportunities by different types of end-users

- *Skills*—develop and implement programs for enhancing computer skills, literacy and effective use of ICTs of the rural population (end users) as well the trainers—a major role for universities.
- *Legal and regulatory framework*—promote and ensure equitable access of ICT at affordable rates for the poor and protection of intellectual property rights of the poor—a major role for the government, community groups within countries, private sector, donors, international institutions, NGOs and universities.
- *Scaling up evidence-based and sustainable models of ICT applications for the poor* (role of universities and independent autonomous institutions)—carry out systematic documentation of various models of e-services and provision of information and knowledge services to the poor:
  - to learn lessons, identify success factors, what has worked and what has not worked, costs and benefits, organization and management arrangements;
  - to develop standardized definitions and indicators for measuring input, output, outcome and impact of ICT for rural development;

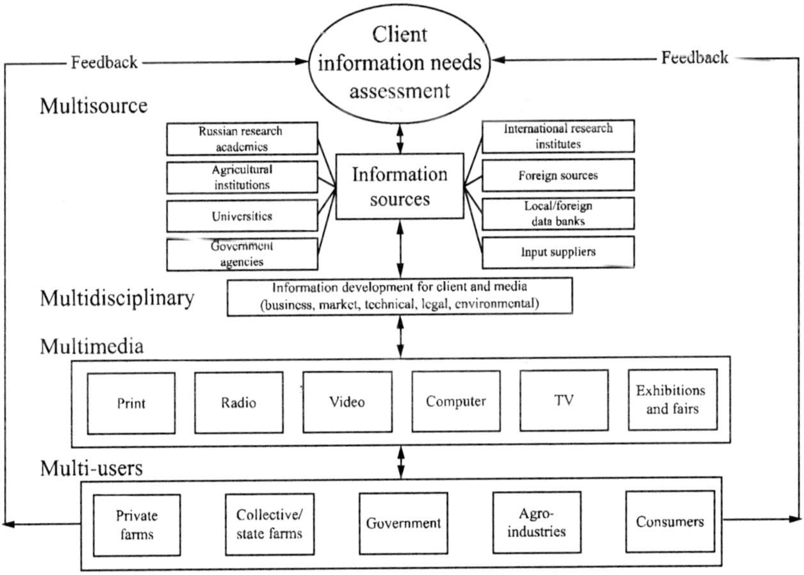

Figure Three **Rural information and knowledge system**

- to develop evaluation methods to assess viability and impact of ICT investments—especially on behavioral and attitudinal changes of the users to bring about efficient and cost effective ways of doing business;
- develop institutional mechanisms between partners to develop criteria, identify, evaluate and scale up sustainable models of ICT activities for improving the livelihoods of the poor.

• *Partnership*—develop partnerships among member governments, universities, international institutions, private sector and others to promote ICT investments for poverty reduction.

What We Hope to See in the Years Ahead

There are a number of developments we hope to see in the years ahead:

• *Interconnected rural information and knowledge centers* within and between countries:
  - tailored to meet the multisectoral and multidisciplinary information needs of local rural population;
  - providing:

    - free; and
    - fee-based information and knowledge services;
  - using a variety of information and communication media.
- *Integrated ICT strategies*—with increasing emphasis on both institution building and infrastructure and interoperability—at national, state, district and community level.
- *Universal adoption of freedom of information laws.*
- *Protection of intellectual property rights of the poor*—and indigenous knowledge as an asset.
- *Increased role of universities and local population to develop and sharing local content in local languages.*
- *Development of information and knowledge markets at the local level.*
- *Public private partnerships*—with increased role of public sector to provide ict connectivity to central nodes in rural areas to stimulate private sector involvement to provide value added demand driven services.
- From more data to less data—and from less wisdom to more wisdom.

Figure Four is representative of the present situation where there is abundant data, which in many developing countries is gathered, processed and analyzed manually, systems to provide information and knowledge in a timely manner are based on antiquated methods and where there is scarcity of wisdom—the more scarce wisdom is the more expensive it becomes. The challenge, therefore, is to reshape the data–wisdom triangle to one of more wisdom and less data, which requires focusing our efforts on both the institutional aspects as well as the information technology infrastructure aspects for promoting economic growth and reducing poverty.

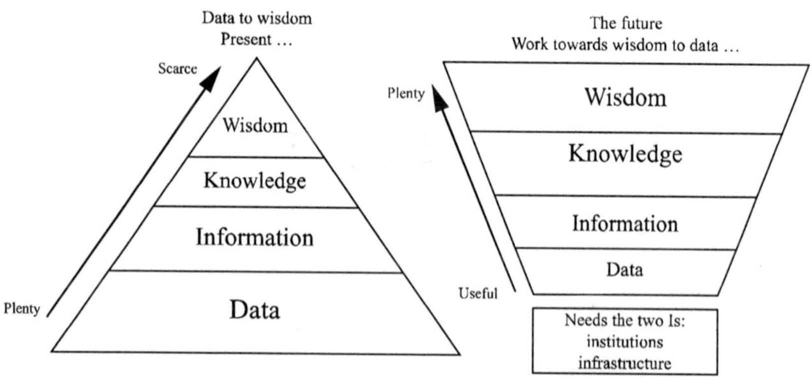

Figure Four **Work towards more wisdom than data**

Notes

1 The views and opinions expressed in this presentation are the author's own and should not be attributed to the World Bank, its management, its Board of Directors or the countries they represent.

2 The country documents, along with the accompanying IMF/World Bank Joint Staff Assessments (JSAs), are made available on the World Bank and IMF websites by agreement with the member country as a service to users of the World Bank and IMF websites (http://www.imf.org/external/np/prsp/prsp.asp).

3 Other definitions used by development institutions are: it consists of hardware, software, networks, and media for collection, storage, processing, transmission and presentation of information (voice, data, text, images) as well as related services (World Bank, UN). ICT is the equipment, algorithms, and techniques for recording, managing, analyzing, and communicating information that people use to conduct their lives at work and at home (USAID). They are technologies that facilitate communication and the processing and transmission of information by electronic means (radio, TV, telephones, computers and Internet) (DIFID).

4 More information is available in the following link to the case study on Russia—Rural information and knowledge system, where this approach has been used: http://topics.developmentgateway.org/edevelopment/rc/ItemDetail.do~1033905.

References

Ahituv, N. and R. Giladi. "Business Success and Information Technology: Are They Really Related", Proceedings of the 7th Annual Conference of Management IS, Tel Aviv University, 1993.

Ahmed, A. *The Role of the Information System in Development*. Studies Series, No. 314 (Baghdad, Iraq: Ministry of Culture and Information, 1982).

Bne Saad, M.H.A. Al-h. "An Analysis of the Needs and Problems of Iraqi Farm Women: Implications for Agricultural Extension Services". Unpublished doctoral thesis (University College, Dublin, 1990).

Brynjolfsson, E. and L. Hitt. "Paradox Lost? Firm-level Evidence on the Returns to Information Systems Spending", *Management Science* (1996).

Dos Santos, B.L., K.G. Peffers and D.C. Mauer. "The Impact of Information Technology Investment Announcements on the Market Value of the Firm", *Information Systems Research*, 4: 1 and 127 (1993): 1–23.

Garforth, Chris and Gwyn Jones. "The History, Development, and Future of Agricultural Extension". http://www.fao.org/docrep/W5830E/w5830e03.htm (n.d.).

Heeks, R. "Information and Communications Technologies, Poverty and Development", Development Informatics Working Paper Series, Paper No. 5, Institute for Development Policy and Management, University of Manchester (1999).

Hitt, Lorin and Erik Brynjolfsson. "Productivity, Profit and Consumer Welfare: Three Different Measures of Information Technology's Value". *MIS Quarterly*: http://ccs.mit.edu/papers/CCSWP190.html (1996).

Markus, L. and C. Soh. "Banking on Information Technology: Converting IT Spending into Firm Performance", in *Strategic Information Technology Management: Perspectives on Organizational Growth and Competitive Advantage*, ed. R. Banker, R. Kaufmann and M. Mahmood (Harrisburg, PA: Idea Group Publishing, 1993): 375–404

OECD. "ICT in PRSPs". Document prepared for the Global Forum on the Knowledge economy *Integrating ICT in Development Programs* held in Paris, France. October 2003.

Parsons, Darrell J. and T.Z. Nkgau. "Using the Internet to Support Information Technology Dissemination in an Information Poor Environment". University of Botswana: http://www.arts.uwa.edu.au/MotsPluriels/MP1300dp&tn.html, (2000).

Strassmann, P.A. *Information Payoff. The Transformation of Work in the Electronic Age* (New York: The Free Press, 1985).

Strassmann, P.A. *The Business Value of Computers* (New Canaan, CT: Information Economics Press, 1990).

United Nations. "Financing ICTD: A Review of Trends and an Analysis of Gaps and Promising Practices". Report of the Task Force on Financial Mechanisms for ICT for Development: http:// www.itu.int/wsis/tffm/final-report.doc (2004).

United Nations. "In Larger Freedom—Towards Development, Security and Human Rights for All". Report of the Secretary General of the United Nations for decision by Heads of State and Government in September 2005. http://www.un.org/largerfreedom/executivesummary.pdf (2005).

World Bank. Information and Communications Technologies (Washington DC: World Bank Group Strategy, 2002).

Wresch, William. *Disconnected: Haves and Have-nots in the Information Age* (New Brunswick, NJ: Rutgers University Press, 1996).

Zijp, Willem. "Improving the Transfer and Use of Agricultural Information – A Guide to Information Technology". World Bank Discussion Papers. Washington, DC (1994).

Chapter Two

Towards a Knowledge-, Science- and Technology-based African Self-development Strategy

Joseph Okpaku Sr*

Introduction: Taking Stock of the African Development Experience

It is time to take stock of the African development experience as it has occurred to date: what does the report card look like? A quick summary might usefully take this form:

- the strategy: poverty management;
- the investment: massive on both sides;
- the outcome: questionable at best;
- the cost to Africa: lost opportunities;
- the beneficiaries: not who you think;
- the consequences: deeper impoverishment and alienation of Africa's strategic intellectual and expert class.

This chapter offers a different perspective on what the African Development Experience could be: it looks towards a knowledge-, science- and technology-based African self-development strategy.

Intellectual Capacity and Development

Societies are built and nurtured on the strength of their intellectual capacity. If you unplug this capacity, societies die; and whether they die in a year or in a century is determined primarily by the residual intellectual capacity that was in place at the time of such hemorrhaging.

Our starting point, then, is the relationship between intellectual capacity and development, and the factors that contribute to this paradigm. A first base is the *ownership of problems*.

---

* President and CEO, Telecom Africa Corporation.

The Right of Ownership of Problems as Intellectual Property

Creativity and innovation derive from problem-solving. If you steal my problem, you cause me two problems:

- you deprive me of the opportunity for creativity and innovation;
- you leave me with the residual guilt of incompetence.

And if you proffer your solutions on my problems and they fail, you blame me. This has been the experience of Africa (see WIPO, 2001).

The Strategic Importance of the Challenge of Problems

The challenge of problems begging for solutions is the main ingredient that feeds the human mind and drives us to excellence. It is the engine that drives development in all societies and at all levels. Without problems to solve, the human mind atrophies. Life without challenges is an oxymoron. People without problems simply die of boredom and ineptitude. Or, in order to avoid such disintegration, they resort to conflict in the absence of better things to do.

The African Development Paradox

Strategic development is the knowledge and capacity building derived from the very process of problem-solving. Therefore, when others solve Africa's problems, it is they, *not* Africans, who are developing. When others mastermind the search for solutions to Africa's problems, they, *not* Africans, are the beneficiaries of African development.

Africans become mere observers on the side streets of their own development. Their knowledge or capacity remains unenhanced, that is if it does not decline in both absolute and comparative terms.

The Consequences of a Poverty Management Development Paradigm

African development remains stalled at the intersection of the conflict of the ownership and the management of the process (see Okpaku, 2002). Africa's self-confidence is undermined and neutralized. Africa's globally competitive expert class is alienated and disillusioned.

That expert class withdraws from the development process, angered by the perception that others less competent, more often than not less knowledgeable and with less compelling obligations to care for the duration, are interposed between them and Africa's political leadership.

From Poverty Management to Knowledge-Based Self-development: Towards a New Paradigm

Let us compare the features of the present poverty management paradigm with a knowledge-based self-development paradigm.

The poverty management paradigm possesses the following characteristics:

- the high cost of subsistence existence with no redeeming feature;
- the threat of entrenching a development assistance dependency and a poverty mentality;
- the unsustainability of building a development strategy that is alien to its intended beneficiaries;
- the strategic flaw in shaping a people's aspirations to the expectations of others;
- the psychological dangers of obliterating a people's confidence in their ability to fend for themselves and to aspire to the greatest heights of human achievement;
- the compelling need to abandon a failed experiment.

Alternatively, a paradigm which moves towards a *knowledge-, science- and technology-based quantum African development* offers a sturdier path:

- whilst poverty management focuses on the least common denominator of a people's capacity, knowledge-based development is built on the cutting edge of its genius;
- poverty management, focused on subsistence, is minimalist; quantum development, being focused on value-addition, aims at exponential, innovative, responsive and versatile productivity and transformation;
- poverty management exploits ignorance, fear and insecurity; quantum development deploys knowledge, science and technology, vision and maximum self-confidence to plumb the depths of possibilities;
- poverty management depresses the people, further deepening their insecurities, whilst quantum development excites people and compels them to reach for the sky and beyond, propelled and empowered by a keen sense of infinite possibilities;
- poverty management addresses hopelessness; quantum development responds to insatiable optimism;
- poverty management involves everyone as a receiver; quantum development involves all the people as creators and innovators;

- poverty management creates dependence; quantum development creates competitive capacity, a key element of political, socio-economic, psychological and intellectual independence that in turn translates into quintessential freedom.

The Place of Knowledge, Science and Technology in African Development

Africa's problem is not one of insufficient resource. If it were, the results should have been different. If you pump all the resources in the world behind poverty management, the best result will be less painful poverty, but poverty still. Africa's problems are strategic, conceptual, and capacity-based. All such problems are susceptible to knowledge, science and technology (see Okpaku, 2002).

The pursuit of these challenges will result in the creation of new or enhanced knowledge, of innovation and intellectual property, themselves the core assets of modern economies. This, in turn, will result in quantum competitive and irreversible development.

The Place of Information and Communications Technology in African Development

In the pursuit of knowledge, science and technology, information and communications technology is a key driver. By virtue of the knowledge base of ICT, the ability of Africans to acquire and deploy it with maximum dexterity at the cutting edge is much greater than is known to Africans or acknowledged by others.

If contemporary society is truly knowledge-based, then Africa is far stronger and better able to drive its own development and global competitiveness than is presently permitted. A map of the global distribution of knowledge will not mimic the global demography of material wealth. The differential between the two is the tension that drives global competition, providing Africa with eminent possibilities.

The Quintessential Leadership Role of African Experts Worldwide: Harnessing the Diaspora.

African experts worldwide have a quintessential leadership role to play. They must drive the process. They already possess the necessary knowledge expertise and hands-on experience to do so. They have the intellectual capacity to do it and the psychological wherewithal to stay the course. They have the cutting-edge capacity to compete globally against the best the world has to offer and more. They have the compelling reasons to do so.

They trained everywhere in the world for decades precisely for this mission. They want to do it; they are dying for the opportunity to do it. They will enjoy doing it, because it is legacy time. This includes Africans at home and abroad, on the continent and in the Diaspora. It also includes African descendants in the global African Diaspora. Joined by non-Africans around the world who care, who are genuinely intrigued by the exciting intellectual challenges and possibilities, or both, working hand in hand with the rest of us in a global partnership search for high-level solutions. The combined human resource capacity to take Africa right up to the frontlines of cutting edge global development and competitive capacity is vast.

The Quintessential Role of African Universities

Universities are the traditional domain of knowledge and transformation. They attract the best minds in society. They are designed to lead change and socio-economic transformation. They are, by tradition, visionary institutions devoted to pushing the limits of human possibilities beyond imagination. Universities are designed for problem-solving and populated by problem solvers.

Specifically, universities are traditionally the centers for the search for high-level solutions to the problems of nature, life and society and the context and manner in which they interact and resolve their often competing demands and attributes. Their main objective is the pursuit of excellence and their tangible accolade is intellectual property.

Universities are the last bastion of innocence against cynicism; the last hope of belief in a better world presently wracked by reckless and callous profiteering single-mindedness. As such, they promote collaborative competition for a common, often noble, cause rather than warfare for winner-takes-all that creates differential development that leads to poverty, social strife and inevitable conflict and violence.

Global Cooperation for Africa's Quantum Development: The Role of Universities Worldwide

From historic times, universities have been the stable for global cooperation. The Internet has made this cooperation much easier and more productive. In fact, it was the *raison d'être* of the Internet. Universities still have the promise of visionary rather than exploitative collaboration. Collaboration amongst universities in Africa and globally holds the best promise of jumpstarting Africa's knowledge and science and technology-based quantum development while reducing the threat of exploitation and the handicap of bias. Information and communications technology offers great tools for this pursuit.

The presence of Africans at the highest levels of science and technology in universities worldwide makes such a collaboration most feasible. The challenge is not for universities to produce paradigms, models or systems and content for African universities, but to collaborate with them to jointly produce them for everyone.

The Telecom Africa Virtual Research Laboratory: An Opportunity for Global Collaboration at the Cutting Edge

In order to jumpstart this global intellectual partnership for Africa's quantum development, and to harness it to enhance overall global human development, we at the Telecom Africa Corporation have embarked on creating the Telecom Africa Virtual Research Laboratory, a secure Virtual Global Intranet to conduct Africa-specific research and development (R&D) online. This global virtual laboratory will allow individuals and institutions worldwide to collaborate in high-level Africa-specific research and development as well as global R&D with important applications for Africa, from wherever they are domiciled, with the flexibility of schedule and the advantage of easy access to their research tools and colleagues. Whenever each specific research reaches the point of physical experimentation, and testing, it will be taken offline and transferred to an appropriate physical laboratory for further development.

The Telecom Africa Virtual Research Laboratory will create substantial benefits, including:

- opportunity to conduct massive and affordable research and development with limited financial resources by substituting a much larger and more versatile expert intellectual resource for the costly physical plant by taking advantage of the benefits of online technologies;
- opportunity to reconfigure Africa's problems as unique opportunities for creativity and innovation, putting a positive spin on problem solving with the promise of new knowledge, insight and intellectual property;
- opportunity for African experts worldwide to engage in research and development for Africa's development without the complexity of having to physically transfer to Africa unless they so desire;
- opportunity for non-Africans interested in Africa's quantum development to engage in the process at their domain of excellence, also without having to physically relocate unless they wish to;
- opportunity to contribute to Africa's cutting-edge knowledge, science and technology research and development;
- opportunity for global corporations, research institutions and universities to join in a unique experiment in scientific cooperation in which the outcome will have a direct impact on the quality of life of millions of people. This should serve in

some measure as a counterfoil to the prevailing struggle for the global control of human knowledge for dominance and the conflicts it engenders;

- opportunity for the exchange of ideas and knowledge among and between African scholars and experts and their global counterparts in the context of a substantive search for solutions to the human challenge;
- opportunity for African experts to contribute their fair share to the global pool of knowledge, science and technology, thus taking their legitimate place in the knowledge world.

Paradigm Shift for African Universities as Strategic Leaders in the Quantum Development Model

To accomplish this paradigm shift, African universities must be restored to the leading role they once played as leaders in masterminding Africa's strategic development model. They must be restructured into knowledge institutions rather than trade schools. They must beef up their research and development capacities. They must take a direct interest in critical socio-economic and development challenges and see them as opportunities for innovation. Their role in development must be enhanced and protected. They must have resources to access global knowledge, to derive from and contribute to it.

Mobilizing the Critical Mass of Africa's Globally Competitive Expertise Worldwide

Africa has the critical mass of expertise to jumpstart the continent's quantum development. People are more interested in joining the drive than is popularly believed.

They must be engaged in the development dialogue as key players, not as afterthoughts. There must be genuine interest in development. They must be protected from exploitation.

African expertise must serve as the lead advisers to Africa's development process. There is a need to identify and quantify this vast globally diffused African expert human resource.

Creating the New Leadership Model for Africa

The new leadership must be holistic: political, academic, scientific, social and cultural, not just political. There are a number of categories of new leaders:

- a new class of leaders;

- current leaders born-again in appropriate knowledge-driven enthusiastic mode;
- others seeking a role in a new and inspired strategic dispensation.

Previous leadership arrangements have not served Africa well: it is time to embrace a new class of African leaders who, besides their visions and leadership qualities, enabled by and with knowledge of technology which can better serve to facilitiate and accelerate the development strategies and processes, and provide continental communications through connecting up Africa for the development, sharing, delivery and diffusion of ideas, experiences, best practices, programmes and services.

The Promise of the New Quantum African Development Paradigm

Africa's quantum development is achievable if we:

- overcome limitations of time and space;
- acquire and manipulate knowledge, information and ICT;
- mobilize human genius to find innovative solutions to pressing socio-economic as well as human challenges such as HIV and deficits of food and clean water;
- build global competitive capacity;
- extend the boundaries of human knowledge;
- reduce conflict and war;
- expand capacity for self-development and self-actualization;
- enhance the creation and equitable distribution of wealth and the diversity of human culture;
- enable all children to pursue their dreams in peace and equanimity, free from the scourge of violence and deprivation.

In doing so we can not only build the New Africa of our dream, but, in the process, also make the world a better place for all.

The Threats to the New Development Paradigm

There is likely to be resistance from those global Development Partners who have not prepared for such a paradigm shift. Resistance of some African leaders who may be threatened by the empowerment implicit in an enlightened people is also likely. Similarly, resistance from current beneficiaries of the status quo is also to be expected.

The fear of failure also represents a threat to the new development paradigm: fear of failure can have major negative consequences for mobilization.

Towards a New African Renaissance

An African Renaissance is our dream for a New Africa characterized by an explosion of genius in an environment of open and shared enthusiasm, hope, creativity and innovation, and a sense of common wellbeing, spread across the continent, emboldened by the self-confidence of a people empowered by the profound sense that there are no obstacles they cannot surmount in order to achieve the African dream. Our African Renaissance dreams of a people's communal love affair with life and the infinite possibilities of Africa's future and the future of all humanity.

To stimulate and sustain this New African Renaissance we must uphold:

- the need for creating an enabling environment of limitless possibilities;
- belief in the durability of knowledge, experience, vision and hope, and the courage to meet the challenge of life and significant development head on with tenacity, faith and camaraderie, enjoying the process and experience every bit of the way;
- belief in the right, responsibility and eminent ability of Africans to mastermind their own destiny, and to contribute their fair share to a common global vision and development.

Global Opportunities and Responsibilities

We need truly global partnerships to make a meaningful difference, and a fairer and more equitable globalization, resulting in a more enriched world with the benefits of Africa's knowledge and expertise—traditional and modern, scientific and human—providing mutual benefits for all and resulting in a better world.

Telecom Africa's Doctrine for Global Engagement

As CEO of Telecom Africa, I have always advocated a doctrine for globalization that simply states that:

Commerce among nations must be:

- fair and equitable;
- guarantee mutual access to each other's market;
- enhance comparative, competitive capacity, in the absence of which an effective affirmative action programme should be in place;
- involve training, research and development.

Competitiveness in a Knowledge Environment

In a knowledge-driven environment in which intellectual capacity becomes the most critical asset, global competitiveness becomes a free-for-all. This is because through the years, the people of the so-called developing world have acquired immense knowledge and capacity through systems and institutions shared with their global counterparts.

Culture and the Pursuit of Self-Actualization

The goals of self-actualization differ from culture to culture—the African vs. the European. There are no universal standards for the strategies for self-actualization, and the parameters for measuring its achievement. Cultural prerogatives must be carefully nurtured and preserved to prevent the profound alienation which results from defining a people's aspirations by the expectations of others.

Clarion Call for the Developing World

There comes a time in the lives of a people when, no matter how embattled, they must find the courage to take their destiny in their own hands, and, armed with their resources, no matter how limited, strike out to shape their own future, with the help of friends, if possible, alone if inevitable. For Africa, that time is now. The African train must leave the station.

References

Okpaku Sr, Joseph O. "Building the Digital Bridge—Challenges, Opportunities and Strategies". Presentation to the United Nations General Assembly Meeting on Information and Communications Technologies for Development, New York. 17–18 June 2002.

Okpaku Sr, Joseph O. "Knowledge And The Translucency Of Government: The Opportunities and Challenges Of eGovernment For Strategic Development". A presentation to the 6th Global Forum on Reinventing Government, Seoul, Republic of South Korea. 24–27 May 2005.

WIPO. "Ownership of Problems, Intellectual Property and the Digital Divide—The Enabling Challenge of Solutions". Speech given at the Second International Conference on Electronic Commerce and Intellectual Property, Geneva. 19–21 September 2001.

Chapter Three

What it's Like Out There: Profiles of Connectivity at African Universities

Nancy J. Hafkin*

Introduction

Despite enormous gains particularly in the few years since the advent of the new century, universities in sub-Saharan Africa are suffering from bandwidth shortages that severely constrain their ability to profit from the potential of Internet connectivity in which they already have made very expensive investments. To illustrate this, this chapter will first present some current first-hand accounts from users of the system. It will then proceed to an analysis of data from a recent survey of the connectivity of African universities. It will conclude with a detailing of the various players working to remedy the situation by securing greater bandwidth for African universities.

I took two "snapshots" to get a good flavor of the ICT situation at two major African universities—Makerere in Kampala and Addis Ababa University. These are both universities that have made enormous investments in the last few years to set up campus-wide networks and are regarded as among the most advanced African universities in information infrastructure. In the case of Addis Ababa, the snapshot was done by e-mail. In the case of Makerere, it was a first-hand visit.

At Addis Ababa University there is a campus-wide network in place, fully connected to the Internet. Graduate students and academic staff have university e-mail accounts with the www.aau.edu.et domain and are allowed to use the network for Internet/e-mail at the libraries and access points at some of the locations in their faculties/departments. The following user observations on the network came from an assistant professor, a graduate student and a branch library head:

From the assistant professor

- It is impossible to use the Internet during working hours. Downloading of a page is nearly impossible.
- It is better to access the Internet in the evenings and weekends (best).
- E-mail is OK because it is not Internet-based.

---

* Director, Knowledge Working.

- The connectivity situation varies from campus to campus.
- It is a frustrating experience for someone who has had an experience of using the Internet in another academic environment (out of AAU/Ethiopia).

From the graduate student:

- The university e-mail account can only be accessed from within the university network (one has to be on the campus).
- Did not experience a speed problem. (He had never worked in a broadband environment; was comparing it to the dial-up access available in town.)
- Graduate students, the only group of students with access, can only do so one hour at a time, if there are other students waiting. In one hour, it is difficult to see more than 4–5 screens. There are no printing facilities available to graduate students. However, students can save on a diskette (if the computer has a diskette drive) or download on a USB drive.

From the head of one of the branch libraries:

- Support service for users of the university e-mail account is not adequate.
- Though not allowed, undergraduate students try to make use of the Internet access by using [illegal] means of getting usernames and passwords.
- Though the university Internet link of the university has been upgraded [to 1MB per second], it is still slow as a result of the large number of connections using this link.

The observations about Makerere University are from my personal experience and from the report of a high-level Cisco Systems computer scientist.

My observations:

- I could not get through to my web-based e-mail of a major US ISP. Even on Hotmail, reading 2–3 e-mails per hour was doing well.
- For several days or parts of days, the network was down entirely.

From the Cisco scientist:

- Doing a "ping" study,[1] he found substantial loss [of packets] and delay in Internet connections, ranging from one-quarter to one-third of all traffic and starting from the MTN distribution router; there was also additional delay and loss in the satellite link.
- The overall diagnosis was "congestive collapse overload" with a loss rate so high that little can be accomplished.[2]

- It is not sufficient to carry some number of bits per second from here to there; one must deliver service. The Internet is useless if at the end of the day it doesn't deliver a useful service, and in Makerere's present situation, it is just barely usable as a service.

As to the Makerere's need for more bandwidth, he concluded that Makerere's need is on an order of magnitude (10 times what it has now). Makerere currently has a 512 KBPS link. Therefore he feels that Makerere needs at least 5 MBPS for current usage.

How representative are these two experiences compared to the rest of Africa, especially sub-Saharan Africa outside of South Africa?

Analysis of Connectivity at 72 Tertiary-level Educational Institutions in Africa

To get a statistical picture of the connectivity situation at African universities, I used the questionnaires collected this year as part of the African Tertiary Institutions Connectivity Survey, being conducted by the African Virtual University. At the end of September AVU prepared a study based on the first 50 replies.[3] As of November 2004, an additional 30 replies (a 60 per cent increase in the available data) had been received) and are accessible on the web.[4]

The following findings are based on my analysis of the 80 replies to the survey that had been received by November 2004. I did not include responses from North Africa, because my primary interest is in sub-Saharan Africa, and I threw out two of the entries that did not make sense (they said they had VSATs or leased lines, but then reported no computers connected to the Internet).

Sources of Connectivity

Of the 72 responses that I looked at, six were using dialup (alone); 40 had leased lines and 26 had VSATs. (Six were using both VSATs and leased lines.) This data is shown in Table Three.

The most common Internet service providers (ISPs) were, first of all, national telecommunication authorities (34.7 per cent) followed by private ISPs, then VSAT companies, educational networks (such as TENET) and bilateral or multilateral sources (including the Sustainable Development Networking Programme (SDNP) of the United Nations Development Program and the Ministry of Cooperation of France).

Table Three **Connectivity source**

Type	No.	%
Dialup	6	8.3
Leased line	40	55.5
VSAT	26	36.1
Total	72	99.9

Table Four **Type of Internet service provider**

Type of service provider	No.	%
National Telecom	26	34.7
Private ISP	24	32
VSAT	16	21.3
Educational network	5	6.7
Bilateral/multilateral	4	5.3
Total*	751	

* Some institutions had more than one ISP.

Bandwidth Capacity

The total bandwidth capacity (uplink plus downlink) of reporting institutions ranged from a maximum of 5 MBPS to a minimum of 56 KPBS. The median was 384 KBPS and the average 829 KPBS. (This median compares to my at-home broadband connection of 3328 KPBS. That means that I have 8.6 times the broadband capacity as the median African university [not user—university!]).

Bandwidth Leaders

Among the universities with the most bandwidth (note: the major South African institutions did not participate in the survey) were the University of Botswana, the Université Cheikh Anta Diop (Dakar), the University of Dar es Salaam and the University of Zimbabwe.

Bandwidth per Accessed Computer

Out of curiosity, I ran the data with a new indicator- bandwidth per accessed computer. I realize this is not very accurate because it assumes that all computers

Table Five **Bandwidth leaders**

Institution	Bandwidth capacity (MBPS) Uplink	Downlink	Total
University of Botswana	1 M	4 M	5 M
Université Cheikh Anta Diop (Dakar)	2 M	2 M	4 M
University Dar es Salaam	1 M	2 M	3 M
University of Zimbabwe	1.5 M	1.5 M	3 M

are being accessed at the same time (this may be the case) and that all are using the same amount of bandwidth (hopefully not downloading music or films!). But it is an interesting indicator of just how much bandwidth the individual user may have to work with. Here the figures, presented in Table Six, are quite daunting. (In this measurement, I took out the dialup access computers.)

Table Six **Bandwidth per Internet-accessed computer**

Measure	KPBS
Maximum	10.7
Median	1.9
Minimum	0.2
Average	3.0

If this measurement has any validity, it seems to indicate that there is not an institution in the survey that has sufficient connectivity for users to do almost anything if all the machines are occupied at the same time, which is frequently the case at most of these universities. It is a strong argument for increased bandwidth.

Best- and Worst-case Scenarios: Bandwidth per Computer

The best cases in terms of bandwidth per Internet-accessed computer are shown in Table Seven. It is interesting that the highest figure for bandwidth/accessed computer was at the University of Hargeisa in Somaliland, in a telecommunications environment that is completely without regulation. As can be seen, some of these high ratings were because the universities had very few connected computers. The worst cases are seen in Table Eight.

Note that all of these cases had relatively large numbers of computers, but clearly the amounts of accessible bandwidth are insufficient to support them.

Table Seven **Bandwidth per Internet-accessed computer: highest ratings**

Institution	Country	Type of connection	Connected computers (N)	Upload	Download	Total bandwidth	Bandwidth per accessed computer (KBPS)
University of Hargeisa	Somaliland	VSAT	18	64	128	192	10.7
Université de Sahel	Senegal	Leased line	100	512	512	1024	10.2
Ashesi Uiversity	Ghana	VSAT	76	256	512	768	10.1
Open University of Sudan	Sudan	Leased line	40	128	256	384	9.6
Université de Yaounde II	Cameroon	Leased line	40	128	256	384	9.6

Table Eight **Bandwidth per Internet-accessed computer: lowest ratings**

Institution	Country	Type of connection	Connected computers (N)	Upload	Download	Total bandwidth	Bandwidth per accessed computer (KBPS)
Gondar University	Ethiopia	Leased line	480	128	128	256	0.5
Egerton University	Kenya	Leased line	500	128	128	256	0.5
University of Asmara	Eritrea	Leased line	500	128	128	256	0.5
Université de Benin	Togo	Leased line	700	128	128	256	0.4
UEM	Mozambique	VSAT	4000	384	1024	1408	0.4
University of Zambia	Zambia	Leased line +VSAT	2000	128	512	640	0.3
Makerere University	Uganda	Leased line	2600	256	256	512	0.2

Costs

Cost/KPBS/Month

The standard measure of bandwidth costs is cost/KBPS/month. Analyzing the costs at these 72 institutions (Table Nine), the median cost came out to be $3.32, with the average at $6.04 and the maximum at $54.69 (calculated by adding uplink and downlink capacity and dividing by reported monthly costs). These figures are all well above the target cost that many advocates of lower cost bandwidth are aiming for: $2.00 or $2.50 per KBPS. It should be noted that included in these calculations are six institutions that self-reported costs of $0 per month for their connectivity. One wonders whether these institutions were either unwilling to reveal cost information or did not have it available to them. If not, there are very benevolent telecommunications authorities or ISPs in their countries!

Table Nine **Bandwidth costs/mo. (US$)**

Measure	Cost per mo.	Cost/KPBS/mo.
Maximum	28,000	54.69
Median	1,500	3.32
Average	3,581	6.04

The institutions with the highest monthly costs per KPBS are shown in Table Ten.

Table Ten **Costs per KBPS/mo.: highest (US$)**

Institution	Country	Monthly cost/KBPS
Makerere	Uganda	54.69
Yaounde I	Cameroon	36.33
Institut de mathematiques et sciences physiques	Benin	26.79
Botswana College of Agriculture	Botswana	15.63

According to my calculations, I pay 0.01 per month per KPBS for my US home connection. That puts the costs per KBPS at Makerere at 5469 per cent of what I pay.

Some others, however, were paying rates that many would regard at quite reasonable. Those that fall into this category are shown in Table Eleven.

Table Eleven Costs per KBPS/mo: lowest (US$)

Institution	Country	Monthly cost/KBPS
University of Science and Technology	Sudan	0.98
University of Mauritius	Mauritius	0.83
Instituto de ciencias et técnicas	Guinea Bissau	0.63
Université Cheikh Anta Diop	Senegal	0.49
University of Namibia	Namibia	0.49
University of Ouagadougou	Burkina Faso	0.39
Université de Sahel	Senegal	0.10
Obafemi Awolowo University	Nigeria	0.01

Table Twelve Bandwidth costs per month and year (US$)

Institution	Country	Bandwidth costs	
		Per month	Per year
Université de Saint-Louis Gaston Berger	Senegal	28,000	336,000
Makerere University	Uganda	28,000	336,000
University of Botswana	Botswana	17,000	204,000
University of Dar es Salaam	Tanzania	10,000	120,000
Universidade Eduardo Mondlane (UEM)	Mozambique	10,000	120,000
Université Yaounde I	Cameroon	9,300	111,600
Total		**102,300**	**1,227,600**

Absolute Costs

The highest bandwidth costs per month were at the following universities shown in Table Twelve. The impact of these figures is felt most clearly when they are annualized. The cost for connectivity at these six institutions is US$1.25 million dollars a year! These are enormous sums for African universities.

Cost per Internet-accessed Computer per Year

I should like to try out another indicator that may be interesting—cost per year per Internet-accessed computer. This provides some striking results: the median cost per year was $80; the average, $181. But one institution (Université de Yaounde II) is paying $2790 per year for each computer accessed to the Internet. Others with high costs per connected machine were l'Institut de mathematiques et des sciences physiques in Cotonou, Benin ($1200) and Université de Dschang in Cameroon ($520). Of those that reported paying something, those with the lowest costs per connected computer were the University of Namibia ($6), Sudan University of Science and Technology ($8), Gondar University in Ethiopia ($10), Université de Ouagadougou ($12); Université de Sahel (Senegal, $12), and the University of Zambia ($12).

The Future: Securing Greater Bandwidth for African Universities

There is clear demand and loud calls for improved bandwidth in the academic and research sectors in Africa. To meet this demand, there appears to be a need for a mechanism for brokering better satellite and terrestrial bandwidth deals for these institutions, which could include a buying club for satellite bandwidth and support for improved bandwidth management. There has come to be growing support for this as well.

Three major organizations are now working together, in varying degrees of collaboration, towards helping African universities increase their bandwidth. These are the Partnership for Higher Education, African Virtual University (AVU) and the International Development Research Centre (IDRC). Additional organizations working in this or related areas are listed in the Annex to this chapter.

The Ford, Rockefeller, MacArthur foundations and the Carnegie Corporation of New York, working together in the Partnership for Higher Education in Africa, established a working group in 2003 to examine the bandwidth situation and options for their partner universities.[5] The background study for this activity was a document entitled, "Securing the Linchpin for Teaching, Learning and Research: More Bandwidth at Lower Cost " (http://www.foundation-partnership.org/linchpin/index.php) presented to a workshop of African universities held in Addis Ababa in 2003. The workshop resulted in the "BandITs" report, which was further discussed at a meeting of vice chancellors and senior staff of African universities in Dar es Salaam in September 2004 when it was agreed to collaborate with the AVU on obtaining improved bandwidth for their respective members. The vice chancellors associated with the Partnership have granted AVU the authority, until end of December 2004, to negotiate on their behalf for improved pricing and increased bandwidth.

IDRC, which has played a major role in supporting connectivity amongst researchers and academics in Africa since the establishment of the ESANET project in 1989, is establishing a project to facilitate collaboration in establishing national and regional research and education networks in Africa. As part of this, IDRC is sponsoring a technical study for establishing a bandwidth purchasing consortium for African research and education institutions (PAREN) to determine the availability and costs of the required bandwidth on the continent, and the cost savings that could be achieved through bulk purchasing and negotiating for discounted bandwidth on behalf of the education and research sector. Consideration of the local regulatory environment in each of the African countries is an important element to see what telecommunications and other policy and regulatory issues constrain market access. In doing this, IDRC is collaborating closely with the Partnership.

African Leadership in the Movement for More and Cheaper Bandwidth

It needs to be stressed that African universities are doing a great deal on their own to move forward on these issues. Professors from Makerere University and the University of Dar es Salaam were chosen by their colleagues from other Partnership universities to co-chair the Steering Committee for increased and cheaper bandwidth created at the Dar meeting. Under the leadership of the University of Jos, Nigerian universities have entered an agreement to form a consortium to share bandwidth.

Given the growing awareness of the bandwidth deficit and high connectivity costs at African universities and the intensification of both African and external action towards correcting this, it appears hopeful that within the next four years African universities will have achieved the order of magnitude increase in their connectivity and will join global research and learning networks for the benefit of African economic and social development.

Notes

1 Fred Baker, "African Ping Studies", October, 2004.

2 TCP will work reasonably well with 2 per cent loss and prefers 1 per cent loss or less. At the point where the system is experiencing a 25 per cent loss, as at Makerere, a significant proportion of the offered load is not first transmissions, but retransmissions, and the applications are forced to not keep a few segments in flight at any given time, but to send one, see if an acknowledgement is received, and then send the request again.

3 "Africa Tertiary Institutions Connectivity Survey Preliminary Insights Sept. 2004", http://www.atics.info/html/about/Initial_response_report1.pdf [accessed 11 November 2004]. More information may be available from Peter Dzvimbo (kdzvimbo@avu.org) and Alex Twinomugisha (alex@avu.org).

4 "Bandwidth connectivity forms." http://www.atics.info/database/view_forms1.php?userid=117&org_id=117 (accessed 11 November 2004).

5 The Partnership supports universities in six African countries (Ghana, Mozambique, Nigeria, South Africa, Tanzania, and Uganda), while the AVU has 24 affiliated campuses in 19 Africa countries (see www.avu.org).

Annex

Additional Sources of Information on Activities to Promote Increased and Cheaper Connectivity for African Universities.

Extracted from Michael Jensen, "IDRC Research Study of Pan African Research and Education Networking (PAREN): Background Information and list of related activities taking place in Africa", October, 2004.

- Members of the NSF in the US and Géant in Europe have indicated they would be prepared to support some sort of initiative to bring better bandwidth the African academic and research institutions. In particular, the High Energy Physics group has been active in this area. Contacts include: Harvey Newman (newman@hep.caltech.edu), Ann Preston (apreston@internet2.edu), Heather Boyles (heather@internet2.edu) and Larry Press lhl@cs.wisc.edu.
- The Millennium Science Initiative (MSI) aims to build capacity in modern science and technology and their uses in developing countries. In Africa, initiatives are planned in Uganda, Cameroon, Botswana and Namibia, and Tanzania. One ministry, typically Science & Technology or Higher Education, takes the lead in promoting the MSI within the government, working closely with the Ministry of Finance to ensure that the MSI is designated a priority item within the country's overall development strategy. Contact information: www.msi-sig.org; Alan Anderson, alan@ias.edu.
- The UN University (UNU) is developing a proposal in collaboration with the International Telecommunication Union to establish an African Universities Network (AUN). Contact information: Barbara Wilson, barbara.wilson@itu.int; Harald Holt. Harald.Holt@grida.no.
- The World Association of Industrial and Technological Research Organizations (WAITRO) is assisting in building the capacity of its 48 members in 25 countries comprising all the major research and technology organizations (RTOs) on the African continent. The Regional Focal Point (RFP) for Africa is managed by the South African Council for Scientific and Industrial Research (CSIR) which has been discussing a proposal for a satellite network to link many of these institutions. Contact information: www.waitro.org; Kobus Roux, kroux@csir.co.za.
- The Internet Educational Equal Access Foundation (IEEAF) is a non-profit corporation created by its member institutions to accept assets donated to the global education community by a broadly defined telecommunication industry and corporate community (www.ieeaf.org).
- The International Center for Theoretical Physics (ICTP) in Trieste, Italy has been assisting with capacity building for improved Internet connectivity in a variety of African universities. The ICTP donation program has maintained a

list of African Universities/Physics Departments for some time and has carried on-site networking training for actors in the region. Contact information: http://www.ictp.trieste.it/~donation/Universities_on_Line.html; Enrique Canessa, canessae@ictp.trieste.it; http://www.collaborium.org, http://wireless.ictp.trieste.it.

- The International Network for the Availability of Scientific Publications is supporting a variety of tertiary institutions in capacity building for bandwidth management and optimization. Contact information: www.inasp.info; Carol Priestley, cpriestley@inasp.info.
- Widernet is a project of the University of Iowa, currently supporting linkages, capacity building and computer donations to Nigerian universities. It has developed an eGranary of digital knowledge delivering over a million digital documents to universities in developing countries. It has also developed a web-based bandwidth test. Contact information: www.widernet.org; Cliff Missen, missenc@widernet.org.
- The Advanced Institute for Mathematical Sciences (AIMS) in Cape Town has been working with the South African Department of Science and Technology to develop a NEPAD proposal to bring connectivity to 20 African tertiary institutions. Contact information: www.aims.ac.za; Neil G. Turok, N.G.Turok@damtp.cam.ac.uk.
- The Association of African Universities (AAU) based in Accra, Ghana, has indicated its interest in supporting improved connectivity within its membership. As part of its 11th annual general meeting, AAU will devote a session to the discussion of the IDRC PAREN proposal. Contact information: www.aau.org.
- Plans are being finalized for the establishment of a Southern African Regional Universities Association. Within the context of this initiative the South African Universities Network, TENET, has been tasked by the SA Dept of Science and Technology to look at the feasibility of establishing a Southern African Research and Education Network. Contact information: www.tenet.ca.za; Oliver Seale, oliver@sauvca.org.za; Ben McGarry, ben@bentvoodoo.com; Duncan Martin, dhm@tenet.ac.za.
- Building on their work to support access to improved bandwidth in eastern European academic and research institutions, George Soros' Open Society Institute (OSI) has indicated its interest in assisting in this area in Africa, and are presently doing so for Malawian tertiary institutions via their local southern African office, OSISA. Contact information: www.osafrica.org; Ashraf Patel ashrafp@osiafrica.org; osisainfo@osiafrica.org.
- Multilateral Initiative on Malaria (MIMCom.Net) is an initiative that aims to give medical researchers in Africa access to a satellite-based research network that enhances communication with other researchers around the world. The initiative is using VSATs, currently in two sites in Ghana and Tanzania and four in Kenya. Potential sites will be established in Uganda and Malawi. Bandwidth

speeds of up to 768 Kbps are being provided. The National Library of Medicine of US government is the principal overseer of the project. www.mim.su.se.

Bilateral and Multilateral Development Assistance Projects

The French Ministry of Foreign affairs has a number of projects supporting tertiary institutions in Africa including:

> Projet COMETES (Coordination et Modernisation des établisdements Technologiques de l'Enseignement Supérieur en Cameroun which will interconnect Universities, provide high-level training in the use of ICTs and develop distance learning. Contact information: Olivier Garro, olivier_garro@yahoo.fr.

USAID is supporting the development of Internet connectivity for many African Universities as part of the Leland Project. Contact information: http://www.info.usaid.gov/regions/afr/leland; Lane Smith, lasmith@usaid.gov.

In September 2004 India proposed to the African Union meeting in Johannesburg to provide Africa with a $50-million integrated satellite and fibre-optic wireless network for improved communication. The network would connect 53 African Union member countries for tele-education, telemedicine, e-commerce and e-governance and e-services. The projected network would bring rural connectivity throughout Africa and could be in position within the next three years.

From IBAUD: www.Ibaud.org.

IBAUD is a not-for-profit organization registered in the USA with an African agenda.[1] The vision of IBAUD is to enable low-cost, high-speed Internet bandwidth to every African academic and research institution. To accomplish this the organization is focusing on four lines of action:

- Obtaining "special" bandwidth licenses for medical/academic institutions in each country
- Creating a "buying club" of research institutions that can negotiate the best price for bandwidth equipment and services
- Assisting participating institutions in utilizing the bandwidth more effectively
- Exploring how the resulting network can be leveraged to increase the effectiveness of research and educational initiatives—especially enabling the dissemination of relevant information to end-users in each country.

IBAUD has a survey of bandwidth prices in Africa on its site at http://www.ibaud.org/html/bandprices/prices.html. It also lists both primary and secondary bandwidth suppliers: http://www.ibaud.org/html/bandprices/Primarybandwidth.pdf and http://www.ibaud.org/html/bandprices/Secondarybandwidth.pdf. It has done a study of the level of competition in the telecommunications sector of African countries: http://www.ibaud.org/html/about/Levelofcompetition.pdf.

Note

1 Unfortunately www.ibaud.org gives no contact information for the organization. The organization is the creation of Roy Steiner, an American living in Zimbabwe. He can be contacted at roy@cyberplexafrica.com.

Chapter Four

Why E-Readiness Matters: The TEEAL and AGORA Resources

Mary Ochs*

Introduction: Access to Library Collections in the Developing World

Many agricultural and health researchers receive their training in Western Europe or in the United States and Canada, relying on large library collections, with their rows of stacks, online databases and electronic journals, to stay current in their fields. Libraries in the developing world have not been able to offer this wealth of scientific information and cannot afford subscriptions to international scientific journals in any meaningful numbers. With the increasing price of journals over the past decade and struggling economies in many countries, libraries in the developing world have reduced subscriptions even further. Some faculty must use information resources that are 10 to 15 years old to prepare their teaching material and do their research.

Many programs have been developed to send print materials to developing world libraries. These programs were expensive to operate and only moderately successful. Information technologies have provided new mechanisms for delivering high quality, state-of-the-art information to libraries all over the world, making the issue of e-readiness a critical one for researchers in developing countries. In the early days of the Internet, some questioned the need for Internet access in the developing world, asking what substantive content was available that would prompt universities to invest in computer and Internet technology. This has changed dramatically with the advent of resources like TEEAL, HINARI and AGORA.

The TEEAL, AGORA and HINARI Programs

TEEAL (The Essential Electronic Agricultural Library, http://www.teeal.org) provides access to the full text of 140 key journals in agriculture and related sciences on CD-ROM. It is often referred to as the "Library in a Box". Since its introduction in 1999 TEEAL has been installed in 99 institutions in 50 countries. It provides access to over 2 million journal pages covering material from 1993 to 2003, with annual updates produced each year. One hundred and nine countries are eligible for TEEAL.

---

* Albert R. Mann Library, Cornell University, Ithaca, New York.

AGORA (http://www.aginternetwork.org) is the sister program to both HINARI and TEEAL and is coordinated by the Food and Agriculture Organization of the United Nations. It is a partnership between FAO, Mann Library, donor agencies and the major scientific publishers. AGORA, or Access to Global Online Research in Agriculture, was developed to provide online access to major journals in agriculture and related sciences. The program currently provides 69 eligible countries with free online access to over 700 journals. Eligibility is based on GNI per capita as at 31 December 2000. By 25 March 2005 430 institutions in 56 countries had registered.

HINARI (http://www.healthinternetwork.org) is the HealthInterNetwork Access to Research Initiative. HINARI provides free or reduced price access to over 2,500 journals in health and medicine. HINARI is a partnership between the World Health Organization, scientific publishers, donor agencies and other partners. Sixty-nine countries are eligible for free access through HINARI and another 44 countries are eligible for reduced-price access.

Objectives of TEEAL, AGORA and HINARI

TEEAL, AGORA and HINARI provide access to a research level library collection for researchers and instructors in agriculture and medicine. By enhancing access to information, many other goals can be achieved. Access to current research literature facilitates high quality and timely research. Without this, researchers can spend time developing research proposals for techniques and topics that have already been proven ineffective. Access to current information also enhances curriculum development. Articles available through these programs can be used on reserve in the library or as part of course reading packets. Researchers can also provide better advice to policy makers in, for example, the Ministry of Health, Ministry of Agriculture or other areas of federal, state or local government.

Reducing the 'publishing gap' is another important goal of these programs. Many researchers in developing countries are at a disadvantage when it comes to getting their own research published. Better access to the research literature can improve the quality of the research produced. More research articles from developing country researchers will be published in international journals and the quality of the articles created for local publications will be enhanced.

Overall, TEEAL, HINARI and AGORA help connect developing-world researchers with the international scientific community. In the long run, we hope that this will result in improved food security and health in the developing world. It may be impossible to show this link for years, but that is the long-term goal of the programs.

Training and Outreach

Training and outreach have been a critical component of the TEEAL, AGORA and HINARI programs. The libraries and institutions that we work with are in various stages of transition to the information age. In many of our training workshops basic skills in using the Internet are covered to ensure that all participants are familiar with the key concepts and skills of Internet use. Additional training focuses on skills needed to use the TEEAL system and the HINARI and AGORA portals. The workshops are designed to train librarians who can then return to their institutions and train others. All three programs work closely together to focus on the interdisciplinary nature of health and agriculture information.

Figure Five AGORA workshop in Harare, Zimbabwe, April 2004

Are These Programs Making a Difference?

Since a number of libraries have owned TEEAL sets since 1999, adequate time has passed to determine whether TEEAL is meeting its objectives. Under the sponsorship of the Rockefeller Foundation, TEEAL undertook a user study. The study consisted of three components:

1 a survey of users;
2 on-site case studies;
3 an analysis of bibliographic citations.

The discussion below will focus on the survey. The following institutions participated in the survey:

Latin America

1 Universidad La Molina, Peru
2 Escuela Agrícola Panamericana/Zamorano, Honduras
3 Universidad Earth, Costa Rica

Asia

4 Institut Pertanian Bogor/ Bogor Agricultural University, Indonesia
5 Center for International Forestry Research, Indonesia
6 Nepal Agricultural Research Council, Nepal

Africa

7 Obafemi University, Nigeria
8 Bunda College, Malawi
9 Africa University, Zimbabwe
10 Kenya Agricultural Research Institute
11 Eduardo Mondlane University, Mozambique
12 Ministry of Agriculture, Tanzania
13 Egerton University, Kenya
14 University of Agriculture, Abeokuta, Nigeria
15 CSIR/INSTI, Ghana
16 Botswana College of Agriculture

Survey coordinators at each institution distributed, collected and returned the surveys to the TEEAL office at Mann Library.

Survey Results

Some of the key findings from the survey are outlined below. The full user study report will be available on the TEEAL website at http://www.teeal.org.

Figure Six highlights key outcomes of the survey. It demonstrates that: 1) access to priced scholarly literature is very important to students and researchers; 2) users are generally very satisfied with TEEAL; 3) TEEAL improves the quality of their

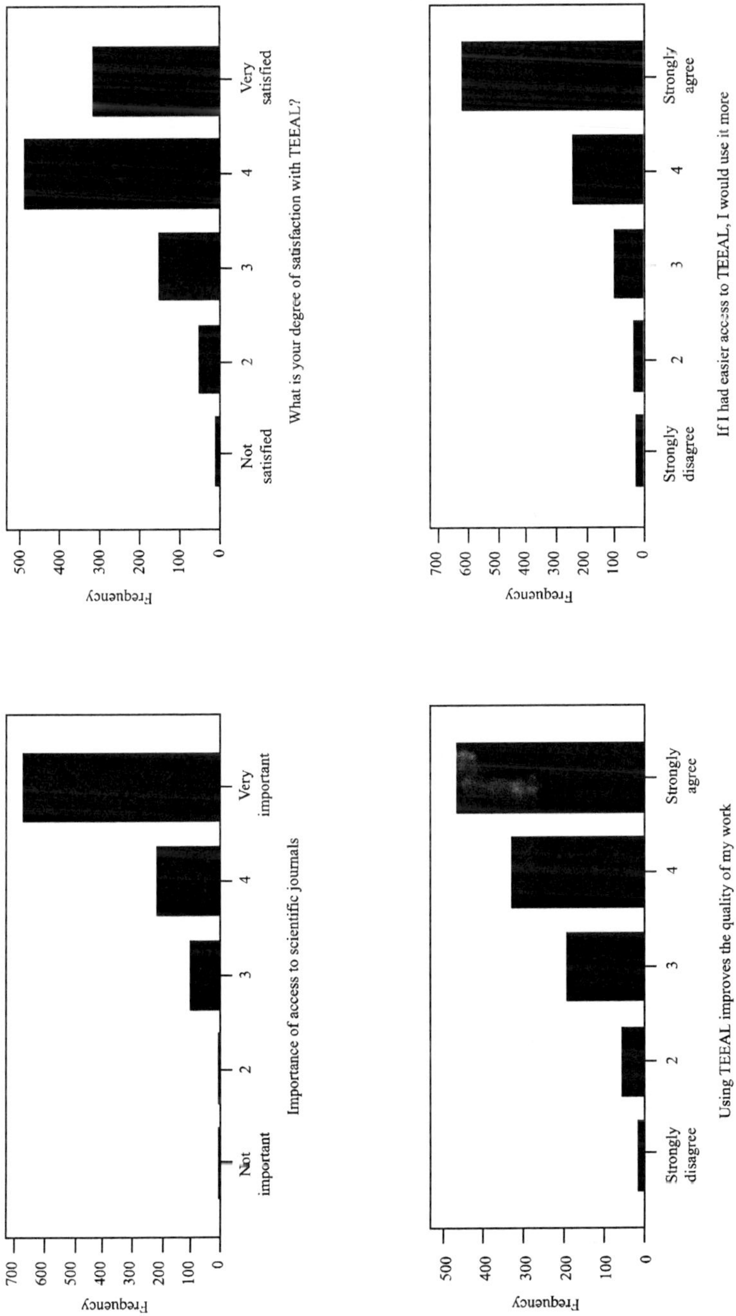

Figure Six General satisfaction with TEEAL

work (approximately 75 per cent of survey respondents answered 4 or 5); and 4) users would use TEEAL more if they had easier access.

Almost all respondents (975 out of 1043) said they were involved in research. Of the 975, 80 per cent found TEEAL useful in their research (Figure Seven) and 66 per cent (Figure Eight) agreed that the literature in TEEAL has influenced their research. Fully 60 per cent of people also felt that TEEAL has influenced ***how*** they search for scientific literature (Figure Nine). About 25 per cent recorded that they strongly agreed with this statement.

Another key goal of TEEAL is to improve the availability of resources for teaching. Not nearly as many survey takers said they were involved in teaching. Fewer than half of respondents answered the questions related to TEEAL and its impact on teaching. Figures Ten and Eleven indicate that TEEAL is not playing as strong a role in teaching as in research. Only 24 per cent of people said that they found TEEAL very useful in their teaching (Figure Ten: 5 on a scale of 1 to 5), although just over half definitely felt it was useful (Figure Ten: 4 and 5 together). However, almost 60 per cent of respondents thought that having TEEAL has improved the quality of their teaching (Figure Eleven: 4 and 5 together). All of the teaching professionals interviewed in the case studies said that they used TEEAL and articles from the journals in their classes.

One barrier to full access to TEEAL, AGORA and HINARI is poor access to computers and high-speed online connections to the Internet. The graphs below show that while access to computers does not seem to be a large problem, access to the Internet is, especially in Africa.

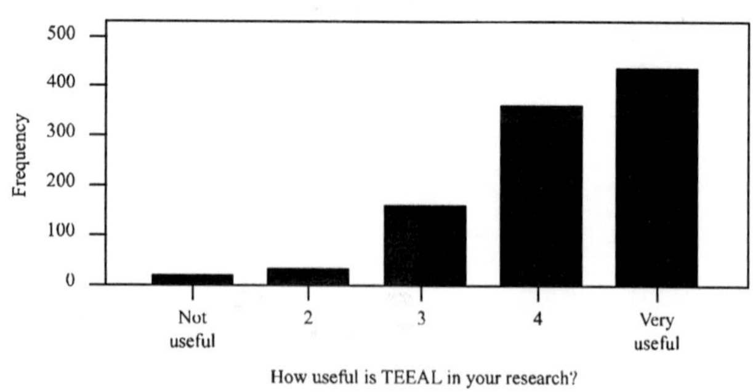

Figure Seven **How useful is TEEAL?**

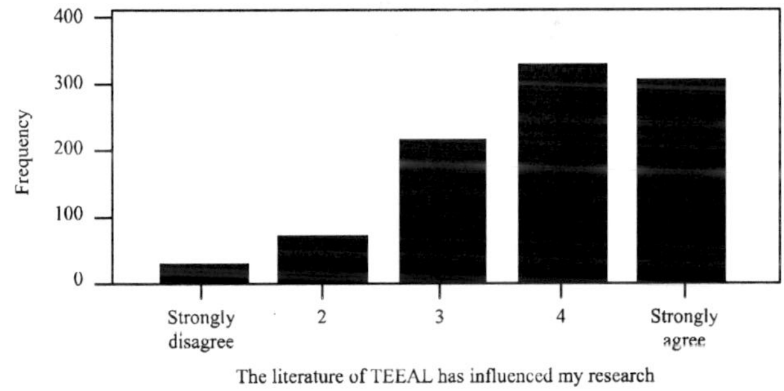

Figure Eight **Has TEEAL literature influenced your research?**

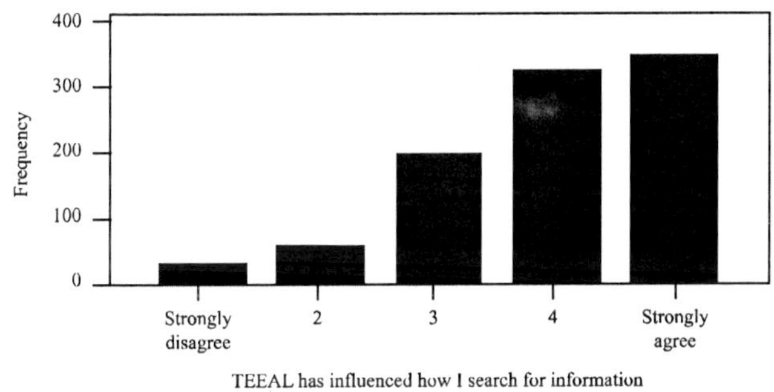

Figure Nine **Has TEEAL influenced how you search for information?**

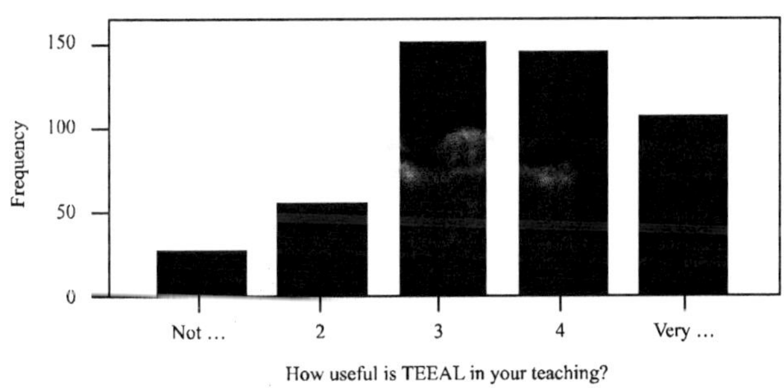

Figure Ten **How useful is TEEAL in your teaching?**

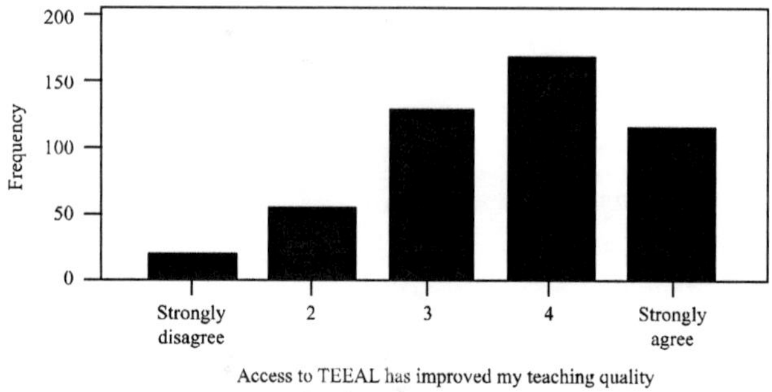

Figure Eleven Has access to TEEAL improved your teaching quality?

Conclusion

Important content for medical and agricultural researchers is now available on CD-ROM and online through TEEAL, HINARI and AGORA. E-readiness is critical for universities and research centers to take full advantage of the valuable content now available. James Grant, Former Director of UNICEF has said:

> the most urgent task before us is to get medical and health knowledge to those most in need of that knowledge. Of the approximately 50 million people dying each year in the late 1980s, fully two thirds could have been saved through the application of that knowledge. (BMJ, 1997)

Through improved technology and programs like TEEAL, HINARI and AGORA, we can get that knowledge to researchers, faculty and extension workers who need it.

Reference

"Meeting the Information Needs of Health Workers in Developing Countries: Editorial", *BMJ* 314:7074: http://bmj.bmjjournals.com/archive/7074e.htm (11 January 1997).

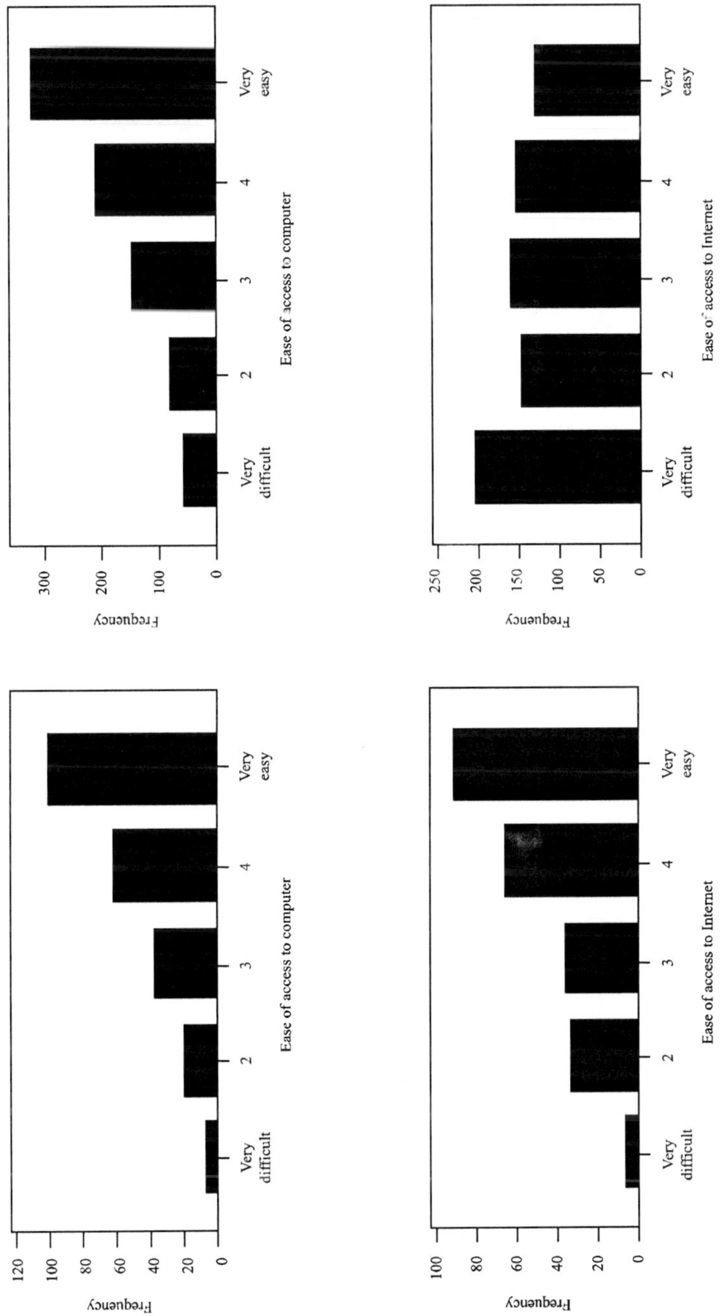

Figure 4.8 **Ease of access to computers and the Internet at all institutions and African institutions**

Chapter Five

The Millennium Development Goals and ICT

Egondu Onyejekwe*

Introduction

In the context of meeting the Millennium Development Goals it is important to recognize that the poor have little or no voice, so can hardly influence the social, political and economic milieu which may be persecuting them. They need stronger voices, they must be heard as they seek basic social services as well as economic stability and growth. Poor countries also need to be heard, as they demand more open markets for trade and technology for development as well as the promised resources from developed worlds that should enable development. For poor people and poor nations to be heard, at least the basic information and communications technology (ICT) infrastructures must be in place. Laying ICT cables for or wireless technology is not enough. A complete infrastructure must have the three "a"s—be available, be affordable, and be accessible to all especially the youth. This chapter explores this agenda for action.

The Millennium Development Goals (MDGs) were the outcomes of agreements and resolutions of world conferences organized by the United Nations (UN) in the early 1990s. The conferences were designed to address that "most compelling" of human desires—the reduction of poverty and to commit the international community to an expanded vision of development—human development. Poverty breeds misery and the vigorous promotion of human development was seen as key in reducing that misery as well as the key to sustaining social and economic progress of nations. The UN member nations also recognized the importance of creating a global partnership for development as they developed the MDGs. There are eight MDGs:

1 eradicate extreme poverty and hunger;
2 achieve universal primary education;
3 promote gender equality and empower women;
4 reduce child mortality;
5 improve maternal health;
6 combat HIV/AIDS, malaria, and other diseases;
7 ensure environmental sustainability;
8 develop a global partnership for development.

---

* Montgomery College, Maryland and President, EARTHMAP

For a complete listing of the goals, targets, and indicators for MDGs, see the Appendix

Overall, these goals are based upon agreement of steps needed to reduce poverty, and on how to achieve sustainable development thus making the goals themselves a commonly accepted framework for measuring development progress. The goals should therefore be seen as being mutually reinforcing and should be viewed together because each of the goals fundamentally addresses an aspect of poverty. The first seven have direct impact on poverty, while the eighth provides a necessary means for achieving the other seven. Achieving gender equality for example will improve the welfare of women and hence children. Enrolling more (or even all) children, especially for girls, in primary education and will reduce poverty and maternal and child mortality. An improved and sustaining environment will definitely allow more people to work and earn a living.[1]

Many of the targets of the MDGs were first set out during the 1990 international conferences and summits. Later compilation gave these goals a new name—International Development Goals. In September 2000 the member states of the United Nations unanimously adopted the Millennium Declaration.

The Millennium Declaration

Here are some excerpts from Press Release GA/9758 of the United Nations on 8 September 2000:

> WORLD LEADERS ADOPT "UNITED NATIONS MILLENNIUM DECLARATION" AT CONCLUSION OF EXTRAORDINARY THREE-DAY SUMMIT
>
> Resolve Action to Strengthen Peace, Development, Human Rights; To Improve UN's Ability to Act on Behalf of Humanity's Priorities
>
> "Only through broad and sustained efforts to create a shared future, based upon our common humanity in all its diversity, can globalization be made fully inclusive and equitable", world leaders stated this afternoon as they unanimously adopted a "United Nations Millennium Declaration" at the conclusion of their Millennium Summit.
>
> The main document to come out of the largest-ever gathering of world leaders, which began on 6 September in New York, the Declaration contains a statement of values, principles and objectives for the international agenda for the twenty-first century. It also sets deadlines for many collective actions.
>
> In an address delivered at the concluding meeting of the Conference, United Nations Secretary-General Kofi Annan told the Summit that it had sketched out clear directions for adapting the Organization to its role in the new century. "It lies in your power, and therefore is your responsibility, to reach the goals that you have defined", he declared. "Only you can determine whether the United Nations rises to the challenge. For my part, I hereby re-dedicate myself, as from today, to carrying out your mandate."

> The document (A/55/L.2) reaffirms Member States' faith in the United Nations and its Charter as indispensable for a more peaceful, prosperous and just world. The collective responsibility of the governments of the world to uphold human dignity, equality and equity is recognized, as is the duty of world leaders to all people, and especially children and the most vulnerable.
>
> The leaders declare that the central challenge of today is to ensure that globalization becomes a positive force for all, acknowledging that at present both its benefits and its costs are unequally shared. The Declaration calls for global policies and measures, corresponding to the needs of developing countries and economies in transition.

After consultations with international agencies such as the World Bank, the IMF, the OECD and other specialized agencies of the United Nations, the United Nations General Assembly recognized the Millennium Development Goals as part of the *road map* for implementing the Millennium Declaration.

As already pointed out in the literature, achieving the MDGs by 2015 will require more focus on development outcomes and less on inputs:

1. it will be crucial to effectively measure national progress towards meeting the MDGs;
2. it will be crucial to engage even more closely with the partners of developed nations in helping governments improve human development; and
3. it will behoove the current planners to invest in today's youth.

Further Analysis

The MDGs establish yardsticks for measuring results for both the developing countries and the rich countries who help to fund development programs as well as for the multilateral institutions that help countries implement them. The tenet of the MDGs rests upon poverty. Again, it is important to reiterate the relationships of the goals. The first seven goals are mutually reinforcing and target all forms of poverty reduction. The last goal—global partnership for development—provides the means to achieve the first seven. In essence, many of the poorest countries will need additional assistance and must look to the rich countries to provide it. Furthermore, countries that are poor and heavily indebted also need to reduce their debt burdens. Virtually all countries will benefit if trade barriers are lowered to allow a freer exchange of goods and services.

Who are the Poor?

So who are the poor? The World Bank gives the following assessment: "It has been estimated that in 2001, 1.1 billion people had consumption levels below $1 a day and 2.7 billion lived on less than $2 a day" (http://web.worldbank.org/WBSITE/EXTERNAL/TOPICS/EXTPOVERTY/EXTPA/ 0,,contentMDK:20153855~menuPK:435040~pagePK:148956~piPK:216618~theSitePK:430367,00.html) According to the World Bank, there are three degrees or categories of the poor.

1 Extreme (or absolute) poverty—households make an income of less than US$1 a day. These people are chronically ill and usually lack most of the basic necessities of life such as drinking water and shelter. This type of poverty is the one that kills and occurs only in developing countries, as illustrated in Figure Twelve.
2 Moderate poverty—households live on US$1 to US$2 a day. Such groups of poor barely meet the basic needs.
3 Relative poverty—households have an income level that is below some defined proportion of the national average.

For the poorest countries many of the goals seem far out of reach because poverty comes in various forms. For the international community, poverty in all its forms

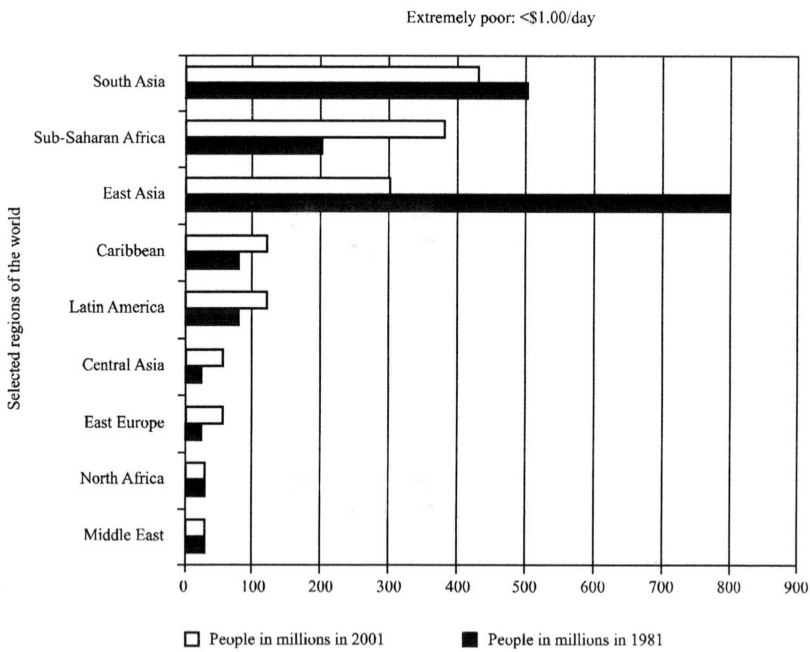

Figure Twelve **Extreme poverty**

Source: World Bank.

presents the greatest challenge. Particularly of concern are the 1.2 billion people who live on less than a US$1 a day, and an additional 1.6 billion who live on less than US$2 a day. Most of the extreme poor live in Asia, while Africa, where about half of the population is among the extreme poor, has the largest proportion (Figure Twelve). The current gulf of divide did not exist a few centuries ago, as shown in Figure Thirteen. But for a few land owners and rulers, poverty was spread across the globe.

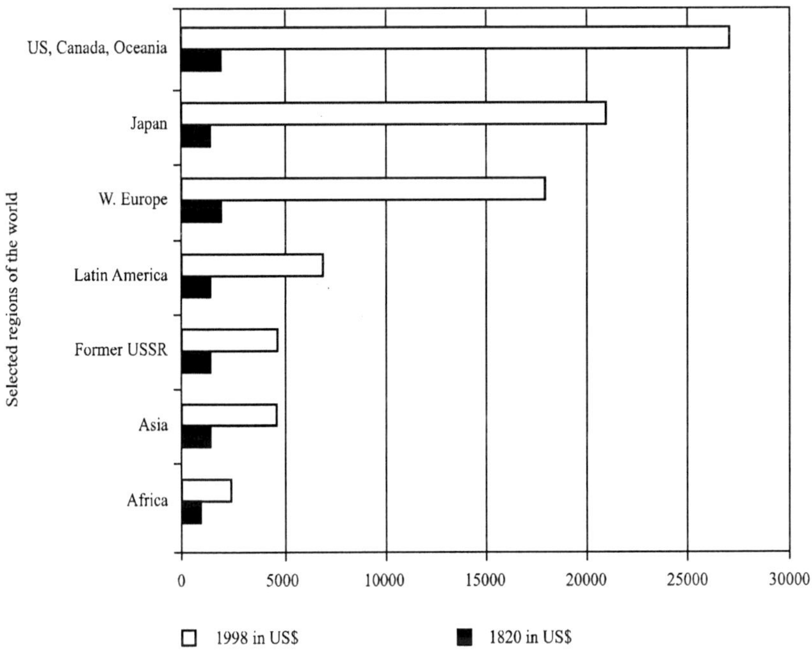

Figure Thirteen Long-term growth in GDP per capita, in 1990 US$

Source: OECD.

Even in better-off countries there may be regions or sub-populations that lag behind, but these groups are in the categories of either moderate or relative poverty. Jeffrey Sachs (2005) tells us that currently eight million people die each year because they are too poor to stay alive. The poor include over 20,000 who die daily as nameless, faceless patients in "hospital wards that lack drugs, in villages that lack antimalarial bed nets, in houses that lack safe drinking water". But Sachs believes that a "provocative plan" can save them. An example of that is what he calls "clinical economics" where he compares good development economics to good clinical medicine.

So, there is really no problem with setting goals to reduce poverty since, if achieved, there will be a better and a more peaceful world for all. The goals, if achievable, will improve the quality of life of those affected. Given this frame of reference, the goals make major strides toward the way forward. Better yet, the international community has made a commitment to the world's poorest and most vulnerable by setting the goals in precise terms. That means that the goals are measured in numbers to ensure accountability. Furthermore, the openness and transparency of these numbers can assist the world community in gauging and charting a course to both achieve the goals as well as track the rate and pace of progress.

The problem is that the international community made far too many assumptions and somehow failed to recognize some of the root causes of poverty and how such great disparity occurred. Sachs (2005) believes that the type of disparity of wealth was orchestrated by the development economics that were imposed by the rich countries on the poorest countries. He likened such an imposition to the 18th century physician who used leeches to draw blood from their patients, often killing them in the process. As in today's practice of medicine, Sachs argues that "developmental economics" must include professional rigor, insight and practicality. Since the sources of poverty are varied and multidimensional, he argues, the solutions must also be multidimensional—and so should include a multitude of areas such as clean water, productive soils, functional healthcare system and even foreign exchange rates. It takes very little to prod the people in poor countries into activating their own economies. But they need help, which is not forthcoming from the developed nations. Figure Fourteen depicts the "giving gap" among the high income countries. The disparity between what a country like the US could give and what it actually gives is very striking.

Furthermore, there is no room for the participation of future leaders in shaping this future, which really belongs to them. Also, numbers are merely numbers and have no relevance to specific human conditions such as emotions and feelings. How can the international community measure happiness or deep anger? What type of statistics or numbers can measure satisfaction, satiation and an uplifted spirit? What does it really mean to halve the number of current poor of the world? Who will remain poor? What causes poverty in the first place? Is all poverty alike? There are too many unanswered questions. Since goals cannot be imposed, the international community adopted another fallacy—that each country should embrace the goals and set their own strategies with their citizens. Also, countries are supposed to work together with the global partners, to ensure that poor people are included in the benefits of development. Can all countries do this? The answer, of course, is no. Time and space do not permit a discussion of many other obstacles that have already been identified. Among them are:

- weak governance;
- bad policies;

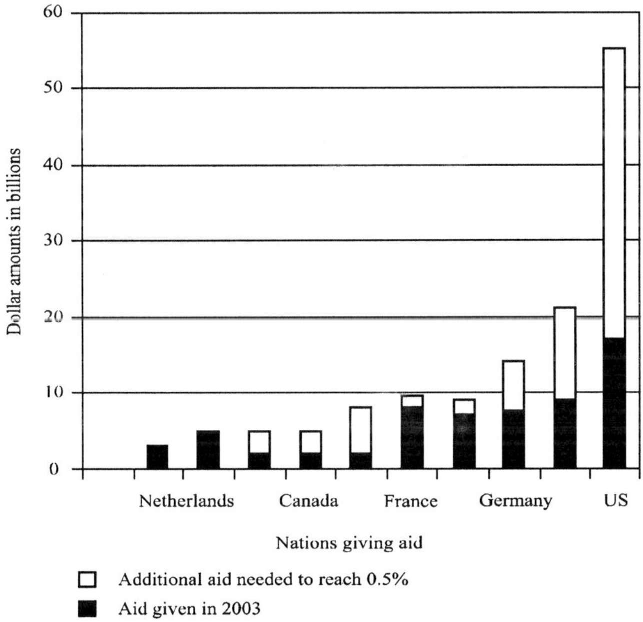

Figure Fourteen The giving gap: additional foreign aid needed to reach 0.5% of GDP in billions of dollars

Source: OECD.

- human rights abuses;
- conflicts;
- natural disasters and other external shocks;
- the spread of HIV/AIDS;
- failure to address inequalities (in income, education and access to healthcare;
- The inequalities between men and women;
- lack of basic infrastructures (for delivery and exchange of goods and services).

For developing countries additional obstacles are:

- limited access to global markets;
- corruption;
- the burden of debt;
- the decline in Development Aid and sometimes inconsistencies in donor policies that also hinder faster progress;
- the blatant exclusion of the youth in the whole discourse.

Many of these obstacles are fundamental and pave the way for cyclic poverty. The Millennium Development Goals are still achievable if countries can:

- eliminate the majority of the fundamental causes (not just the manifestations) of poverty;
- spend efficiently—by avoiding waste and ensuring that the mechanisms for accountability are always in place;
- spend effectively—especially on those activities that are aimed at human social and economic development, rather than, say, for excessive military capacity and or on environmentally disastrous projects;
- spend wisely—not committing public resources to activities that can be best undertaken by private sector;
- spend within the country—rather exporting the country's wealth to foreign bank accounts, which can never be reclaimed by the country when the leader dies;
- groom new leadership.

The Report Cards

The results with charts are available and some countries have made some progress. Poverty reduction is indeed occurring in many nations except mainly for countries in sub-Saharan Africa. China, for example, has been able to reduce its 360 million number of poor in 1990 to about 210 million in 1998. Korea, Malaysia and Morocco are among the select countries that halved the proportion of their people living in poverty in less than a generation. The Indian states of Haryana, Kerala and Punjab have also halved the number of people living in poverty. About a dozen more countries—including Botswana and Mauritius—reduced poverty by a quarter or more in a generation. Mauritius also decided to cut its military budget and redirected most of the cut to health and education. Now, a Mauritian has access to sanitation and to 98 per cent safe water. In Mauritius, 97 per cent of the births are attended by skilled health staff. Many Latin American countries have also moved closer to achieving gender equality in education. These are but a few examples that show that the MDGs are achievable goals. Because these are well-documented experiences, other countries can learn much from them, for if it has been done once it can be done again. But note too that these are also examples of nations where basic infrastructures are in place to enable the achievement of these goals.

On the other hand, in countries such as Sudan conflicts are reversing the gains in social development. The spread of HIV/AIDS is also impoverishing individuals, families and communities in other parts of India, sub-Saharan Africa and elsewhere in the world. Sustained economic growth, an essential ingredient for long-term poverty reduction, still eludes about half of the world's nations. For over 30 nations of the world real per capita incomes have fallen over the past 35 years. Even when and where there is growth, it tends to remain in isolated communities.

For these goals to be achieved there is a need for not just hard work, but a rethinking of current directions.

The poor have little or no voice, so can hardly influence the social, political and economic milieu which may be persecuting them. They need stronger voices: they must be heard as they seek basic social services as well as economic stability and growth. Poor countries also need to be heard, as they demand more open markets for trade and technology for development as well as the promised resources from developed worlds that should enable development. For poor people and poor nations to be heard at least the basic information and communications technology (ICT) infrastructures must be in place. Laying ICT cables or wireless technology is not enough. A complete infrastructure must have the three "a"s –availability, affordability, and accessibility to all especially the youth.

Voices and Choices for Poor Countries and the Poor

Empowering poor nations and their people is the starting point. Developing countries especially those in sub-Saharan Africa need to be heard. They must participate in the global discourse and hence in globalization. Poor countries need the empowerment to be heard. They should have unrestricted access to open markets for trade, technology and ideas to guide their internal decisions and goals.

Poor Countries and Globalization

The growing importance of trade is depicted in Figure Fifteen. Trade has grown faster than global output for the past 40 years. The problem is that heavily protected economies and those dependent on commodity exports like the developing countries have lagged behind or suffered from price fluctuations. While more and more countries are beginning to recognize the advantage of open trade, which boosts their exports and increases their capacity to import, many are still too impoverished by old trade policies which do not give them an exit route.It is common knowledge that globalization will offer enormous opportunities to the developing countries because it inherently provides better ways of tapping the world's knowledge, better technology for delivering products and services and better access to the world's markets.

However, not all countries are enjoying the possible benefits of globalization, because many of the poor nations have a legacy of poor policies and poor performance. Some also have very poor governance. Some are entangled in corruption and bad government practices. Others invest their capital in buying military equipment—usually from the high income nations who should be discouraging such efforts. So far too many of the poor countries are being left behind in trade, finance, technology and ideas. These are precisely the things that could help them grow and reduce the cycle of poverty.

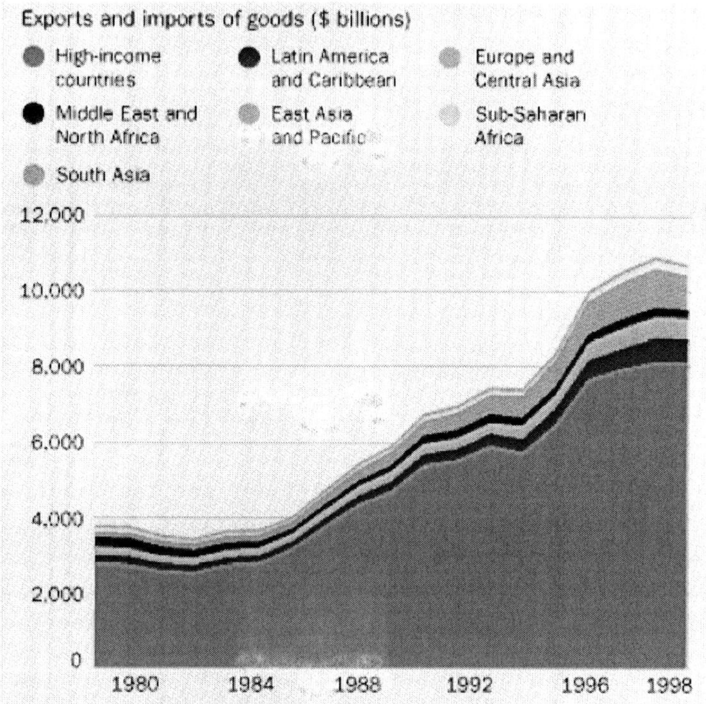

Figure Fifteen The growing importance of trade

Source: A Better World For All 2000.

On the other hand, the rich and developed countries have to lower their tariffs and other trade barriers such as unfair pricing of agricultural products from developing countries and subsidy for farmers in advanced countries. The high-income countries can also play other roles beyond reducing tariffs and other trade barriers to imports from developing countries. They can provide the much-needed assistance to build the capacity for the less developed countries to trade effectively.

These will help developing countries to streamline their systems for the flow of imports, exports and finance. Developing countries can also be in better positions for doing international trade and business by being strategically positioned to manage their inflation, interest and exchange rates. They can also learn to maintain consistent policies in order to be credible to both domestic and foreign investors. Therefore taking advantage of the opportunities provided by globalization requires action by both the rich countries that currently enjoy the benefits and attributes of globalization, and the poor countries who ironically do not, and perhaps do not even know what they are missing.

Empowering the Poor

Besides empowering poor nations, poor people also need to be empowered. Their empowerment comes in various forms, such as providing universal primary and perhaps even secondary education to the poor and providing opportunities for women. It has been documented that investing in education, especially girls' education, produces one of the highest payoffs in development. Part of this empowerment also means that developing countries have to deliver high-quality and cost-effective services to the poor—healthcare, water, sanitation and other basic services. Another part of this is ensuring action to reduce malnutrition, with a special focus on women of childbearing age and young children. Many developing countries have begun to lose the 'safety nets' that were in place for the vulnerable before the arrival of devastating diseases such as HIV/AIDS and other life crises. These social safety nets need to be restored, especially in times of crisis when the poor are most vulnerable.

Above all, the poor need to be empowered by opening political space for poor people to organize. Democratization is not just simple rule by the majority. It must include the poor and minorities in all aspects of political participation, from cabinets, legislatures and civil services to local governments. Such an inclusive democracy promotes an independent judiciary, an open civil society and a free media. An inclusive democracy can go a little beyond to ensure respect for human rights and make governments accountable for their promises and actions.

Who will represent the problems of the poor better than the poor—after they have been sensitized to alternative routes out of poverty? When the poor have been exposed enough, they will demand policies that go beyond the purely economic to ones that focus on the real needs of the poor. This is one way to ensure that the poor achieve at least minimum social standards and universal access to basic social services.

ICT—The Enabler

In today's world the best way to hear the voices of and provide choices for poor countries and poor people is through information and communications technology (ICT). Globalization has no meaning in the absence of ICT. For example, in today's world a trader in an East or West African country who needs to know the world price of a given good such as cocoa can do so with a cellular phone. So too can a trader in East and West Europe. These activities are all possible because the cost of telecommunications has plummeted in the past two decades. But for whom has it plummeted? It is ironic that the developing countries who can ill-afford high communications costs are those excluded from communication or limited in the way they can communicate by the sheer cost of the use of the technology.

A British-based communications group—RoadPost—for example, provides international cellular, satellite and Internet services. For what it calls its oneRoam

World Cell Subscription it divides the world into four major areas it calls zones. From Figure Sixteen, we can see that the zones are:

Zone 1—all the regions in green, plus a few select other countries;
Zone 2—mainly the regions in yellow, plus a few other countries;
Zone 3—all but a few of the countries in blue; and
Zone 4—mainly the regions in red.

Please see the appendix for exceptions to these color codings.

All the subscription costs are listed in US dollars:

Zone 1—the world basic price for airtime (both incoming and outgoing calls to anywhere in the world) isUS$1.49/minute;
Zone 2—the world basic price for airtime (both incoming and outgoing calls to anywhere in the world) isUS$2.99/minute;
Zone 3—the world basic price for airtime (both incoming and outgoing calls to anywhere in the world) isUS$4.49/minute;
Zone 4—the world basic price for airtime (both incoming and outgoing calls to anywhere in the world) isUS$5.99/minute.

Furthermore, globally the Internet offers e-mail, online training and infinity of resources on the Web. Again, these resources have become a reality for some,

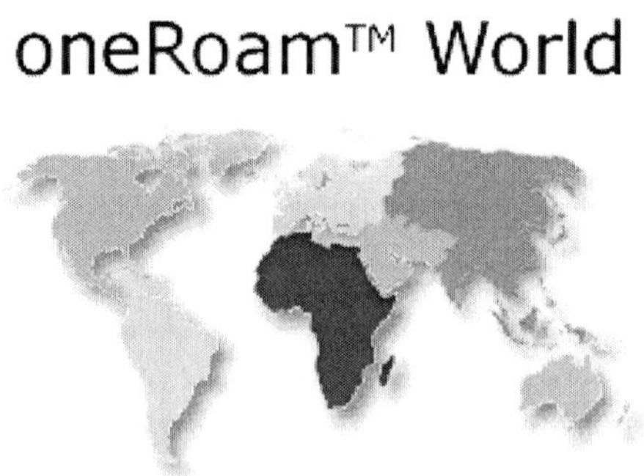

Figure Sixteen oneRoam World Cell Subscription zones

Source: RoadPost http://www.roadpost.com/cellular/subscription/world.asp.

especially those in the developed and rich nations. The sources of most of the research for this chapter came from almost free access to the web and the multitude of sources that this author can access freely from the Web. This virtually free access to Internet material is clearly not available in many developing countries.

For poor countries and poor nations to have a say in any of these factors, including pricing structures that are out of reach for those who can ill afford it, there has to be a way to make these services available and affordable. The international community therefore faces the major challenge of plugging in all of these groups: youth; all of civil society; all of developing country business; and all of the developing countries' governments and leadership into these networks that offer so much. If the international community is serious about the successful outcome of the MGMs, then they should push towards ICT access for all. Grasping such an opportunity will require huge overhauls of current telecommunications in these countries and/or major investments in telecommunications.

Once the cable (or cable-less) networks are in place, there should be a commitment towards bridging the digital divide so that the poorer and less developed countries can cross the divide. Figure Seventeen illustrates the distribution of personal computers per 1,000 population in the different regions of the world. Although the data only goes up to 1998, it is very revealing, because for the high-income countries there is a linear growth, while for the less developed countries the distribution of personal computers may rise and fall.

Capacity Building—College Students are the Missing Link

One of the major (perhaps unintended) outcomes of the international community developing the Millennium Development Goals is that it brings out existing global disparities very vividly. Also, the insufficient capacities in the developing and many poor countries to engage in programmes that could be slated for success become glaringly obvious. An attribute of the development goals that has resonated across the world is that they have also helped to focus global attention on the fight to eliminate abject poverty from the world.

Progress toward the Millennium Development Goals is measured by 48 quantitative indicators. Most of these 48 quantitative indicators are derivatives of national statistical systems. Furthermore, countries have set national goals that are not included in the MDGs. Moreover, effective statistical systems exist to monitor progress toward the goals. But even more profound is that they underpin development by providing the basis for rational decision-making, macro-economic management and the efficient allocation of scarce resources. Despite the greater demand for statistics, there is still a critical shortfall in national and international efforts to develop appropriate and sustainable statistical capacity. Again, these have led to the development of more meetings and more papers including a global action plan for statistics, which entails the preparation of national statistical

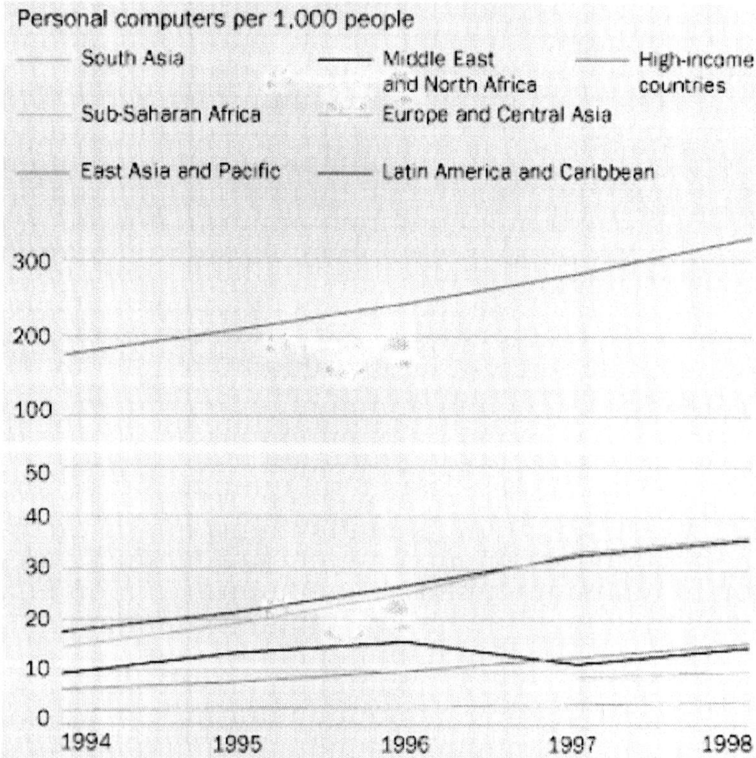

Figure Seventeen Closing the digital divide is essential for being competitive

Source: A Better World For All 2000.

development strategies for all low-income countries by 2006 and the urgent need for improvement in monitoring the MDGs by 2005. The World Bank's Statistical Capacity Building website has more information in this area. There are many more such programmes.

The 'missing link' in all of these efforts is the isolation of colleges and institutions of higher learning where the students are able and eager to participate. Even more potent is the fact that academia harbors future leaders both for the rich and for the very poor countries. The opinion of this author, then, is that there should be universal ICT availability and access for all enrolled college students in the developing countries. For students in the rich countries access to the Internet—e-mail, web and web servers—is a non-issue. Even elementary and high school students in rich countries have access not only to personal computers at home and at school, but also to the Internet.

Yet many college students in sub-Saharan African countries do not have access to the Internet. Either the computers are unavailable, or when they are available in the schools the networks are not working, or when the networks are working, there is no electricity, or when electricity is available it fluctuates, or when all of these are in place, the cost is exorbitant. Most African college students therefore do not have direct access to the Internet, either at home or at the colleges and universities where they obtain their degrees. This includes students who are studying Computer Science, MIS, IT and so forth. None of these or other students can afford e-mail even if they can go to cyber cafes.

Their potential cannot be realized unless they become immersed in the global discourse. Furthermore, these are the future leaders of the world in whose hands rest the future of the globe. For the MDGs to become successful, we must invest in college students in the developing nations, and we must do it now.

Note

1 To view the full United Nations document on Millennium Development Goals indicators' definitions, sources and methodology, go to http://www.developmentgoals.org/UNDG%20document_final.pdf.

References and Background Materials

Sachs, Jeffrey. "The End of Poverty", *Time Magazine* 165:11 (14 March 2005): 42.

http://www.developmentgoals.org/UNDG%20document_final.pdf.

http://www.paris21.org/betterworld/home.htm. "A Better World for All 2000".

http://www.un.org/millennium/.

www.worldbank.org.

www.undp.org.

www.un.org.

www.oecd.org.

Appendix

A complete listing of the goals, targets, and indicators for MDGs

Goals and targets		Indicators	
Goal 1	*Eradicate extreme poverty and hunger*		
	Target 1: Halve, between 1990 and 2015, the proportion of people whose income is less than US$1 a day below national poverty line)*	• 1	Proportion of population below US$1 (PPP) a day[a]
		• 1a	Poverty headcount ratio (percentage of population
		• 2	Poverty gap ratio (incidence × depth of poverty)
		• 3	Share of poorest quintile in national consumption
	Target 2: Halve, between 1990 and 2015, the proportion of people who suffer from hunger	• 4	Prevalence of underweight in children (under five years of age)
		• 5	Proportion of population below minimum level of dietary energy consumption
Goal 2	*Achieve universal primary education*		
	Target 3: Ensure that, by 2015, children everywhere, boys and girls alike, will be able to complete a full course of primary schooling	• 6	Net enrollment ratio in primary education
		• 7a	Proportion of pupils starting grade 1 who reach grade 5[b]
		• 7b	Primary completion rate*
		• 8	Literacy rate of 15 to 24-year-olds

Goals and targets		Indicators
Goal 3	*Promote gender equality and empower women* Target 4: Eliminate gender disparity in primary and secondary education preferably by 2005 and in all levels of education no later than 2015	• 9 Ratio of girls to boys in primary, secondary, and tertiary education • 10 Ratio of literate women to men ages 15–24 • 11 Share of women in wage employment in the nonagricultural sector • 12 Proportion of seats held by women in national parliament
Goal 4	*Reduce child mortality* Target 5: Reduce by two-thirds, between 1990 and 2015, the under-five mortality rate	• 13 Under-5 mortality rate • 14 Infant mortality rate • 15 Proportion of one-year-old children immunized against measles
Goal 5	*Improve maternal health* Target 6: Reduce by three-quarters, between 1990 and 2015, the maternal mortality ratio	• 16 Maternal mortality ratio • 17 Proportion of births attended by skilled health personnel

Goals and targets		Indicators
Goal 6	*Combat HIV/AIDS, malaria, and other diseases*	
	Target 7: Have halted by 2015 and begun to reverse the spread of HIV/AIDS	• 18 HIV prevalence among pregnant women ages 15–24
		• 19 Condom use rate of the contraceptive prevalence rate[c]*
		• 19a Condom use at last high-risk sex*
		• 19b Percentage of 15–24-year-olds with comprehensive correct knowledge of HIV/AIDS[d]*
		• 19c Contraceptive prevalence rate
		• 20 Ratio of school attendance of orphans to school attendance on non-orphans ages 10–14
	Target 8: Have halted by 2015 and begun to reverse the incidence of malaria and other major diseases	• 21 Prevalence and death rates associated with malaria
		• 22 Proportion of population in malaria-risk areas using effective malaria prevention and treatment measures[e]
		• 23 Prevalence and death rates associated with tuberculosis
		• 24 Proportion of tuberculosis cases detected and cured under directly observed treatment short course (DOTS)

Goals a nd targets		Indicators
Goal 7	*Ensure environmental sustainability*	
	Target 9: Integrate the principles of sustainable development into country policies and program and reverse the loss of environmental resources	• 25 Proportion of land area covered by forest • 26 Ratio of area protected to maintain biological diversity to surface area • 27 Energy use (kilograms of oil equivalent) per USS1 GDP (PPP) • 28 Carbon dioxide emissions (per capita) and consumption of ozone-depleting chlorofluorocarbons (ODP tons) • 29 Proportion of population using solid fuels*
	Target 10: Halve, by 2015, the proportion of people without sustainable access to safe drinking water and basic sanitation	• 30 Proportion of population with sustainable access to an improved water source, urban and rural • 31 Proportion of population with access to improved sanitation, urban and rural
	Target 11: Have achieved, by 2020, a significant improvement in the lives of at least 100 million slum dwellers	• 32 Proportion of households with with access to secure tenure

Goals a nd targets		Indicators
Goal 8	*Develop a global partnership for development* Target 12: Develop further an open, rule-based, predictable, nondiscriminatory trading and financial system (includes a commitment to good governance, development, and poverty reduction—both nationally and internationally)	Some of the indicators listed below will be monitored separately for the least developed countries, Africa, landlocked countries, and small island developing states Official development assistance • 33 Net ODA total and to the least developed countries, as a percentage of OECD/DAC donors' gross national income
	Target 13: Address the special needs of the least developed countries (includes tariff-and quota-free access for exports enhanced program of debt relief for HIPC and cancellation of official bilateral debt, and more generous ODA for countries committed to poverty reduction	• 34 Proportion of bilateral, sector-allocable ODA of OECD/DAC donors for basic social services (basic education, primary health care, nutrition, safe water, and sanitation) • 35 Proportion of bilateral official development assistance ODA of OECD/DAC donors that is untied • 36 ODA received in landlocked countries as proportion of their gross national incomes • 37 ODA received in small island developing states as proportion of their gross national incomes

Goals a nd targets	Indicators
Goal 8 cont'd	
	Market access
Target 14: Address the special needs of landlocked countries and small island developing states (through the Program of Action for the Sustainable Development of Small Island Developing States and 22nd General Assembly provisions)	• 38 Proportion of total developed country imports (by value and excluding arms) from developing countries and from least developedcountries, admitted free of duty • 39 Average tariffs imposed by developed countries on agricultural products and textiles and clothing from developing countries • 40 Agricultural support estimate for OECD countries as a percentage of their gross domestic product • 41 Proportion of ODA provided to help build trade capacity
	Debt sustainability
Target 15: Deal comprehensively with the debt problems of developing countries through national and international measures in order to make debt sustainable in the long term	• 42 Total number of countries that have reached their HIPC decision points and number that have reached their HIPC completion points (cumulative) • 43 Debt relief committed under HIPC initiative • 44 Debt service as a percentage of exports of goods and services

Goals a nd targets	Indicators
Goal 8 cont'd	Other
Target 16: In cooperation with developing countries, develop and implement strategies for decent and productive work for youth	• 45 Unemployment rate of 15- to 24-year-olds, male and female and total[f]
Target 17: In cooperation with pharmaceutical companies, provide access to affordable, essential drugs in developing countries	• 46 Proportion of population with access to affordable, essential drugs on a sustainable basis
Target 18: In cooperation with the private sector, make available the benefits of new technologies, especially information and communications	• 47 Telephone lines and cellular subscribers per 100 population • 48a Personal computers in use per 100 population • 48b Internet users per 100 population

Notes

* These indicators are proposed as additional MDG indicators, but have not yet been adopted.

[a] For monitoring country poverty trends, indicators based on national poverty lines should be used, where available.

[b] An alternative indicator under development is "primary completion rate."

[c] Among contraceptive methods, only condoms are effective in preventing HIV transmission. Since the condom use rate is only measured among women in union, it is supplemented by an indicator on condom use in high-risk situations (indicator 19a) and an indicator on HIV/AIDS knowledge (indicator 19b). Indicator 19c (contraceptive prevalence rate) is also useful in tracking progress in other health, gender, and poverty goals.

[d] This indicator is defined as the percentage of 15- to 24-year-olds who correctly identify the two major ways of preventing the sexual transmission of HIV (using condoms and limiting sex to one faithful, uninfected partner), who reject the two most common local misconceptions about HIV transmission, and who know that a healthy-looking person can transmit HIV. However, since there are currently not a sufficient number of surveys to be able to calculate the indicator as defined above, UNICEF, in collaboration with UNAIDS and WHO, produced two proxy indicators that represent two components of the actual indicator. They are the percentage of women and men ages 15–24 who know that a person can protect herself from HIV infection by "consistent use of condom," and the percentage of women and men ages 15–24 who know a healthy-looking person can transmit HIV.

[e] Prevention to be measured by the percentage of children under age five sleeping under insecticide-treated bednets; treatment to be measured by percentage of children under age five who are appropriately treated.

[f] An improved measure of the target for future years is under development by the International Labour Organization.

Chapter Six

ICTs, Universities, and Development: Toward eQuality

Maria A. Beebe*

Introduction

This chapter is about ICTs, universities and development. I will start with an overview of sustainable development and a quick summary of the Millennium Development Goals (MDG) for 2015. Then I will discuss the leadership role of African universities as they are called upon to contribute to sustainable development. After briefly defining ICTs, I will summarize some of the trends with regard to ICTs and African universities. Using NetTel as a case study, I will highlight the possibilities of using ICTs to develop the capacity of African universities to strengthen ICT/telecommunications policy and regulation in order to improve access to ICTs and utilize ICTs for development. Finally, I will challenge the reader to use the human and social capital found in US universities to develop strategic US and African partnerships that build on each other's comparative advantage and that contribute toward eQuality in order to contribute to achievement of the millennium development goals. What is envisioned is engagement between African and American universities—away from a one-way process wherein one transfers its expertise to the other, toward *commitment to sharing and reciprocity*; where partnerships are two-way streets defined by mutual respect among the partners for what each brings to the table.

Sustainable Development

Leaders concerned about sustainable development suggest that our ability to meet the needs of the future depends on how well we balance social, economic, and environmental objectives—or needs—when making decisions today. Sustainable development encompasses economic equity, social progress, and environmental protection (see Figure Eighteen). In part to integrate sustainable development principles into national policies and programmes, Millennium Development Goals (MDG) for 2015 were set by the member states of the United Nations.

The MDG targets for increasing economic equity are: to reduce by one-half the proportion of people living on less than a dollar a day, and to reduce by one-half the

---

* Center to Bridge the Digital Divide, WSU.

Social Progress
Goal 2: To achieve universal primary education for both girls and boys Goal 3: To eliminate gender disparity in primary and secondary education, preferably by 2005, and at all levels by 2015 Goal 4: To reduce child mortality (reduce by two thirds mortality rates of children under 5) Goal 5: To improve maternal health (reduce by half the maternal mortality ratio) Goal 6: To win the fight against HIV/AIDS, malaria and other diseases

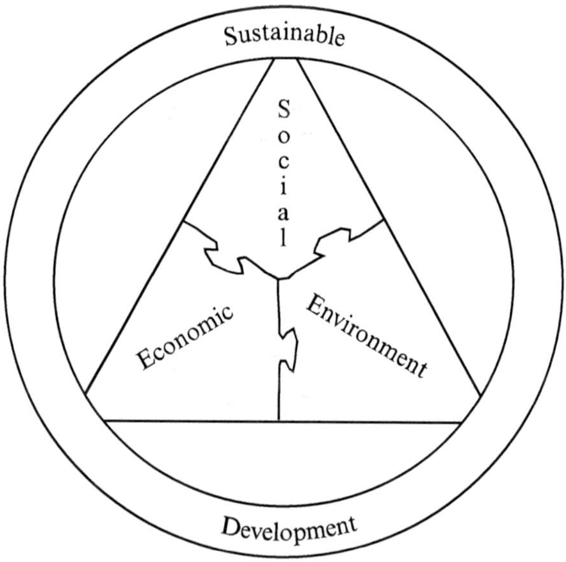

Economic equity Goal 1: To eradicate extreme poverty and hunger	**Environment** Goal 7: To ensure environmental sustainability
Goal 8: To develop a global partnership for development	

Figure Eighteen Millenium Development Goal

Source: adapted from http://worldbank.org/depweb/sustain.htm, proportion of people who suffer from hunger. For social issues, the MDG targets are: in education, to achieve universal primary education for both girls and boys and to eliminate gender disparity in primary and secondary education, preferably by 2005, and at all levels by 2015; and for health, to reduce child mortality, improve maternal health, and win the fight against HIV/AIDS, malaria and other diseases. For environmental sustainability, the MDG targets include integration of the principles of sustainable development and reversal of the loss of environmental resources, as well as sustainable access to safe drinking water and basic sanitation by reducing by one-half the proportion of people without sustainable access to safe drinking water and by achieving significant improvements in the lives of slum dwellers.

Achievement of the MDG requires national ownership by governments as demonstrated by policy and regulatory responses to structural constraints, by the willingness of the private sector to invest in basic infrastructure, and by the engagement and resourcefulness of local communities coupled with the development of global partnerships for development. Equally important are policy changes in rich countries, such as open market access, open access to technology, debt relief, more effective aid, and follow-through on commitments that are necessary to sustain development.

Stated as an eighth goal is the intention 'to develop a global partnership for development' that primarily speaks to developed countries with regard to tariffs and quota-free access to exports from developing countries, debt relief, and measures to make debt sustainable. The eighth goal also suggests areas of cooperation with regard to decent and productive work for youth, affordable essential drugs in cooperation with pharmaceutical companies, and making available the benefits of new technologies, especially information and communication technologies (ICTs), in cooperation with the private sector. ICTs not only facilitate by electronic means the creation, storage, management and dissemination of information, but also offer a range of communication and knowledge applications. ICTs as enablers of development are being mainstreamed into national, regional (as in the case of the New Partnership for Africa's Development [NEPAD], particularly its e-Africa commission), and global development strategies. The challenge is figuring out how to better utilize ICTs to meet MDG for economic growth, social progress and environmental protection, and how to nurture the leadership role of universities in the US and in Africa toward realizing the promise of ICTs for sustainable development.

Universities and Sustainable Development

The fundamental mission of universities is in teaching, research and service. Mazrui (2003) emphasizes the symbiotic relationship between a sustainable university and a society with the will to maintain sustainable development.

Universities are now expected to contribute to society by widening access to higher education, continuing professional development, supporting applied research, contributing to local economic impact, and improving social inclusion. Higher education institutions can play a leadership role to develop capacity to manage sustainable development. The International Association of Universities (IAU) calls on universities to develop and build bilateral, regional and international networks or partnerships in research, courseware, development of information services, and ICT expertise.

African universities, like universities elsewhere, are being challenged to contribute to social and economic equity while protecting the environment; to deliver an expanding array of programmes to a diverse set of students and other clients, while coping with very real resource constraints; and to address internationalization, transnational education, and trade in education services.

The critical role of African universities in research, evaluation, information transfer, and technology development to national social progress and economic growth has been recognized by African leaders, more recently by the New Partnership for Africa's Development (NEPAD). The March 2003 COREVIP of the African Association of Universities (AAU) discussed the role of African higher education institutions as partners in development. Although most African universities embrace the concept, there needs to be greater clarity as to what an African perspective to development should be. This development perspective should accomplish two things: inform national development policies and priorities, and give guidance toward a development orientation in the teaching/learning, research and service programmes of universities (Ekong, 1996). However, several challenges need to be overcome, including: (a) governance with regard to linkages with external stakeholders, especially financial dependence on governments and internal management of the institution (Ekong, 1996); and (b) dependence on knowledge and knowledge application processes from elsewhere, which Mazrui links to the rise and fall of intellectualism. Mazrui (2003) suggests that the rise and fall of intellectualism in universities is related to independence or dependence on government, along with striking a balance between cultural closeness with the society in which the university is embedded and with the wider world of scholarship and science. The challenge, according to Fraser-Moleketi (2003), is twofold: "How do we understand the particularity of 'African' without losing sense of universal/widely shared knowledge, experience and history", and how to factor in sufficient distinction and diversity within the concept of "African". Thus, Mazrui (2003) recommends the notion of re-Africanizing the African university through three strategies:

- adapting the university teaching curriculum, research and service more firmly to local linguistic, cultural and economic needs;
- diversifying educational and cultural links not just with the west, but also with the rest of African cultures, as well as with Indian, Chinese and Islamic civilizations and languages; and

- recognizing that Africans must be not just receivers of knowledge, but also givers of knowledge.

These strategies must be viewed in relation to the explosive developments in science and information and communication technologies (ICTs).

IT, ICTs: What Are They?

But first, let us examine a short description of information communication technologies (ICTs). As currently used, ICT is a shorthand to denote a wide range of services (telephone, mobile telephone, fax, e-mail, SMS, FTP) applications (teleworking, distance learning, videoconferencing) and technologies (old technologies, such as radio and television and new technologies, including fixed and mobile wireless communication). These array of equipment and software, linked by telecommunication's networks allow people to access, analyse, create, exchange and use data, information and knowledge in ways that, until recently, were almost unimaginable. The term *ICT* is used almost interchangeably with *the Internet*. The Internet and its applications (the most well known being the World Wide Web) is a shorthand for the infrastructure that brings together people, in different places and time zones, with multimedia tools for data, information, and knowledge management in order to expand the range of human capabilities. With convergence, all communication devices will compute and all computing devices will communicate (Figure Nineteen). Such a diverse set of technologies offers a challenge and an opportunity for us to 'think outside the box', as ICTs could be considered both as an economic sector by itself and as an enabler for growth, development, innovation, competitiveness and cooperation.

ICTs and African Universities

The Association of African Universities (AAU), along with the World Bank, acknowledges in *Revitalizing Universities in Africa* (1997) a 'declining quality of university education' as a result of resources dwindling while enrolments are growing. Yet there are positive signs, as most African institutions have started to implement plans to ensure sound institutional management, transparent and accountable governance, a thriving intellectual environment, a modicum of ICTs facilities for faculty members and students, and above all, effective leadership. Universities have started to develop institutional strategic plans with stakeholder involvement. Increasingly their strategic plans are being used to renegotiate relationships with government. Universities are starting to build capacity for teaching and research at an international standard in one or more academic areas crucial for their country's economic or social advancement, foster and reward research, develop

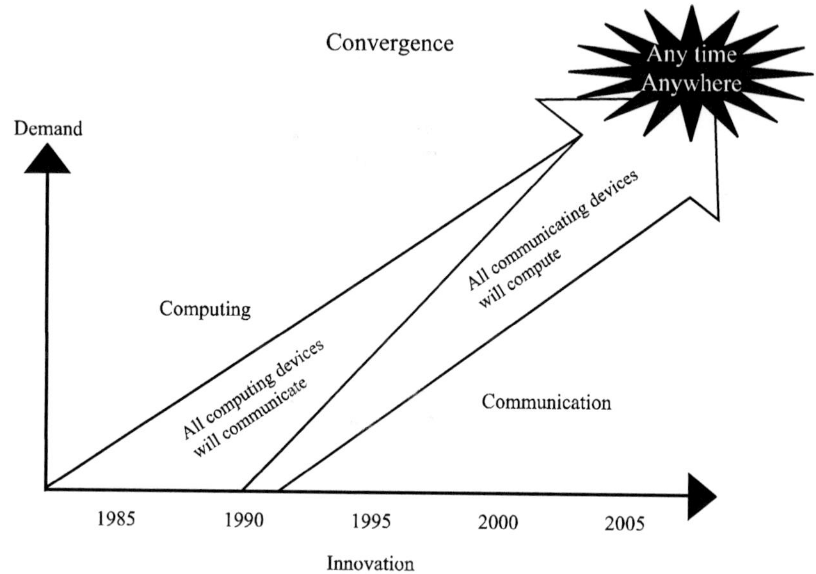

Figure Nineteen Convergence of ICTs

management information systems, and devise management training courses for all university managers.

This developoment is reflected in an emerging literature. *AfricaDotEdu: IT Opportunities and Higher Education in Africa* (Beebe, 2003) highlights the challenges faced by African universities as they begin to realize the promise of ICTs. Part 1 looks at the evolution of the Internet in Africa, the institutional policies that contribute to the development of the Internet, and the relationships among higher education, economic growth, and IT. Part 2 looks at regional initiatives, such as the African Virtual University, African digital libraries, community learning centers, distance learning, open content, institutional policies, and eLearning. Another set of studies examines the use of IT that is not specific to the functions of higher education institutions but has implications for developing new curriculum in higher education institutions—for example, e-commerce and e-government (Moloketi, 2003). Another useful resource produced by the Bandwidth Task Force Secretariat, University of Dar es Salaam, is *ICTs for Teaching, Learning and Research—A Workshop for African Universities: Securing the Linchpin* (2002).

The evidence is that ICTs are being reflected in university strategic plans and institutional guidelines. More and more African universities are seeing the benefits of adding "e" to "learning". Universities like Eduardo Mondlane University (Mozambique), Makerere University (Uganda), Obafemi Awolowo University

(Nigeria), and University of Dar es Salaam (Tanzania) have ICTs institutional guidelines that are aligned to their university strategic plans.

The use of ICTs for university management of financial, personnel and educational resources is exemplified by the University of Pretoria's Client Services Centre. The Client Services Centre includes the following services: all general inquiries regarding University of Pretoria, residence, applications, payments, study financing, student accounts, student and personnel cards, parking discs, course consultation, and a computer laboratory for all registered students to access the Virtual Campus. Another example is the University of Western Cape's integrated information strategy.

Increasingly, library services are being digitized and viewed as a critical part of Africa's development. Mbambo (2003) defines a digital library as containing the following attributes: service to a specified community, digitally presented data, organized structure or organization, efficient information provision services, efficient control of resources, and collections which can include objects as well as texts. Furthermore, Mbambo (2003) envisions making African scholarship available through digital libraries.

During the last 10 years, distance learning, also known as open learning, has moved from a peripheral form of educational delivery to 'one that is a central pillar in many countries' and institutions' educational plans' (ADEA, 2002). Rumajogee (2003) summarizes four generations of distance learning, the first being correspondence courses, with behaviorist views on teaching, lack of contact, and summative evaluation. The second is multimedia, which still relies on print, integrates broadcast media (radio and television) and closed-circuit audiovisual materials (audio and video cassettes), some face-to-face tutorials, telephone counseling and, to some degree, use of computer software. The third generation, relies on audio and video conferencing to ensure greater interactivity, but deprives learners of the flexibility of time, place and pace. The fourth generation distance learning institution relies on the Internet and encourages the elaboration of multidisciplinary knowledge (see Box Three).

New forms of collaboration are starting to emerge among higher education institutions in Africa. Despite less than perfect access to ICTs, African higher education institutions are embracing learning networks to respond to the challenges posed by a rapidly changing and increasingly interdependent world. Despite the tremendous policy, infrastructure, and human resources constraints, learning networks in African higher education and training sectors are similar to those being set up elsewhere (see Box Four).

E-mail has made it easier for African researchers to share information, communicate, and exchange knowledge with each other and with colleagues outside Africa. ICTs, including tools for collaboration, have made it easier to share datasets, publish weblogs, and get prompt feedback and reviews from peers. This access to new research tools and communication systems is already showing an impact on the substance of research.

Box Three: Distance education in Africa

Saint (1999) notes that:

1. Botswana, Cameroon, and Zambia are using a university-based Internet system to support interactive regional study centers for distance learners.
2. Tanzania, Botswana, and Zimbabwe have established new tertiary institutions wholly dedicated to distance education. The Zimbabwe Open University already enrolls nearly 10,000 students in nine programmes and recently launched a master's degree in education for in-service teachers.
3. Côte d'Ivoire, Congo, Togo, and Benin are in various stages of setting up university-based distance education programmes.
4. Nigeria's Centre for Distance Learning (Abuja) offers B.A. and B.S. degrees in 14 subject areas.
5. Madagascar has pioneered the use of audiocassettes for university programmes in law and the social sciences.
6. In Senegal, distance education supports teacher training and Master's degree programmes in health and law.
7. The Confederation of Open Learning Institutions in South Africa (COLISA), led by the University of South Africa (UNISA), is developing Internet-based courseware, a web-based student-teacher interaction system, and a series of local Internet access points for students.

Earlier we envisioned engagement between African and American networks; away from a one-way process in which one transfers its expertise to the other, toward *commitment to sharing and reciprocity*; where partnerships are two-way streets defined by mutual respect among the partners for what each brings to the table. Knowledge exchanges and learning partnerships must be fundamentally different from traditional technical assistance projects, in which benefit flows are perceived as being largely one-way. Instead, the principles of development cooperation must apply, with all partners sharing and benefiting from the relationship, increasing the likelihood of sustainability over time.

The concept calls for networking higher education institutions through reciprocity or partnership agreements. Agreements may cover a variety of activities and collaborative mechanisms, such as content sharing, shared delivery via eLearning, collaborative research, and outreach. Inherent in the above are collegial peer relationships among partners, with each recognizing and respecting the strengths and contributions of the others.

It is important to underscore that institutions must be willing to participate to bring about a desired development objective: to increase the leadership role of universities in sustainable development by sharing ideas, committing time and

Box Four: Transnational collaboration and Africa

Beebe (2003) notes the following forms of transnational collaboration that are starting to emerge in Africa:

1 Establishing remote campus branches away from the main institution to provide educational programmes to students from other countries. For example, Monash University in Australia has campuses in South Africa and in Malaysia.
2 Twinning or partnership agreements between institutions in different countries to offer joint programmes that involve reciprocal agreements or articulation of credits between institutions. For example, the Réseau Africain de Formation à Distance (RESAFAD) programme delivers teacher-training courses from France in conjunction with universities in Benin, Burkina Faso, Guinea, Mali and Togo.
3 Education business partnerships. Cisco, in partnership with African universities and donor programmes, such as the United Nations Development Programme (UNDP) and the Leland Initiative of USAID, has established several Regional Networking Academies in Africa—Central African Republic, Chad, Côte d'Ivoire, Congo, Ghana, Kenya, Mali, Malawi, Mozambique, Namibia, Niger, Nigeria, Rwanda, Senegal, South Africa, Togo, and Uganda.

resources, making decisions, and taking action. A necessary condition is an overall plan by institutions to ensure sound institutional management, transparent and accountable governance, a thriving intellectual environment, a modicum of facilities for faculty members and students, and above all, effective leadership.

Since capacity enhancement involves individuals who make up institutions that shape the institutional environment, partnerships or networks must involve all stakeholders; for example, in NetTel@Africa policy makers, regulators, operators, NGOs, and academics from 20 countries in Africa and the US form the network. The network partners abide by the following principles of networking: local leadership; global engagement; mutual benefit—interdependent networking; shared objectives; and mutual respect for one another.

NetTel@Africa: A Case Study

NetTel@Africa is the network for capacity building and knowledge exchange in ICTs and telecommunications policy, regulation and applications. The overall goal of NetTel is to make the provision of ICTs and telecom services more accessible and more affordable.

NetTel came about as a response to a request for training and capacity building made by the Telecommunications Regulators Association of Southern Africa (TRASA). Since most of the regulators at that time came from an engineering background, the request was for engineers to understand the need for policy and regulation, for policy makers to understand the technical aspects of what they are making policy about and what they are regulating, and for both engineers and policy makers to understand the financial implications of their policy decisions and technology choices. In addition to the interdisciplinary requirements, two options on who would provide the training were considered: option 1, buy the training from the US; option 2, build capacity in the region to provide a more sustained capacity-building programme in the region. The first is a short-term view and the second a longer-term view. TRASA chose the second option—go for the longer-term, more sustainable option. So through a participatory process, the network came about: The regulators and practitioners in the field identified the knowledge requirements for a good regulator; the academics from Botswana, Kenya, South Africa, Tanzania, and Zambia were invited to design an interdisciplinary curriculum on ICTs policy, regulation and applications; and US academics and regulators played a supportive role as peers. And because neither the African nor the US universities had a full curriculum on ICTs/telecoms policy and regulation, it became necessary to combine forces and work toward a common curriculum. With an initial eight African academic and training institutions, four US resource partners, and regulatory bodies and associations, it was necessary to have multiple leaders and coordinators. University of Dar es Salaam was tasked to be the academic coordinator, and the Center to Bridge the Digital Divide at Washington State University was tasked by the key donor agency—USAID—to act on its behalf as the executing agency.

Because the key players are distributed across Africa and the US, the use of ICTs is central to our work and central to the teaching/learning environment. We use KEWL, an online learning management system developed by one of the network partners, the University of Western Cape. KEWL is based on open source principles, and there is a spin-off initiative called AVOIR with regard to building capacity in software development. With a combination of using CDs for static content, logging on for discussion forums, and having face-to-face discussions among those who are in the same location, we identify what we are doing as eLearning, defined as the effective teaching and learning process created by combining digital content with local community and tutor support along with global community engagement.

NetTel has a coordinated quality assurance process which is African-led—academics, with a supportive role by US academics and by practitioners/experts from Africa and US who assisted with identifying knowledge requirements, pilot testing of materials, peer review of materials, and participating as online guest experts and mentors.

The first semester of courses was held during February-July 2004, with the second semester held during August-December 2004. What are noteworthy are the changes that are occurring at the institutional level, as these transformative changes represent one level of impact (see Table Thirteen below). Collaboration rather than competition among the university partners has become the priority. Partner universities have become co-developers of content rather than mere users of content developed elsewhere (old syllabi have been replaced and new material developed with links to digital resources). Delivery is across national borders and across time zones. Instead of knowledge being hoarded, it is shared, and the paradigm shift from a traditional to a restructured educational setting is starting to manifest itself. A second level of impact analysis during the next six months is expected to verify that institutional changes that are happening are reflective of the following principles of good teaching and learning practice: encouraging contacts between students and faculty, developing reciprocity and cooperation among students, using active learning techniques, giving prompt feedback, emphasizing time on task, communicating high expectations, and respecting diverse talents and ways of learning. NetTel@Africa will continue to pay close attention to quality on the line benchmarks, including institutional support, curriculum and instruction (course development, teaching/learning, course structure), student support, faculty support and evaluation, and assessment benchmarks.

Table Thirteen Institutional changes that had to happen within institutions to make NetTel@Africa possible—these changes may be transformative in scope

Area	From	To
Business approach	Competitive	Cooperative
Content	User	Developer
Delivery	Within institution	Across borders
Educational processes	Discipline specific	Multidisciplinary
Focus	Internal processes	Collaborative processes
Flexibility	Restrictive	Flexible
IT System	Defined by producer inflexible	Defined by user, adaptable
Knowledge attitudes	Hoarding	Sharing
Learning	Confined	Open
Pedagogy	Teacher-centered	Learner-centered
Perspective	Narrow	Broad
View of other institutions	Suspicion	Trust
Quality control	Internal	Shared

Source: Keats and Beebe, 2004.

The ultimate impact of interest to NetTel is improved educational outcomes. Based on Kirkpatrick's four-level model of evaluation (1994), the notion is to monitor not only reactions, new learnings or behavioral changes but also results that are aligned to improvements in ICTs/telecommunications policy, improvements in investments in the sector, and improvements in the performance in the sector.

From the students who participated in the Semester 1 courses, reactions are generally favorable about the eLearning experience, the quality of the content, the delivery platform, and the *perceived* value and transferability to the workplace. The lecturers and the students are in agreement about the need to improve interaction with one another through setting clear standards for prompt feedback, emphasizing time on tasks, respecting deadlines, using the discussion forums more productively, and e-mailing lecturers when learning materials or exercises are not clear. Overall the experience has been positive.

One of the early results since the roll-out of the first set of courses this year is that the "students" who are practitioners or regulators are seeing the benefits of the use of ICTs for their own capacity building and experiencing the frustrations of low bandwidth and the cost of dial-up or telecentres, a situation which they as ICTs and telecoms regulators can correct.

Why Focus on ICTs/Telecommunications Policy and Regulation?

Prior to the mid-1990s, telecommunications in Africa were primarily state-owned monopolies. They were usually undercapitalized and the penetration of service was very low, while prices for long-distance service and highly subsidized local calls were overpriced. In the mid-1990s the terrible performance of state-owned providers combined with internal pressures for political change and restructuring and external pressures from international donors made it necessary to launch telecommunications sector reforms.

Despite the initial reluctance to liberalize telecommunications services, some African countries introduced some important regulatory changes. In general, telecommunications was split from postal services. In some cases, along with the privatization of the state-owned monopoly provider, competition was introduced and an independent regulatory body created. At the same time, many African countries opened the market to cellular entrants. Along with the decrease in the cost of wireless technology and pent-up demand for services, a rapid expansion of mobile subscribers followed. As a result, there were more wireless subscribers than wireline subscribers in the region by 2001.

In doing a regression analysis (based on a sample of 14 African countries and 16 Latin American countries), Wallsten (1997: 1) suggests positive relationships between (a) "competition—measured by mobile operators not owned by the incumbent" and "increases in the per capita number of main lines, payphones, and connection capacity, and ... decreases in the price of local calls" and (b) "privatization combined with an independent regulator' and 'telecom performance measures". However, privatization by itself is associated with few benefits, and shows a negative relationship with main line penetration (Wallsten, 1997: 12–13).

While policy is important, additional conditions necessary for regulation to be effective, as noted by Smith and Wellenius (1999: 3–4), include broader country governance, strong administrative traditions and substantial professional cadres capable of handling complex regulatory concepts and processes. To be effective, regulators must have adequate *de facto* authority, including support from key stakeholders.

To summarize: one result is strengthened institutional capacity of academic institutions to do telecommunications research, develop IT curriculum, and use IT for teaching and learning; another result is strengthened capacity of regulatory and policy bodies. Enhancing the capacity of regulatory bodies and key players in the sector is expected to give the longer-term results of improved investment climate, improved delivery of ICTs and telecommunications services to the public, and improved consumer satisfaction. Ultimately we expect that increased accessibility and affordability will contribute to sustainable development, as in increased access to better education.

Challenges: ICTS in Africa

To a large extent the challenges that are facing NetTel mirror the broader challenges related to ICTs in Africa.

The Cooperative Association for Internet Data Analysis (CAIDA) compared five demographic measures (country area, population, GDP, number of telephone lines, number of Internet Service Providers [ISPs]) against three measures of Internet resources (number of Autonomous Systems [ASes], address prefixes, announced address space), stratified by continent with substratification by country (http://www.caida.org, 2002). Their findings indicate that the United States, with only 7 per cent of the population, dominates the allocation of Internet address space. North America and Europe combined contain over 80 percent of the ASes and nearly 75 per cent of the ISPs. Asia, Africa and South America, with more than 75 per cent of the world's population, use only slightly more than 10 per cent of Internet resources.

When compared with the rest of the world, access to basic telecommunications infrastructures, and hence to the Internet, for Africans is bleak. Factors that have isolated Africa from international networking are well documented (Saint, 2001). These interrelated factors include:

1 policies and regulatory frameworks on telecommunications and other related sectors that constrain infrastructure development;

2 infrastructure development that is at the world's lowest level. For example, only 2 per cent of world telephone lines are in Africa and there were more cellular telephones in Thailand at the beginning of 2002 than in the whole of Africa;
3 lack of human capacity for economic and social growth, specifically scarcity of African specialists in telecommunications.

Policies that are related to ICTs take-off are interrelated and should be reviewed and revised as cross-cutting issues. These policies include: a favourable entrepreneurial environment for local or foreign owned computer vendors, assembly plants, software manufacturers, and technical support specialists; physical infrastructure, including master infrastructure development for electricity, solar, phone lines, and security; telecommunications policies, including liberalization, universal service funds from licensing fees and e-rate (discounted rate for schools and libraries); and trade policies for procuring equipment, including reducing red tape and import taxes for procuring equipment for local computer assembly plant(s).

The International Internet bandwidth (http://www.telegeography.com) that shows the narrow bandwidth that Africans have to work with is shown in Figure Twenty. Intra-African connectivity to the rest of the world http://www.comet.columbia.edu/~nemo/netmap/ (Semret, 1998) indicating the need for intra-regional connectivity is shown in Figure Twenty-one.

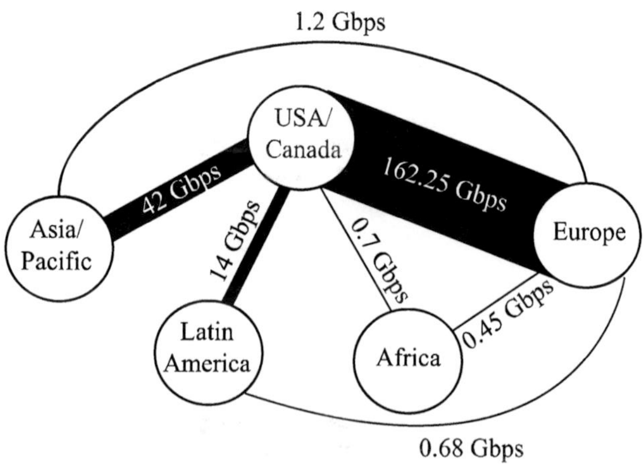

Figure Twenty **International Internet bandwidth**

Note: Gbps = gigabits (1,000 Mb) per second.

Source: TeleGeography, www. telegeography.com.

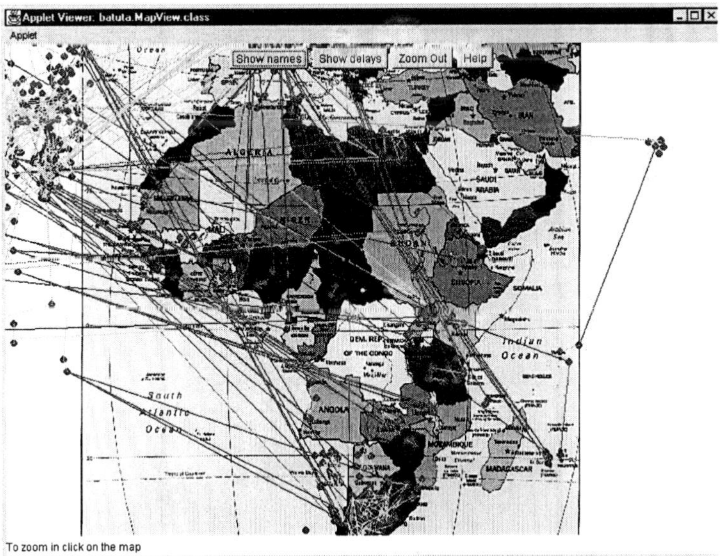

Figure Twenty-one African connectivity to the rest of the world

Finally, the areas for capacity enhancement include those that are related to the policy required for ICTs to take-off. These are:

- infrastructure development, bandwidth management;
- software and open source development;
- content development;
- policy research;
- intersect between telecoms policy and education and training policy, such as implications of universal service obligations on eEducation policy.

6 Opportunities for US Universities: Toward eQuality

> We must be the change we wish to see in the world.
>
> Mahatma Gandhi

As stated earlier, the eighth MDG is to develop a global partnership for development. A specific target is making available the benefits of ICTs, in cooperation with the private sector, and, I might add, the not-for-profit academic sector. The challenges with regard to policies, infrastructure and capacity building seem daunting. An added challenge is discerning how to better utilize ICTs to meet MDG for economic growth, social progress and environmental protection; and, how to nurture the leadership role of universities in the US and in Africa toward realizing the promise of ICTs for sustainable development.

How do we ensure e-quality not just for Americans but also for Africans? American universities represent a tremendous source of human and social capital. In the spirit of *Ubuntu* ("I am because we are"), we can put our collective strengths together to address the millennium development goals in collaboration with African universities. We must do so consistent with Mazrui's recommendations. As Americans we must not just be givers of knowledge, but also receivers of knowledge from our African colleagues. Engagement with our African colleagues must be reciprocal, defined by mutual respect for what each brings to the table.

Bibliography

Association of African Universities (AAU). "Draft Strategic Plan" (Accra: AAU, 2002).

Association pour le Development et L'Education en Afrique (ADEA).) "Distance Education and Open Learning in Sub-Saharan Africa: A Literature Survey on Policy and Practice Association for the Development of Education in Africa." ADEA (April, 2002).

Association of African Universities (AAU). "Revitalizing Universities in Africa: Strategies for the 21st Century: Final report" (Arusha: COREVIP '99, 1999).

Bandwidth Task Force Secretariat, University of Dar es Salaam. *Securing the Linchpin: More Bandwidth at Lower Cost: An Investigation for the Partnership for Higher Education in Africa* (New York, NY: Partnership for Higher Education in Africa, 2004).

Beebe, M. "Partnerships, Alliances and Networks for E-Learning", in *AfricaDotEdu: IT Opportunities and Higher Education in Africa*, ed. Maria A Beebe, Kouakou Koffi Magloire, Banji Oyeyinka and Madanmohan Rao (New Delhi: Tata McGraw-Hill Publishing Company, Ltd., 2003): 69–89.

Ekong, D. "The Future of Universities from an African Perspective." Paper presented at the Symposium on The Future of Universities, 5 December 1996, Santiago, Chile (1996).

Jensen, M. (2003) "The Evolution of the Internet in Africa", in *AfricaDotEdu: IT Opportunities and Higher Education in Africa*, ed. Maria A Beebe, Kouakou Koffi Magloire, Banji Oyeyinka and Madanmohan Rao (New Delhi: Tata McGraw-Hill Publishing Company, Ltd., 2003): 43–68.

Keats, D.W. and Maria Beebe. "Addressing Digital Divide Issues in a Partially Online Masters Programme in Africa: the NetTel@Africa Experience", ICALT 2004 Proceedings (2004).

Kirkpatrick, D.L. *Evaluating Training Programs: The Four Levels* (San Francisco, CA: Berrett-Koehler, 1994).

Mazrui, A. "Towards Re-Africanizing African Universities: Who Killed Intellectualism in the Post Colonial Era". *Alternative: Turkish Journal of International Relations*, 2: 3 and 4 (Fall and Winter 2003): 135–63.

Mbambo, B. (2003) "Digital Libraries in Africa: A Review of Developments since 1996", in *AfricaDotEdu: IT Opportunities and Higher Education in Africa*, ed. Maria A Beebe, Kouakou Koffi Magloire, Banji Oyeyinka and Madanmohan Rao (New Delhi: Tata McGraw-Hill Publishing Company, Ltd., 2003): 190–205.

Moloketi, F.G. "Africanising Public Administration: Issues of Leadership and Good Governance." Colloquium/Anniversary of the School of Public Administration at the University of Pretoria (2003).

Rumajogee, A. (2003) "Distance Education: Issues and Challenges in Sub-Saharan Africa", in *AfricaDotEdu: IT Opportunities and Higher Education in Africa*, ed. Maria A Beebe, Kouakou Koffi Magloire, Banji Oyeyinka and Madanmohan Rao (New Delhi: Tata McGraw-Hill Publishing Co. Ltd., 2003): 292–313.

Saint, William. "Tertiary distance education and technology in Sub-Saharan Africa." ADEA Working Group on Higher Education (1999).

Saint, William. "The World Bank and Higher Education in Africa." Governance and Higher Education in Africa Conference, University of Florida, Gainesville, FL (2001).

Smith, Peter L. and B. Wellenius *Mitigating Regulatory Risks in Telecommunications*. Washington, Bank. Note 189 on Public Policy for the Private Sector (1999).

Wallsten, S. (1999) "Telecom Reforms in Africa and Latin America." *Economic Reform Today* 2.

Websites

http://www.caida.org
http://www.comet.columbia.edu/~nemo/netmap/
http://www.telegeography.com

Chapter Seven

Universities as Alternate Incubators of Information Communication Centers for Ghana's Development

Benjamin K. Addom*

Introduction

It is evident that the increasing use of the Internet worldwide which has exploded throughout recent years is not only responsible for enormous changes in the developed countries but also has repercussions on the developing nations including Ghana. Unfortunately, using ICTs in Ghanaian universities *for university work* (teaching, research and outreach) is still a luxury. ICTs are new communication technologies being used to improve the existing "old" technologies, and cost-effectively and efficiently aid information delivery and exchange. For example, the most important impediment to Ghana's agricultural development does seem to be issues relating to lack of appropriate and useful information that could help the Ghanaian farmer improve production, storage and marketing activities.

The World Summit on the Information Society (WSIS) is one in the recent series of global meetings sponsored by the United Nations. Concerning information communication technologies, the final report released from the first phase of the Summit in December 2003 at Geneva has identified a significant role for information and communication technologies in strategies for African development (WSIS, 2003: 7). The report notes that the New Partnership for Africa's Development (NEPAD), endorsed by the heads of the G8 industrial countries, "includes a strong focus on the dual strategy of ICT Development and ICT for Development" (Okpaku, 2003).

Regarding ICT development in the university context, the Partnership for Higher Education in Africa (PHEA) organized a workshop for African universities in July 2002 titled "Securing the Linchpin, ICT for Teaching, Learning and Research" in Addis Ababa. The participants explored the role of ICT in higher education, noting that ICTs "are essential to the running of universities" (PHEA, 2002). In this research, we went a step further to include faculty outreach (activities which go outside the walls of the universities) in the e-readiness assessment. The study has revealed a very good "ICT posture"[1] of the faculty members of the surveyed institutions towards *ICT for Development* programs but due to poor ICT human resources, facilities, and inadequate academic programs in computer sciences,

* Cornell University.

faculty members are not using ICT in teaching, research, and outreach. A unique innovative initiative is, therefore, going to be part of the study in which the National Service Scheme of Ghana will be used to support the human resource capacity in sustaining the ICT for Development projects in Ghanaian communities through a "university-based community telecenter" model. The concept of university-based community telecenters takes its root from the sustainability challenges facing these rural information centers that are seen as potential channels for reducing rural poverty in the developing world.

E-Readiness Assessment

The first step being taken in almost all approaches to the measurement or assessment of the digital divide problem is to consider a country's ability or "readiness" to integrate information and communication technology and e-commerce in order to provide a platform that can be used for regional comparisons and forecast. According to Colle (2004), e-readiness is a concept usually applied to nations—and it refers to a nation's inventory of ICT resources for operating in a modern Information Society. He concluded that typically included in e-readiness of nations are such items as service providers, networking facilities, favorable ICT policies, appropriate human resources and telecommunications competition. Not usually included in e-readiness assessments are universities, which, all over the world, have a very critical role to play in every country's development efforts.

Colle (2004) has identified the following five elements, as critical in addressing the e-readiness of any university and these elements have been tackled in detail in this project:

1 Human resources: Does the university have a personnel (staffing) system that supports ICT in both the teaching program and outreach initiatives, personnel such as programmers, media production people, web page designers, and digital technicians?
2 ICT facilities: This is the most visible part of e-readiness. It is the connectivity issue. Are there computers and network connections to take advantage of the existing digital resources and to create new digital resources? Are there media production facilities for recording audio and video materials?
3 Academic programs: Are there academic programs that invite students to study and apply ICTs to the challenges that face the nation and the community, and their development? Are there research and internship opportunities that thrust students and faculty members into the ICT-for-development environment—reaching beyond the walls of the "ivory tower"?
4 Outreach policies: Is there institutional support for a "university without walls"? Does the university allow, encourage or reward members of the faculty to become involved with appropriate communities so that professors and lecturers

can contribute to the vitality and sustainability of community-based institutions such as telecenters or extension systems?

5 Faculty posture. Does the university have a faculty (professors and lecturers) who are in-tune with the new digital world; do they have the inclination to be innovative and aggressive in the application of ICTs to learning and outreach; is there an ICT "champion" in the institution (Colle, 2004)?

Problem Statement

The *sustainability* of community telecenters is a worldwide issue nowadays. The desire to use these new technologies to improve the living conditions of the rural people has overshadowed consideration of the strategies necessary to actually make these centers work. Below are some statements made by ICT Champions that point to the problem:

> Only one out of every one hundred telecenters is really useful for the local community where they have been set up, in terms of supporting development and social change. Thousand of telecenters have been planted during the past five years and millions of dollars have been invested in buying computers and ensuring Internet connectivity; however, every time we are to mention the successful experiences, the same five or six places come into mind. In other word something smells very bad in cyber land ... (Senthikumaran amd Arunachalam, 2001: 3).

> From 1994 through 2001, Canada's Community Access Program funded the establishment of over 8,000 telecenters, yet today we know very little about what happened to these centers (Proenza, 2003: 10).

> Not all the centers that have been established are still in operation. In Argentina, for example, between August 1999 and June 2000 a total of 1,281 Community Technology Centers (*Centros Tecnologicos Communitarios* or CTCs) were installed. A year later, only about 72% of these CTCs were still working, and no one knows how many CTCs remain open today (Proenza, 2003: 9–10).

This situation is not different in Ghana as the efforts being made in respect of "ICT Development" (ICTD) and other "ICT for Development" (ICT4D) projects are uncoordinated. The effect is reflected in many ICT for Development (ICT4D) projects that have inappropriate/irrelevant content; are very expensive; unaffordable and inaccessible to the rural poor; have little or poor monitoring, or evaluation and research into the usefulness of the projects to the beneficiaries, demonstrate underutilization of ICTs for further research, and have poor ICT human resource development, resulting in unsustainable projects.

It is discouraging and disturbing to note the insignificant role the universities are currently playing in this sector, despite much being done to provide ICT facilities and develop the human resource base in order to handle the facilities (ICT4D) within the universities. At the same time, isolated and uncoordinated ICT projects are springing up both in the urban and rural communities of Ghana brought into being by individuals, private enterprises, non-governmental organizations and government institutions. However, it is apparent that little has been done to tie in the human resource development institutions – the higher education institutions in Ghana- that are a potential source of middle and high level manpower of the country and a research base for improvement of ICT programs necessary for *sustainable*, *cost effective*, *affordable* and *appropriate* services to all, especially the marginalized. A recent article in the General News of Ghana webpage (23 March 2004) with the caption "Government to Prevent Proliferation of Inadequate Computer Schools" gave a picture of the real and chaotic situation on the ground. According to the article, "on behalf of the Sector Minister, the Ministry of Communication and Technology would come out with measures to check the proliferation of inadequate computer training schools in the country." The statement promised that the Ministry was working in collaboration with the National Accreditation Board to ensure the standardization of information and communication technology education in Ghana (Ghana Web, 2004). The following discouraging statement also appeared in the Plan for National Information and Communication Infrastructure (NICI) of Ghana 2000–2005 project document:

> In Ghana academic institutions have not been well identified to lead in areas of ICT so they cannot serve as a reference point for the new emerging ICT technologies. It is important that some special and organized growth channels be identified to bring up the knowledge levels of Ghanaians (ECA [Economic Commission for Africa], 2000).

Universities and institutions of higher learning are playing the leading role in the development and application of ICTs in the industrialized countries. For example, the Association of African Universities (AAU) notes that the history of the Internet clearly shows the leading role played, and which is still being played, by the Higher Education Institutions (HEI) in the developed countries. In many cases the HEIs are in the forefront of the development and usage of ICT especially, the Internet. A dozen or so of the US HEIs are already enjoying the benefits of the Internet with the speed in the Gbps range (AAU, 2000). Meanwhile, Ghana is still trying to find some other specialized channels for this task of bringing the knowledge level of ICTs and its application to its people.

Paradoxically, what telecenters need for institutionalizing ICT for development is what universities potentially have: that is the potential to offer resources such as relevant content, human resources, practical research, training capacity and the ability to sustain these telecenters.

Aims and Objectives

The overall goal of this study was to conduct an e-readiness assessment of Ghanaian universities (human resources, physical infrastructure, hardware and software facilities, academic programs, teaching and research, connectivity, and outreach activities), the result of which would be used as a baseline to develop a detailed action plan for both the universities and Ghanaian communities. When implemented, this could move the country towards achieving its information and communication technology For Accelerated Development (ICT4AD) goals. The specific objectives of the project therefore include the following:

- identify the ICT human resource base in the universities;
- assess the physical ICT infrastructures in place in these universities;
- identify the available hardware and software facilities present in these universities;
- assess academic programs related to ICT and student internship activities;
- identify ICT policies in place for faculty's outreach activities;
- propose a program of study that will incorporate teaching, research and outreach from these universities to rural communities, and incorporate linkage to Ghana's National Service Scheme (NSS).

The Research Process

Unit of Analysis or Sample Size Selection

The selection of the sample size was based on certain deciding factors within the scale of the survey operations such as time, cost, operational constraints and the desired precision of the results. As a result, a moderate sample size, which is sufficient statistically and operationally, was estimated and chosen. The data were collected from seven higher education institutions in Ghana spread within six of the 10 regions of the country, from the southern border of Cape Coast to the northern sector of Tamale. These are:

1 University of Cape Coast, Cape Coast;
2 Ho Polytechnics, Ho;
3 University of Ghana, Legon;
4 Kwame Nkrumah University of Science and Technology, Kumasi;
5 Tamale Polytechnics, Tamale;
6 University of Education, Winneba;
7 University for Development Studies, Tamale.

These institutions were selected based on their involvement in agricultural science programs for students. Each of them has some form of agricultural training either through extension, production, or agricultural education. It should be noted that all the institutions are public and under the control of the Government of Ghana. The sample size thus covers all the teaching and research staff of the Faculties of Agriculture in the seven institutions. Following upon prior research on the population size, an estimate of 250 booklets was prepared and delivered for the survey. Out of this number, 194 were completed and returned and are analyzed in this discussion.

The Data Collection

The "Mailed Survey" method of data collection, described by Diem (2002) as that which uses a printed questionnaires mailed or delivered to the respondents and permits them to respond at will and return the result by mail, was combined with the "Hand Delivered" method outlined by Statistics Canada (2003) in which self-enumerated survey questionnaires are hand-delivered to people and mailed back by the respondent after completion. A set of questionnaires with detailed instruction from the Cornell Development Communication Research Group (DCRG) was delivered through coordinators to the respondents. A second questionnaire was designed for completion by one administrator from each of these seven institutions. The data for this round of research were collected in the form of one to one interviews in which the administrators were further interviewed on some ICT policies and programs of their universities.

There was a coordinator for each institution who was responsible for the interview, distribution and retrieval of booklets for that institution. The coordinators were selected and trained in advance and introduced to the various Deans of Faculties before the dispatch of the survey questionnaires from Cornell. The completed questionnaires were picked up by the coordinators and mailed back to Cornell.

Summary of the Results and Discussion

In this section of the chapter, we present the results of these surveys and discuss them.

ICT Human Resources Level in Ghanaian Universities

The survey produced a useful and informative profile of the respondents.

From the results presented above, the opportunities for strengthening the ICT human resource base in Ghanaian universities may be located in the following potentials as well as challenges:

Table Fourteen General profile of the respondents

Number of institutions	7
Total number of respondents	194
Number involved in teaching	166
Number involved in research	178
Number involved in outreach	129
Mean age range	41–45 years
Number of male	174
Number of female	19
Number of respondents holding PhD degree	86
Number of respondents holding Masters degree	70
Number of respondents with other degrees	37
Respondents from the field of agriculture	172
Respondents from non-agricultural fields	17
Number of Senior Lecturers	57
Number of Lecturers	84
Number of Teaching Assistants	13
Others (research staff)	34

Table Fifteen Summary of ICT human resource level at the universities

Variables	% on the low side	% on the high side
Experience with the use of PC	20	80
Experience with the use of Web	38	62
Experience with the use of e-mail	30	70
Use of e-mail for outreach	92	8
Use of websites for outreach	97	3
Use of CD for outreach	96	4
Level of computer skill	27	73
Use of web design private company	33	66

- Table Fourteen shows good academic qualification by the faculty members—86 of the respondents holding a PhD and 70 of them holding a Masters degree;
- from the interview conducted with the administrators, it is obvious that the universities have some level of staff to assist faculty in computer use, hardware maintenance, software development and other areas such as graphic design and webpage development;

- most of the respondents have good exposure to computers, e-mail, and websites with their potential impacts but significantly have little experience with the use of these technologies in their university work;
- the level of computer skills, though perceived by the respondents as "good," appears not to be enough. This can be inferred because when given the options to choose between their universities and private companies for solving technical problems, the greater percentage prefers going outside the university as compared to those who would visit their university technical unit (Table Fifteen);
- the low use of these technologies—compact disk (CD), websites and e-mail for their university work—indicates that respondents have either little knowledge and ability or opportunity to use them for their university work (Table Fifteen).

It could be inferred from the above discussion that the seven institutions involved in the survey have basic computer literacy such as exposure of the faculty to computers, e-mail, Internet websites, and of using Microsoft Word and other spreadsheets for data entry and record keeping.

Infrastructure Facilities, Access and Connectivity in the Universities

There is a huge unsatisfied demand for ICT facilities in these seven Ghanaian universities as revealed by the results from the survey.

Table Sixteen Summary of ICT infrastructure level at the universities

Variables	**% on the low side (N=194)**	**% on the high side (N=194)**
Physical access to computer	20	80
Physical access to Internet websites	38	62
Quality of connectivity	70	30
Satisfaction with speed of Internet	92	8
Frequent of use of Internet with students	97	3
Frequent of use of Internet materials for class	96	4

The result from the interview conducted with the administrators revealed that, generally, the seven institutions have a student population of about 57,000 and only 1,600 computers are available for independent student use. This low computer to student ratio does not allow faculty to to communicate regularly with students through e-mail or the Internet.

The physical access to computers, Internet connectivity, speeds of the Internet and the frequency of use of these technologies measure the level of ICT infrastructure in the universities. Less than 30 per cent of the respondents have their own assigned office computers, while a majority either have shared computers or have to go to their departmental laboratory to use computers. Only three out of the seven institutions have public computer facilities. The difficulty of access increased from computers through e-mail to Internet websites. This reflects the unavailability and poor connectivity of Internet facilities at university level: only three out of the seven institutions have a digital network within their universities.

Table Sixteen shows that a very high percentage of respondents often have difficulty with connectivity and are not satisfied with the speed of the Internet they use. The difficulty with connectivity would impede the ability of the respondents to use computer/websites to prepare materials for class and deliver lecturers to the large number of students currently in a given class.

It is, however, worth noting that all the seven institutions have some form of computer laboratory for instruction. This could act as the basis for improving the ICT facilities in these universities. Other facilities indicated as available include radio broadcasting transmitters and dial-up and broadband telecommunication networks. Audio and video recording facilities are available in some of the universities, and web pages with agricultural information were found to be present in four out of the seven institutions.

Academic Programs

Academic programs in any university are the bases for the production of the required manpower needed by the society for development. Higher education in Africa needs to play a more aggressive role in preparing these human resources. The result from the e-readiness assessment from the seven institutions in Ghana (Tables Seventeen and Eighteen) has revealed that academic programs related to ICT are at the initial stage.

Table Seventeen Some academic programs in the universities

Some academic programs in the universities	Yes (N=7)	No (N=7)	Don't know
Computer operation	5	2	0
Community/rural development	6	1	0
Research methods	7	0	0
Extension/communication methods	7	0	0
Information and communication technology	6	1	0

Referring to UNESCO (2002), these universities have made a transition from the "Emerging stage" to the "Applying stage" where the institutions have understood the potential contribution of ICT to learning, and administrators and teachers are

Table Eighteen Student internship programs

Student internship programs	**Yes (N=7)**	**No (N=7)**	**Don't know**
Internship is a requirement in my university	7	0	0
My university offers opportunity for internship	7	0	0
My university encourages students internship	7	0	0
Students are rewarded for internship work	4	1	2

beginning to use ICT for tasks already carried out in university management and in the curriculum, although teachers still largely dominate the learning environment. There is, therefore, the need to move from this applying stage to the "Infusing stage" and then, finally, to the "Transforming stage" where a range of computer-based technologies in laboratories, classrooms, and administrative areas are applied, and universities use ICT creatively to rethink and renew the university organization.

Other programs relating to the objectives of this research are community and rural development, research methods, and extension and communication methods. These are programs that can help transform ICT development in the universities into *ICT for Development* activities. Results from the interview with the administrators indicate that student internship is a requirement by all the universities, and the institutions offer students the opportunity and encouragement to do internship outside campus during vacation. However, only three out of the seven institutions have agreed that students are rewarded either in the form of academic credit or money for the internship. This is likely to be a hindrance since students prefer or may need to work for money most of the time during the vacation.

ICT Policies on Outreach

There is unsatisfied demand in the immediate communities around these institutions as well as rural and more remote areas, which will need the use of information and communication technology services. This could be done through an extension of student internship and the involvement of university staff in external programs.

Results from the interviews (Tables Nineteen and Twenty) show that respondents do not see a lack of community interest or a lack of need for outreach into these communities as obstacles to outreach and extension. Only two out of the seven institutions have indicated a lack of faculty interest and no mandate from the universities as obstacles to outreach. Lack of time for outreach was also not seen as an obstacle confirming the result from the questionnaire. The main obstacles identified are lack of resources, cost of outreach programs and lack of incentives from the universities.

Table Nineteen Position of Faculty on Outreach Work

Position of Faculty on outreach work	Percentage (N=7)	
	Agreed	Disagreed
Outreach is an important part of my work	93	7
Personal interest in outreach	95	5
Doing outreach work is gratifying	67	33
I gain prestige from doing outreach work	87	13
I have the time to do outreach work	98	2
Social norm—people think I should do outreach	78	22
The use of Internet in outreach will be expensive	31	69

Table Twenty Position of the Universities on Outreach Work by Faculty

Position of the universities on outreach	Percentage (N=129)	
	Agreed	Disagreed
My university requires me to do outreach	81	19
My university encourages outreach work	85	15
My university rewards faculty for outreach work	29	71

The following results from the survey questionnaire (Table Twenty-one) also pose the challenge for improving the ICT policies and implementations on outreach by the faculty in these universities. A very high percentage of the respondents agreed that outreach is an important part of their university work, they have personal interest in doing outreach work, outreach is a requirement from their universities, and they have the time to do outreach work in addition to their teaching and research work. On the other hand, an equally high percentage *disagreed* that using ICT to do outreach can be expensive and that their universities have the ability to invest in ICTs for their future outreach activities.

It could be inferred from both the interview and the questionnaires that the faculties of agriculture staff of these seven institutions have been involved in outreach activities. Their incorporation of ICT into faculty outreach work will markedly improve their work and give an added value to their immediate communities.

The Posture of ICT among the Faculty Members in the Universities

The posture of ICT in these universities is very high. Though the skill and use of these new technologies by the faculty are low, they still see the importance of ICT in their university work. About 90 per cent of the respondents see the importance of

Table Twenty-one Summary of ICT posture by the university faculties

Summary of ICT posture by the university faculties	% on the low side	% on the high side
Computer is important in my university work	4	96
The use of websites is important in my university work	8	92
The use of e-mail is important in my university work	11	89
If I have access to the Internet I will use it for my work	10	90
Computers are useful in my university work	6	94
Internet websites are useful for my research work	13	87
E-mail is useful for my research work	19	81
The Internet has no benefit to my work	97	3
My university is able to invest in Internet for outreach	63	37

ICTs (computers, e-mail, Internet) in their university work. Eighty-seven per cent of the respondents see the usefulness of the Internet websites in teaching, research and outreach while 94 per cent believe that the use of computers in their university work will increase their productivity. Not only do they see the importance and usefulness of these tools but they also believe that the society expects them to use it for their work. Eighty per cent of them agreed that people think they should use ICTs for their work.

A high percentage of the respondents have the intention to use these tools for their university work in the future when they have access to them. They are ready to try new technologies such as ICTs in doing their work if they have access to it. Some of the comments made by the respondents during the interview also attest to that fact that they are readily awaiting for the tools in order to use them for their work. The availability of ICT would enhance the status of and opportunity to undertake outreach: as one respondent stated “Extension is a third mandate for every lecturer in the university. Percentage time allotted is low as compared to teaching and research mandates”. The routine availability of ICT in the universities would better enable university staff to meet the third mandate.

Implications of the Results for Development

The results of the study have far-reaching implications for both the universities and their communities. Its implications for these two institutions (universities and rural communities) are summarized below:

1 for these institutions to be able to keep pace with the current information age:
  - the existing ICT situation in the universities must be improved (ICT development);

2 for the ICT development in the universities to be useful to a broader society:
  - the capacity of the universities needs to be strengthened to be able to reach out to their communities through rural development programs (ICT for development);
  - this could be achieved through development of an academic module that combines the technical and social sciences/education aspects of ICT4D;
  - the establishment of ICT4D centers in the communities with direct support from the universities—University-Based Community Telecenters (UBCT) needs to be undertaken and;
  - the use of National Service Scheme of Ghana with constant faculty outreach programs to these centers to contribute to their sustainability needs to be initiated.

The Proposed Action

Stage I—Building the ICT Capacities of the University

The proposed ICT development in the universities builds upon the existing infrastructure facilities identified through the e-readiness assessment and other feasibility studies to be conducted. This is shown at the left-hand side of Figure Twenty-two and may include:

- the supply of new/used computers to these institutions through international collaboration with other Western universities;
- upgrading the communication network systems such telephone lines, bandwidth, radio transmitters, etc. on the campuses;
- building more physical infrastructure like computer laboratories for classroom instructions, and training centers on the campuses specifically for development programs;
- improve upon the technical training in information and communication technologies system of both the students and faculty for teaching, research and outreach work.

Stage II—Strengthening Academic Programs in the Universities for Development

The second phase of the proposed plan continues in the universities and entails the development of an academic module involving ICT and rural development programs. This involves linking the ICT development in the first phase with the conventional extension and rural development and educational programs currently going on in the universities as identified through the survey. This will be done through:

- the strengthening of the current fields of extension and rural development;
- introducing research methods and other social sciences courses such as Development Sociology and development Communications that combine the expertise from the social sciences and the information and communication technologies.

This is also shown at the left-hand side of Figure Twenty-two within the university.

Stage III—Implementation of the Project in the Rural Communities

The third stage of the proposed action moves from the university to the rural community to transform the academic module in Stage II into ICT for Development projects with strong support from the universities. This project may be referred to as "university-based community telecenters". The telecenters may be sited within strategic locations in the administrative districts of Ghana, either in the district capitals or rural communities close to the district capitals *but not* in the regional capitals. The centers will also be multipurpose in nature to accommodate the information needs of the majority. The telecenters will be university-based because:

- students doing internship or practical attachments in the communities during the long vacation while in the universities will be posted to these centers (shown by the plain arrow from left to right in Figure Twenty-two);
- students return to their universities to complete their programs of study after 2–3 months of internship in the centers (shown by the plain arrow from right to left in Figure Twenty-two).
- graduates serving their National Service year in the rural communities at the end of their four-year programs in the universities will be specifically posted to these centers annually after their training (shown by the thick bottom arrow from left to right);
- outreach/extension or distance education activities by the faculty will be constant and continuous to these centers with frequent feedback to the universities (shown by the top thick arrow from left to right).

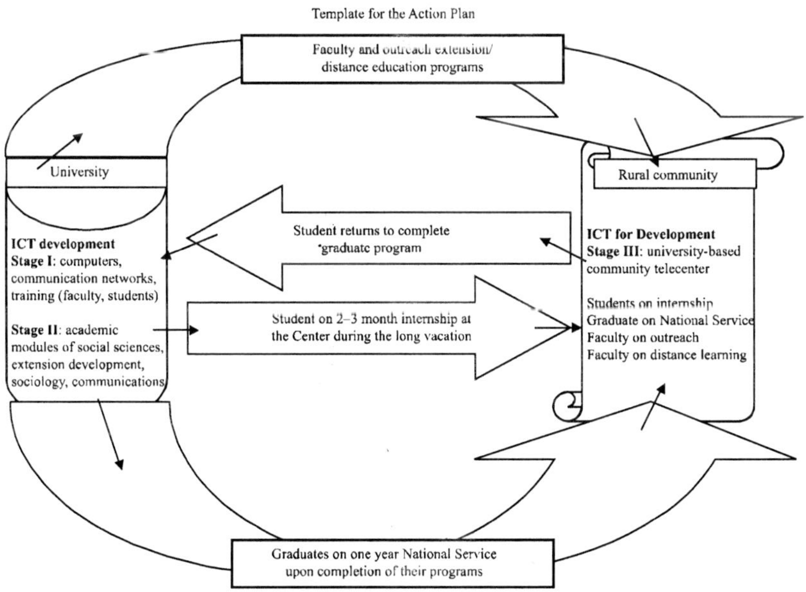

Figure Twenty-two Template for the action plan

Figure Twenty-two gives a sketch of the various stages involve in the proposed action to build the ICT capacity of the universities and transform it for rural and community development.

What Makes the Proposed Framework Different from Others?

The proposed action plan is unique as a result of the following features that are likely to make the centers more affordable, accessible and sustainable.

The Role of the Universities

According to the Ghana National ICT Policy and Plan Development Committee Report (2001), tertiary education facilitates the main channels where most of the country's human resources are developed; they tend to nurture human resources that are deployed in the country's economy. There is no doubt that tertiary education is a requisite for national development. The use of the country's universities will lead to the use of qualified but affordable labor at these centers drastically reducing the cost of operation and maintenance.

Various ICT champions have pointed out the danger of invading local culture with foreign cultures as a result of the emergence of these technologies (Ballantyne, 2001: 1; Batchelor, 2002). The second stage of the framework is designed to reduce this danger by using the local universities to deal with issues of relevant content of information to the needs of the communities.

A more comprehensive approach for universities getting involved in ICT-related activities proposed by Roman and Colle (2003) could be adopted to make the centers more unique. The universities will be used to:

- conduct continual research on community information needs so that appropriate information resources can be developed;
- conduct on-going e-readiness studies at the regional and community levels and interpret their results for regional and local policy formulation and action;
- convert their own research and academic knowledge into education, information, and training packages suitable for community use;
- mobilize, interpret, integrate, and package information from external authoritative sources and tailor it to the needs of populations in surrounding communities;
- build curricula that train students in the application of ICTs to development problems and reward faculty members for participation in this type of program;
- design and execute ICT training programs for various community groups, especially those that are likely to be bypassed by conventional ICT training;
- provide on-going monitoring and evaluation support to the telecenter and ICT initiatives;
- prepare a new generation of "champions" in various sectors to use and support the application of ICTs and telecenters for community development and poverty alleviation;
- actively contribute to the Country Gateway (information portal) system;
- orient university officials and faculty to ICT-for-development so they can support ICT initiatives, build ICT-related curricula and research programs, and be opinion leaders in this area;
- initiate "university-based" telecenters similar in approach to the school-based telecenters of World Link for Development (WorLD), but exploit the opportunity to use them as learning and research labs for ICT4D (Roman and Colle, 2003: 401–2).

A Perfect Partner for ICT Development: The National Service Scheme of Ghana

Overview

The Ghana National Service Scheme (NSS) is a public organization under the Ministry of Education of Ghana. The Scheme was established by a Military Decree

N.L.C.D. 208, 1973 with the responsibility of providing manpower for the public service, educational institutions and the urban oriented industrial and commercial establishments. This perspective of National Service Scheme was initiated by an Act of Parliament, Act 426 (1980) and brought into force in 1982 by the government of the Provisional National Defense Council (PNDC). The Scheme in Ghana is necessary and useful and, according to a NSS document National Service Today (NST), students suggested, welcomed and gave support to the National Service program when it was established in 1973 (NST, 1987).

Aims and Objectives of the Scheme

The rationale behind the establishment of the Scheme stems from the fact that:

- increasing urbanization of educated youth seems to have produced a group in which the majority is out of touch with the living conditions and the problems of the larger portion of society;
- there was the need to ensure that the priority sectors of national life always had adequate personnel to keep them running;
- graduates are obliged to do some minimal service for the people whose efforts financed their education;
- there was the need to make the educational system more meaningful to the majority of Ghanaians by allowing the new graduates to integrate into the larger society;
- theories can be translated into practical actions through internship activities by the national service persons;
- as Ghana's future leaders, it is essential that graduates' academic education is rounded off with practical application, and with opportunities to test and develop their skills of planning, innovating, exercising initiative, and thinking wisely and creatively about the country's development needs.

The Scope of the Scheme

Presently, the Scheme covers all graduates from the country's five public universities, ten polytechnics, and other diploma awarding colleges of education. The human resources available to the scheme now are large. This potential is enormous for the mobilization of the rural communities and for the injection of skill and talent into many spheres of the economy given the right orientation, spirit and support. This is especially so considering the academic background of the group deployed under the Scheme—engineers, doctors, social scientists, educationists, and artisans.

Eligibility and Duration

Under the National Service Act 426, a Citizen of Ghana who has attained the age of 18 years or more is eligible to do National Service. By this Act, the minimum duration of the scheme was increased from one year to two years, and National Service was made mandatory for all able-bodied men and women of at least 18 years. However, the Scheme as currently being practiced is a modification of the law as it covers only 18-year-olds at the terminal points in the school system of technical institutions, polytechnics, the universities, and other professional institutions. The service year begins from November/December of every year and continues to September.

Sectors of Deployment

Education

The sector that benefits most from the scheme is the educational sector. The scheme supplies teachers to broaden the base of the formal educational system at all levels. The service posts 70 per cent of its personnel to teach from the pre-school level through to the tertiary level. The service also provides support for the Ministry of Education in the non-formal educational sector. In addition, the Scheme has helped to initiate the establishment of a few community schools, which are managed, and run by the respective communities. Subjects taught are very practical and of direct relevance to the development of the communities concerned.

Community Improvement Unit (CIU)

The community development service is one of the cardinal programs of the "National Service Year," and provides one of the major areas of assessment of the personnel's performance. It is a wide area that tests the corps member's enterprise, creativity and devotion to the ideas of welfare service to community. As part of their community development service, corps members over the years have worked on projects such as construction of culverts, bridges, clinics, community halls, and mass literacy, design of farm implements, agricultural extension, legal air, basic health, water resources, etc., which have won appreciation and admiration from communities.

Information Sector

The NSS is also involved in the production of material to aid the transfer of information. The audio-visual section has documentation on:

- National Service today;
- experience of National Service personnel;
- the role of National Service personnel in Primary Health Care Program;
- training for service, among others.

At the moment, these services are made possible through equipment assistance from the Government of Ghana, Voluntary Service Overseers (VSO) and UNICEF.

Problems

The Scheme has survived for all these years but with numerous problems. The main problem has been finance, which has reduced the scope of coverage of the scheme and has limited its activities. A review of the Law (Act 426, 1980) under which the Scheme operates has been commissioned to examine the Scheme and recommend ways by which it could be self-financing and more sustainable.[2]

The Role of the National Service Scheme

The National Service Scheme of Ghana could provide a perfect partner for the development and operation of community telecenters in Ghana. The use of the scheme has the potential to result in more affordable, accessible and sustaining centers for the rural people through the following mechanisms:

- Human Resources: The guaranteed annual supply of well-qualified graduates to the telecenters which will provide adequate personnel to keep the centers running.
- Social Accessibility: The perception of science and technology as foreign and the ICTs as culturally damaging could be made acceptable and useful to the ordinary people of the country through the National Service persons. This would be achieved through the training that would be offered during the second stage of the project.
- Financial Accessibility: Since the Scheme obliges those graduates that have trained at the expense of the Ghanaian taxpayer to provide their services to the state in recompense within a national service framework, their services in the communities are not fully compensated financially. They are made to serve the people whose efforts financed their education. The cost of maintenance of these human resources will be less since the personnel will be on allowance but not salary.
- The supply of these graduates from the universities to the centers will help in achieving the aims of the Scheme by putting the highly educated youth in touch with rural conditions and problems.
- The system of ensuring that continuing students do internship in areas of their study makes the educational system more meaningful to the majority of Ghanaian as well as to the student themselves. Theories learnt in the classroom could be translated into practical activities and feedback brought back into the classroom upon their return.

- The National Service-University-Telecenter system will contribute to the professional development of students who, in their careers, will be able to use ICTs to help the country take up its role in the Information Society of the twenty-first century.

Recommendations

In conclusion, this chapter has demonstrated that there is a need to strengthen the ICT skills, facilities and connectivity at Ghana's public universities. It has indicated how any such improvements could usefully be harnessed to outreach programs with benefits for the rural communities of Ghana. It has proposed the development of telecenters which integrate university ICT training with service to the wider community making use of university internships and the National Service Scheme. It has shown a way of utilizing the ICT potential and leadership potential of the universities in serving the wider goals of ICT for Development. The proposed framework was developed from the baseline survey conducted in agricultural faculties in the seven higher education institutions in the country but could be applied to all of Ghana's universities and all of their faculties. However, for a deeper investigation into other fields within the universities and other universities within the country which were not covered in this survey, further research work is recommended.

Acknowledgment

The author would like to thank Dr Royal D. Colle, Department of Communication, Cornell University and Dr Raul Roman, Research Association, Annenberg Research Network on International Communication, Annenberg School for Communication, University of Southern California.

Notes

1 University faculty (professors and lecturers) who are in-tune with the new digital world; who have the inclination to be innovative and aggressive in the application of ICTs to learning and outreach; faculty members who are ICT "champion" in the institution.

2 The overview of the National Service Scheme given above is adapted from a paper presented at the 3rd Global Conference on National Youth Service, Papua New Guinea in 1996 on the theme "National Youth Service: A Global Idea for Local Action" by B.G. Hikah from Ghana.

References

AAU. Summary of On-Line Discussions on ICT in Higher Education Institutions in Africa. Association of African Universities, Technical Experts Meeting on the use and Application of Information and Communication Technologies in Higher Education Institutions in Africa, University of Dar Es Salaam Dar Es Salaam, Tanzania. 21 April–8 May 2000: http://www.aau.org/english/documents/aau-ictreport-p4.htm.

AAU. Core Program of Activities 2001–2004: http://www.aau.org/coreprog/0104/index.htm (2003).

Ahiabenu, K. "Rapid Growth in Internet Use despite Cost Constraints: Balancing Act News Update": http://www.balancingact-africa.com/news/back/balancing-act54.html (2004).

Ajayi, G.O. *Information and Communication Technologies: Building Capacities in African Universities* (Trieste, Italy: National Information Technology Development Agency, Federal Ministry of Science and Technology at ICTP, 2002).

Ballantyne, P. *Collecting and Propagating Local Development Content*. Research Report No. 7 (The Hague: International Institute for Communication and Development, 2002).

Baryamureeba, V. "Human Resource Development and Retention Capacity of ICT/Computer Science Professionals in a Third World Country". Paper presented at a workshop on the establishing a regional master of Science in Computer Science Degree Program, 10–11 February, Makerere University Uganda (2003).

Batchelor, S. *Using ICTs to Generate Development Content*. Research Report No. 10 (The Hague International Institute for Communication and Development, 2002)

Best, R., F. Abbott and M. Taylor. *Teaching Skills for Learning*. Library and Information Research Report 78 (London: The British Library, 1990).

Budhiraja, R. and S. Sachdeva. "E-Readiness Assessment (India)": http://unpan1.un.org/intradoc/groups/public/documents/APCITY/UNPAN014673.pdf (2002).

China Daily. "Funds for Poor Areas to Surge this Year". 4 May: http://www.china.org.cn/english/2004/May/94619.htm (2004).

Claude, K.J. *ICT Development in Ghana: Use of ICT for Education, Research and Development in Ghana: Challenges, Opportunities and Potentials* (Tamale, Ghana: Second Sight Enterprise, 2004).

Colle, R. Draft Project Proposal on the E-readiness of African Universities, unpublished (Ithaca, NY: Cornell University, 2004).

Colle, R. and R. Roman. "Communication Centers and Developing Nations: A State of the Art Report": http://www.devmedia.org/documents/banga.htm (1999).

Colle, R. and R. Roman. "Content for ICT Initiatives". Prepared for the International Congress of Information Conference *Information, Knowledge and Society.*

Challenges of New Era. Havana International Conference Center, Cuba, 22–26 April (2002).

Colle, R. and R. Roman. "ICT4D: A Frontier for Higher Education in Developing Nations", *African and Asian Studies* 2:4 (Leiden: Koninklijke Brill NV, 2003a).

Colle, R. and R. Roman. "Challenges in the Telecenter Movement," in *Closing the Digital Divide*, ed. S. Marshall, W. Taylor and X. Yu (Westport, CT: Praeger, 2003b).

Colle R.D. and L. Yonggong. "ICT Capacity-Building for Development and Poverty Alleviation. Enhancing the Role of Agricultural Universities in China". Paper prepared for the Third Asian Conference for Information Technology in Agriculture, Beijing, 26–28 October (2002).

Daily Mirror. "ADB says ICT can Help Reduce Poverty in Asia" A seminar on the theme "Unlocking the ICT Potential in Asia": http://www.dailymirror.lk/inside/IT/020513.html (2002).

Diem, K.G. "Using Research Methods to Evaluate your Extension Program", *Journal of Extension* (on-line), 40:6: http://www/joe.org/2002december/a1.shtml (2002).

Dzidonu, C. "A Blueprint for Developing National ICT Policy in Africa. Information Technology Policy Framework for Ghana. Report of the Technical Group—from Poverty Reduction to Wealth Creation—Building Consensus on Vision for Ghana". ATPS Special Paper No. 5 (2002).

ECA. "Plan for National Information and Communications Infrastructure of Ghana 2000–2005 – Ghana", ILO: http://www.logos-net.net/ilo/150_base/en/init/gha_2.htm (2000).

ERNWACA-Ghana. "ICT in Education in Ghana: Workshop to Develop Terms of Reference for Transnational Study on Education and ICT". Education and Research Network of West and Central Africa (ERNWACA), 27–29 March, Bamako, Mali (2003)

ESCAP. Expert Group Meeting on Government Policies and Strategies on Information and Communication Technology (ICT) for Rural Poverty Reduction in Asia and the Pacific Region, Bangkok Thailand, 27–28 November (2003).

Fuchs, R. "If You Have a Lemon, Make Lemonade: A Guide to the Start-up of the African Multipurpose Community Telecenter Pilot Project", Ottawa, International Development Research Center (IDRC): http://www.idrc.ca/acacia/outputs/lemonade/lemon.html (1997).

Ghana ICT Policy Document. National ICT Policy and Plan Development, Republic of Ghana, Committee (n.d): http://www.ict.gov.gh/ (2001).

Ghana Web. "Government to Prevent Proliferation of Inadequate Computer Schools". General News of Tuesday, 23 March: http://www.ghanaweb.com/GhanaHomePage/NewsArchive/artikel.php?ID=54517 (2004).

Hikah, B.G. 3rd Global Conference on National Youth Service Papua New Guinea. National Youth Service: A Global Idea for Local Action. Paper on Ghana: http://www.acys.utas.edu.au/ianys/proceedings/1996/paper-18.html (1996).

National Service Today (NST). A Bulletin of the National Service Secretariat, Accra, Ghana. Volume 1, May (1987).

Okpaku, J. (ed). *Information and Communication Technologies for Africa's Development: An Assessment of Progress and Challenges Ahead* (New York: UNICT Task Force, (2003): 23–4.

PHEA. "Securing the Linchpin, ICT for Teaching, Learning and Research. The Partnership for Higher Education in Africa". Addis Ababa: http://www.foundation-partnership.org/linchpin/ (2002).

Proenza, F. "ICT-enabled Networks, Public Sector Performance and the Developoment of information and Communication Technologies", in *Connected for Development: Information Kiosks and Sustainability*, ed. A Badshah, S. Khan and M. Garrido (New York: United Nations, 2003).

Roman, R. and R. Colle. *Content Creation for ICT Development Projects: Integrating Normative Approaches and Community Demand* (Information Technology for Development, IOS Press, 2003).

Senthilkumaran, S. and S. Arunachalam. "Using ICTs in Development: What Have We Learnt from our Experience in Pondicherry?" M.S. Swaminathan Research Foundation, Motorola Dispatch Solution Gold Award 1999 and Stockholm Challenge Award 2001 Chennai 600 113, India (2001).

Statistics Canada. "Statistics: Power from Data! Data Collection Methods": http://www.statcan.ca/english/edu/power/about/about2.htm (2003).

University of Cape Coast (UCC). Data Processing Unit, UCC, Cape Coast, Ghana, 34th Congregation Basic Statistics, March (2004).

UNDP. Towards an Open Information Society: Global Meeting on ICT for Development, Ottawa, 9–11 July: http://ictd.undp.org/it4dev/gpm/background.html, (2003)

UNESCO. World Declaration on Higher Education for the Twenty-First Century: Vision and Action Higher World Conference on Higher Education, Paris, Final Report, 5–9 October (1998).

UNESCO. Information and Communication Technologies in Teacher Education. A Planning Guide. Division of Higher Education: http://portal.unesco.org/education/en/ev.phpURL_ID=18592&URL_DO=DO_TOPIC&URL_SECTION=201.html (2002).

World Bank. "Constructing Knowledge Societies: New Challenges for Tertiary Education," *Direction in Development*. World Bank Report (Washington, DC: World Bank, 2002).

World Bank. "World Bank to Set up Regulatory Environment for W-Prosperity." Cyber India Online Limited (CIOL):: http://www.ciol.com/content/nasscom/coverage/103021202.aspk (2003).

WSIS. Plan of Action: WSIS Geneva 2003–Tunis 2005. "Building the Information Society: A Global Challenge in the New Millennium", November: http://www.itu.int/wsis/documents/doc_multi-en-1161|1160.asp (2003).

CHAPTER EIGHT

WORLD COMPUTER EXCHANGE: AN INVENTORY OF ACTIVITIES

Timothy Anderson

Introduction

This chapter describes the activities of World Computer Exchange (WCE), especially focussing on its work in Africa. This insight into the workings of WCE is given in a context where WCE is one of six international educational NGOs selected to participate in the Global ICT pilot initiatives of the World Economic Forum.

Its mission is:

> To act as a partner in helping bridge the global digital divide for youth, promoting cultural understanding between students in developed and developing countries, and building local capacity for the use of information and communication technology in education.

How does this mission translate into activities? What form do these activities take? The rest of this chapter sets out these activities for us so that we can get a better grasp of what is needed in the process of bridging the global digital divide in respect of youth.

The Work of the WCE

WCE is the largest North American non-profit provider of donated used computers to connect youth in developing countries and has shipped 16,000 donated used computers in 66 shipments to Partners to connect 1,550 schools with 700,000 students in 31 countries. With 320 formal Partner organisations in 51 developing countries, WCE has 125 volunteer Program Officers and teams of online support volunteers in technology, telecenter management and content and hundreds of volunteers gathering working computers, technical volunteers and sister-schools in 30 US and Canadian cities.

In terms of international organizations, WCE works with a large span of relevant agencies: to give an idea of this span, WCE works with UNDP, UNESCO, UNICEF, USAID, Asha, World Economic Forum, YES, iEARN, SchoolNet and Peace Corps volunteers.

---

* President and Founder, World Computer Exchange.

Its services include:

- *capacity building assistance*: WCE leads a consortium of Strategic Allies to help its in-country partners and universities build ICT capacity in teacher training, technology maintenance, telecenter management—as well as the development, adaptation and sharing of local educational content;
- *supplying of computers*: WCE provides low-cost computers and software to Partners to connect young people to the Internet years earlier than would otherwise be possible;
- *cultural exchanges*: WCE brokers sister-school collaborations and online website development connections to help improve understanding among young people in different countries.

WCE recognizes that simply providing the computers is only the first step towards helping underprivileged communities begin to bridge the global digital divide. WCE also provides capacity building assistance in other forms such as help with teacher training, curriculum development, telecenter management, and technology maintenance.

In undertaking its activities with its partners, WCE employs a clearly identified threefold approach:

- to help our Partners (NGOs, business and governments) to find ways to make Internet access for youth sustainable;
- to use WCE's Program Officers, teams of online support volunteers and 20 global strategic allies to leverage resources and services for our partners;
- to act as a quiet, respectful, and transparent broker helping Partners to build their ICT in education capacity.

In turn, WCE requires its Partners to:

- commit to the understanding that the primary use of most of the donated computers is to connect poor youth to the Internet;
- present a sustainable implementation plan that shows capacity and a draft list of interested schools and centers;
- pay WCE's sourcing and administrative cost of US$49 per Pentium I and/or US$37 per Power Mac plus shipping ($64 each for all-PII and III mixed shipments plus shipping);
- agree to final disposal of equipment in a way that minimizes damage to the environment.

Each of these elements is important in meeting sustainable social and environmental goals.

Schools, centers, libraries and orphanages are recruited by WCE Partners who train, instal and evaluate. The participants must agree to protect, maintain, and connect computers to the Internet for poor youth (for example, by charging fees for adult use after school hours). They must also help youth in the school, library, or orphanage or center to form partnerships with sister-schools, file semi-annual reports and develop a cultural and historical website.

WCE operates in 51 countries with 320 formal Partner organisations: Afghanistan, *Bangladesh*, *Bénin*, *Bolivia*, *Bosnia*, Burundi, *Cameroon*, Côte d'Ivoire, Democratic Republic of Congo, *Ecuador*, *El Salvador*, Ethiopia, *Georgia*, *Ghana*, *Guatemala*, *Guinea*, Guyana, Haiti, *India*, Iraq, Jordan, *Kenya*, *Liberia*, *Lithuania*, Macedonia, *Madagascar*, *Malawi*, *Mali*, *Mexico*, Moldova, Mongolia, Morocco, Mozambique, Namibia, *Nepal*, *Nigeria*, *Pakistan*, Paraguay, Perú, Philippines, *Rwanda*, *Sénégal*, Sierra Leone, *South Africa*, *Sri Lanka*, *Tanzania*, Togo, *Uganda*, *Viet Nam*, *Zambia*, and Zimbabwe.[1]

The container contents shipped to the recipients comprise:

- 200 (20 ft) or 400 (40 ft) used Pentium and/or Power Mac desktops and laptops including: colour monitor, mouse, keyboard and US-style power cords;
- networking gear, parts, speakers, 110 volt printers (one for each 10 computers), scanners, extra hard drives and software from donor companies and individuals.

The WCE Partner provides warehouse, duty waiver, 220 volt transformers for printers, appropriate wall plugs, local software installation, repairs for 10 per cent of the computers after shipping, and delivery to the schools involved in the scheme.

Ongoing Evaluation

Ongoing evaluation is built into the WCE program: for three years after the computers arrive, WCE gathers and posts data and pictures on their status, use and impact. Each Partner is expected to visit each school once a year and students in each school report to WCE online each year. WCE volunteers and staff visit Partners and some schools and Partners write a summary report once a year.

Schools Program

A number of high schools in the US are involved with the work of the WCE. In Washington DC, for example, students from two high schools manage computer donation events. A team from Thomas Jefferson High School is going to Ecuador to provide website development training. They are seeking a Youth Venture grant. In Seattle, students from four high schools help with computer testing and packing.

A team from Ballard High School visited the Republic of Georgia thanks to Rotary funding to provide technical support. In New Haven, a team of students from St Bernard High School each year configures servers-in-a-box for some of WCE overseas schools. In San Francisco, students from several high schools help with computer testing and packing. In Boston, a team formed of students from three high schools works together to test equipment and pack pallets for shipment. Several schools across the USA have formed sister-school partnerships to help schools that have recently received computers from WCE. A new, more intensive project is being developed with several schools in Canada interested in becoming sister-schools with schools in developing countries that have received computers from WCE.

"Internet Ambassadors"

The WCE and its Partners recognize the value of ambassadorial visits by participating students from North America. For example, students from US or Canadian schools plan school trips to an interested WCE recipient Partner. WCE provides introductions between school and Partner and the school works out insurance details with the Partner. The North American students stay in homes of interested parents and contribute a small amount to family food budget. The Partner arranges for transportation and for participation in projects. During their visit, the ambassadors provide training in website development or use of Internet in education or help with network maintenance.

WCE's Request for Business Involvement

WCE makes a number of requests to businesses and entrepreneurs, among which is Sponsorship of the last third of the sourcing and shipping costs of a container shipment. They are also asked to donate working Pentium laptops and desktops as well as network gear, parts, software and printers. In addition, employees are encouraged to make a contribution, donate their personal computers, or volunteer to provide online support in technology, content and telecenter management.

There are a number of options open to businesses who would like to offer sponsorship:

- *container sponsors*: funding the last one-third of the sourcing and shipping funds needed to deliver 400 computer sets to connect 12,000 students in 30 schools or libraries, at a cost of US$10,000;
- *city sponsor*: funding for WCE to start a sister-school program with the Sponsor's city's schools—US$5,000;
- *trip sponsor*: sending a WCE volunteer to help train teachers, evaluate and trouble-shoot technical problems—US$2,000;

- *lab sponsor*: providing a full computer laboratory for a school or library in a developing country—US$750;
- *computer sponsor*: providing a computer for a school or library in a developing country—US$50.

Those wishing to offer local help can:

- donate working Pentium II or better computers;
- help WCE locate donated warehouse space;
- volunteer to help us gather and test computers;
- help find financial sponsors to help our partners;
- help WCE recruit interested sister-schools locally;
- help WCE find universities interested in partnering with universities in Africa.

Working Models: Recycling Centers

A key feature of WCE's activities is to be found in its working collaboratively with recycling nonprofits and businesses. Some of the models that WCE uses with these Recycling/Reuse Allies demonstrate a number of different working models:

- *Total Reclaim* in Seattle—test selected computers in their stream for WCE—WCE pays part of salary and they let WCE accept, test and palletize in their facility;
- *WITS* in St Louis and *STEP* in Houston—jointly market a single donation and testing program by shared volunteers for donated computers to go both to local schools and to be shipped to schools internationally;
- *ElectroniCycle* in Massachusetts and *Computer Recycling Center* in California—pay for missing pieces of equipment that WCE needs.

WCE is also leading a consortium of allied organizations in an e-Waste Initiative to provide best-practices materials for groups in developing countries to be used as simple tools for orienting people to the need for environmentally appropriate recycling and for the development of a business plan for a pilot e-Waste recycling center to be tested in Africa. The African e-Waste Recycling Pilot is working with the Basil Action Network, CIDA, UNESCO, UN Environment Program, environmentalists, Yale Recycling, University of Dakar, Computer Aid International and American Retroworks.

Access for All

WCE has 30 partners with implementation plans and two-thirds of the necessary funding for the sourcing and shipping of 10,600 computers ready to connect nearly 300,000 youth—all that is needed now is less than $1 per student to connect them!

WCE works within many developing countries to help 'connect the dots' horizontally within the country—among local educators, entrepreneurs, NGOs, donors and international NGOs.

Most of WCE's partners employ used computers from us during the school day for youth and then afterwards for the community on a fee basis—to help cover the school's connectivity costs. The implications for sustainability are clear: the technology can be used to secure an income which supports its maintenance.

We encourage all African schools that receive WCE computers to join the resource networks of SchoolNet, YES, and iEARN. These provide important contexts and training for the effective use of the technology and for enhanced and sustainable access to resources.

Working with Universities

WCE has learned about the potential of university involvement in ICT in education by working with university partners in Bolivia, Georgia, Viet Nam and Bangladesh. Based on these experiences, WCE asked African universities if they would be interested in developing a capacity-building initiative together. The resulting initiative is based on the assumption that it is valuable to have universities in Africa increase direct practical involvement in solving today's issues and to build the capacity at interested universities in the area of ICT in education so they can build this capacity in primary and secondary schools in their areas. WCE recruited a consortium of experts and organizations with the skills to respond to needs of universities in teacher training, evaluation, local content development, telecenter management, technical support, and environmentally-appropriate disposal.

African Universities Initiative

On a continent faced with massive immediate challenges ranging from health and HIV/AIDS to ineffective governance and war, education remains a key component for a better future in Africa. Africans themselves identify education and computer literacy as priorities, viewing them as mechanisms for bootstrapping themselves out of a cycle of poverty and dependence. They see the potential of well-developed ICT capacity as an avenue through which they can begin to improve their economy and make the leap into a technological society.

African formal education systems are taxed by minimal resources and extensive responsibilities. They often lack the confidence of the private sector and civil society and require genuine institutional reform. The combination of limited financial and political support for change, the size of the system and its great complexity make clear the need for new and alternative approaches.

The promise of ICT attracts individuals and institutions from across sectors and classes, marshalling their interest in a way that traditional education reform does not. In this way, the potential for the use of ICT to alter the status quo is unparalleled. Using technology to attract and facilitate connections and interaction among communities, regardless of where they are located or who they are, can promote flows of information and knowledge, creation of ideas and initiatives, and ultimately a healthier society.

This initiative was developed to respond to the following challenges faced by the universities:

- many well-intentioned but underfunded African universities are striving to respond more effectively to the educational and development problems facing their communities;
- most African universities lack the communication and information technology that can enhance instruction for their students;
- among the African universities with education faculties most face challenges in their ability to teach future teachers how to use the Internet to improve learning in primary and secondary classrooms and to develop local online content;
- most African universities would benefit if their entering students had more expertise with computers and the Internet;
- many African university students would benefit from more practicums in computer and network maintenance, local content development, and the management of small entrepreneurial businesses like community telecenters.

Participation in AUI will help African universities to increase their capacity for understanding of and teaching and training in ICT in education, while building deeper ties with their communities and reinforcing their own relevance. Schools will benefit from outside interest and ideas, helping them to offer richer and more diverse learning opportunities to their students—and teachers. Local communities will also benefit from the increased connectivity available to them, creating additional opportunities in terms of lifelong learning, entrepreneurship, social communication and other factors influencing quality of life. As a result, we expect that this initiative will impact the short- and long-term educational and economic conditions at the local and regional levels.

WCE is now launching our largest project to date, the *Africa Universities Initiative (AUI)*. As a result of this program, 200,000 students in over 300 African universities and high schools will benefit from improved IT access and development.

The initiative that was developed as part of the World Economic Forums's Global Digital Divide Initiative is called the African Universities Initiative (AUI) has as its objective that ten universities in Africa build up their ICT capacities in the following areas and each in turn assists 30 nearby primary and secondary schools to build their ICT capacities:

- teacher training in the educational use of the Internet;
- management of telecenters in schools;
- distance learning;
- computer and network maintenance by technology students;
- development and sharing of local online learning content;
- online multinational educational projects;
- environmentally-safe disposal of "dead" computers.

The *African Universities Initiative* begins with 10 selected universities from 10 African countries. Each of the 10 AUI universities will identify areas in which they need additional capacity building. Depending on these areas, they will either get assistance from one of the other AUI universities or from a member of the *AUI Consortium*. Each university, in turn, will use this new capacity to have their students undertake practicums to build these same skills among the teachers in 30 nearby 'adopted' schools. As part of this initiative, low-cost computers will be provided to all educational institutions involved, enabling ongoing Internet access all students in the program.

The 10 universities involved in the initiative are:

- D.R. Congo: University of Lubumbashi at Mbuji Mayi;
- Ghana: University of Education at Winneba;
- Kenya: Jomo Kenyatta University of Agriculture and Technology;
- Malawi: University of Malawi, Chancellor College;
- Mozambique: Eduardo Mondlane University;
- Nigeria: University of Nigeria at Nsukka;
- Sénégal: Universite Cheike Anta Diop;
- Togo: l'Universite de Lome;
- Uganda: Makerere University;
- Zambia: University of Zambia.

WCE is leading a diverse, international *AUI Consortium* of 12 educational NGOs that each bring unique expertise in helping university leaders to shape a vision of the future educational use of technology, knowledge of the use of information and communication technology (ICT) in education, training teachers in the use of online collaborative projects, the development of local online content, youth resources in each country and substantial contacts in North American liberal arts colleges.

This AUI Consortium of WCE Strategic Allies comprising the Africa Network of US liberal arts colleges, the Center for Democracy and Development (Nigeria), COMETE (France), the International Technologies Group (Harvard Law School), iEARN in nine of the 10 countries, InterConnection for web development, SchoolNet in nine of the 10 African countries, the United Nations Volunteers to recruit volunteers, WiderNet (University of Iowa and *e-Granary*), the World Education Corps in Ghana (Nigeria and Uganda) and the Youth Employment Summit (YES) in all 10 countries.

African and US College Partnerships

WCE works with the Africa Network to recruit interested US colleges to form Partnerships with 10 African universities around curriculum material sharing, distance learning collaboration, student scholarships, faculty exchanges, student community service to help gather computers and adapt content for local needs.

The Role of AUI Specialists

The AUI specialists play an important role in the coordination of activities in many directions—they:

- coordinate resources for AUI within AUI university;
- coordinate resources from the AUI Consortium;
- are the eyes and ears and undertake due diligence for AUI;
- guide evaluation at 30 primary and secondary schools;
- coordinate with other WCE Partners in-country;
- coordinate content, telecenter and technical resources;
- assist with working with the Partner university;
- communicate with WCE for other nine AUI country teams.

The Role of AUI Consortium Members

Likewise consortium members have an important role to play—they:

- help build capacity in the area where the specific organisation has skills;
- commit to being listed and involved as part of an AUI team in countries where they are located;
- agree to occasional use by WCE as eyes and ears on the ground to help with due diligence in considering potential WCE Partners in countries where they are located;

- meet with AUI University in countries where they are located to determine the role they would like to play with them as part of AUI;
- inform WCE on appropriate strategies for WCE in countries where they are located.

AUI Fund Raising

The total AUI budget required is US$5 million. At the time of writing, in-kind commitments in hand stand at US$3.35 million and the WCE is therefore seeking US$1.65 million or US$165,000 per university. The testimonies to the need for the partnership work of WCE are clear: and so is the need for the budget to move forward.

This initiative will have fundamental, lasting and far-reaching impact on the information technology infrastructure in Africa. It will result in improved communication and collaboration between African universities and between universities and high schools. It will build IT capacity in 300 educational institutions in 10 different African countries and, in its first two years of operation alone, will directly impact on over 200,000 students.

> The work of WCE has been invaluable for developing countries willing to harness the digital opportunities emerging from the nascent global networked economy. Since July of 2000, our initiative, the UNDP Sustainable Development Networking Program, which we launched in 1993, has been a close partner of WCE and helped identify key local partners and stakeholders, and finance the actual shipment of computers to Bangladesh, Cameroon Nigeria, DR Congo, and Benin. We look forward to continue our partnership with WCE to find innovative ways to address the digital divide with action oriented interventions. (Raúl Zambrano, Senior ICT for Development Policy Advisor, UNDP)

> The digital divide is one of the most popular topics at meetings of the international development community. The World Computer Exchange is one of the few organizations that actually does something about the problem. This effective non-profit group has sent thousands of donated computers to the developing world. It is helping to equip and train the people who will soon narrow the digital divide'. (J. Brian Atwood, Dean, Hubert Humphrey Institute of Public Affairs, WCE International Advisory Council, Former USAID Administrator)

> It has been very interesting to watch the quick development of World Computer Exchange. They have been effective at improving the image of used computers in many of the countries of Africa. The consulting process and the 25 questions that WCE asks their partners to think about are very helpful in training NGOs in sustainable IT development. (Lane Smith, Coordinator, USAID Leland Initiative)

Note

1 Italics = shipments have already been made (31 countries).

Chapter Nine

The Challenge: Universities and ICT Incubation[1]

Royal D. Colle*

There is a young woman named Nigar who lives in a mostly Muslim slum in New Delhi. Separated from an abusive husband, Nigar and her two children struggle against the poverty that engulfs her home. It is through a local telecenter that she and other women in the community are breaking the isolation of their ghetto lives and learning about health and gaining vocational training including the use of computers. The Nigar story speaks to the first Millennium Development Goal: to reduce extreme poverty and, more specifically, to *cut in half the proportion of people living on less than a dollar a day and those who suffer from hunger.* Nigar demonstrates how telecenters can play a role in harnessing ICTs for education.[2] This chapter suggests that, universities in developing nations should play a stronger role in supporting telecenters as community learning institutions.

A report released at the World Summit on the Information Society in 1993 identified a significant role for information and communication technologies (ICT) in strategies for African development. The report notes that NEPAD[3] includes a strong focus on the dual strategies of *ICT Development* (ICTD) and *ICT for Development* (ICT4D). In this chapter we argue that universities in developing nations are potentially important players in both of these NEPAD strategies, and that the 'eReadiness' of universities is a vital issue in community development. The eReadiness of universities is clearly relevant to the global creation and distribution of knowledge, which, in turn, is a core challenge in the world's thrust toward the Millennium Development Goals.

First, a clarification. We apply the NEPAD terms to universities this way:

- *ICT development* in the university context refers to building media and digital facilities to support a university's internal functions, along with an academic and research program that prepares students to function effectively in an information society in both the public and the private sectors;
- *ICT for development* refers to the university applying ICTs in programmes outside its walls in the service of communities and the nation. *We know of no convincing evidence that universities spontaneously move to ICT4D after, or while, achieving ICTD.*

Most African universities themselves are just beginning to get organized for the ICT environment. In fact, one observer contends that the current weak state of

---

* Cornell University (USA)

most African universities accounts for the lack of good Africa-relevant educational content on the Web (da Costa, 2000). As digital technologies shape the new frontier for information and communication in this twenty-first century, higher education institutions in the Africa and Asia can become a more powerful force in applying them to education, training and development issues rather than abandon them to commercial interests.

With the exception of technical connectivity issues, computer training and distance learning courses for college level students, the record of higher education in information and communication technologies for development is dismal.[4] The record of university involvement with ICTs and the Millennium Development Goals also is virtually invisible. With regard to supporting and helping sustain community telecenters in particular, universities are widely perceived as irrelevant, *if they are even considered at all.*

Recently we raised this relevance issue in India when the National Alliance for Information and Communication Technologies for Basic Human Needs came into being in May 2004. The National Alliance set a goal of bringing all of India's 600,000 villages into the modern "information society" by 2007, the sixtieth anniversary of the nation's Independence. The National Alliance hopes to achieve its "Mission 2007" primarily through the creation of a network of Rural Knowledge Centres (telecenters) across the country. When we proposed to an Alliance leader that the agricultural universities in India be explicitly included in the planning as partners for the knowledge centers, we received this terse emailed response:

> The universities have failed miserably in many respects. Most university faculty have no clue to life outside the campus nor have they any social concerns. Sorry for being very forthright or even blunt.

The issue is summed up by a recent two-year study commissioned by the World Bank and UNESCO. The study concluded that the contribution of higher education to social and economic development in developing countries has been "disappointing to date" including a failure to advance the public interest. One of the major obstacles, said the report, is that "the social and economic importance of higher education systems is insufficiently appreciated" (World Bank, 2000: 93).

Universities and Telecenters

Telecenters are important in the discussion of ICTs and education because they are emerging all over the developing world: Taiwan, Vietnam, China, India, Latin America, and, of course, Africa. Typically a multi-purpose community telecenter is a public facility in the community that affords people the opportunity to use computers, networks, copiers, scanners, telephone, community, printed materials and audio and video resources for information searching, communication, training and entertainment. The services are free or available at an affordable cost. The primary mission of a telecenter is community service as compared to a cybercafé whose primary mission is profit. A telecenter has staff—often volunteers—who actively assist the public in resolving information and communication problems. Ideally, the telecenter management also collaborates with other institutions such as those in agriculture, health, government, and education to mobilize information, training and distance learning resources.

We went beyond the rather general indictment of academics illustrated by my email correspondent and looked at five dimensions of what we called *university e-readiness*, or the conditions that are significantly relevant to ICTD and ICT4D. These included:

- ICT facilities and network access for the university community;
- personnel available to support design and production of digital materials such as CDs, webpages and distance learning (training) packages;
- academic programs including field experience that prepare students for applying ICTs to community development;
- university policies that apply to faculty participation in outreach programs;
- faculty ICT posture: for example, what is their disposition regarding the use and efficacy of ICTs in education and learning.

Telecenters can be a local institution that parallels the local school system, providing a learning resource for reaching people like Nigar in the New Delhi slum and millions of others, mostly in rural areas, who have been overlooked by the conventional education system.

Let us be specific about the connection between universities and telecenters. First a very large percentage of telecenters struggle for survival. The reasons vary but prominent among them is the failure for telecenters to be *demand-driven.* And this happens because telecenter people often lack an understanding of the communities' information, education and training needs, and also often lack the know-how and resources to build the content and services that could respond to those needs. We can identify four specific ways in which higher education can contribute to the sustainability of telecenters that, unlike cybercafés, have a community development mission.

Research

Research helps telecenters become demand-driven. Research can identify communities' needs for information and related services. Research must be a long-term process, not a single start-up activity, because needs change over time, especially if the community is developing. Telecenters generally have neither the skills, time, motivation nor interest in systematic research about the communities around them. Telecenters also need research to evaluate continuously how well they are serving the needs of their communities. Many universities have research capabilities that could be applied to these telecenter needs. Students and university faculties in a range of disciplines (from computer science to rural sociology) can apply their knowledge and training to ICT-related research that will better link telecenters to their communities.

Local and Relevant Content

Too much content on the web is not relevant to farmers and other rural people,nor to the young women in the New Delhi slum. It is a common problem around the world, where externally-generated information often dominates locally-tailored material. This is where credible, useful and user-friendly information needs to be crafted. The UNDP has suggested that the most important reason for the failure of telecenters is their lack of suitable content. Universities such as agricultural universities have access to science-based information that could be tailored to regional, provincial and local agronomic, social, linguistic and cultural characteristics, and could be matched with many of the education and training requirements related to the Millennium Development Goals. Also, universities are in a good position to design and administer distance learning and self-paced learning packages that people can use to negotiate successfully in contemporary society. Returning once again to the Delhi slum, we find that Nigar studied embroidery on a six-week course at the telecenter and ended up teaching embroidery in the community. In south India the Tamil Nadu University of Veterinary and Animal Sciences has produced video CDs on subjects ranging from remedial measures for infertility in cattle to "Cream, Butter and Cheese", all designed for rural populations.

Information Management

People in telecenters need to be trained in how information can contribute to development. We have found telecenter managers who know a lot about computers but do not know how to link telecenter potential to health clinics for community health education, or to schools, agricultural extension or local government. Likewise, telecenters need to make their communities aware of the value of information, such as agricultural marketing, micro enterprise management or the chances for more education through distance learning. Awareness of the value of information will help the communities realize the value of the telecenter. Logically, universities have the capacity to teach and train, and these skills could be applied to these telecenter-related information awareness and information management needs.

Human Resources

Telecenters need volunteers who can help make them good places to visit—volunteers who can help people search and understand the basic rewards of a digital experience and help those people navigate the various media in the telecenter. A major challenge for telecenters is to "gain, train, and retain" volunteers. Those in touch with today's young people are aware that they—especially college students—generally have the media and digital skills to be good volunteers in a telecenter. Volunteers are important in welcoming persons in special groups such as women and the elderly who are frequently shut out of access to ICTs and telecenters by culture. Universities have human resources such as students who could serve as telecenter interns and faculty members who could serve as content and development advisors.

Benefits to Universities

Universities and telecenters have a logical affinity. In addition to the benefits that they can bring to telecenters, the universities can benefit themselves from an affiliation with telecenters. Three ways are described below.

1 Telecenters provide universities with a means of reaching beyond their "ivory tower" to extend their knowledge and learning resources to the surrounding communities and to other populations in the region. This includes translating, adapting, localizing and repackaging information from external sources to fit the agronomic and cultural characteristics of those local communities. This function is especially vital to the worldwide priorities identified in the Millennium Development Goals. Ultimately this makes universities more relevant and better candidates for support from the public and private sector.

2 Telecenters provide a laboratory for faculty and researchers to carry out ICT and extension-related research and development (R&D) projects especially involving issues ranging from HIV/AIDS to small business enterprises and poverty alleviation, and to universities' involvement with these issues. Telecenters as extensions of the classroom can also strengthen student understanding of issues ranging from computer applications and community development to eGovernment and eCommerce.

3 Telecenters provide a learning environment for students as telecenter volunteers to gain practical experience in helping people in the community. In some countries college graduates have a public service obligation for one or two years. While it is often associated with military service, attention can be drawn to adding community service in telecenters as a means for discharging this obligation. Benjamin Addom, a recent Cornell graduate student, has done a Masters project that includes a proposal and plan to apply Ghana's service commitment to telecenters.

It is important to note that an active, visible and successful university ICT4D programme can have two additional outcomes. One is the simultaneous building of the university's own internal ICT infrastructure—that is, its ICTD—which will contribute to the quality and efficiency of its academic and administrative functions. And second is the reshaping of its relationship to the outside world as a more active agent of change. This addresses the observation of the Task Force on Higher and Society that "Unlike primary and secondary education, [regarding universities] there is little in the way of a shared vision about the nature and the magnitude of the potential of contribution of higher education to development" (World Bank, 2000: 93).

Precedents

We conclude this chapter by returning to the judgment that universities, especially in developing nations, are irrelevant. We need to emphasize cases in which universities *are* relevant. Two examples from India are:

1 a 1969 initiative in which the Ford Foundation helped build the capacity of the G.B. Pant University of Agriculture and Technology (then in Uttar Pradesh) to produce radio programs for Indian farm families. Radio was the major "ICT" of that time. In producing complete radio programs and delivering them on tape to an All India Radio station (in Rampur), the university became the first non-governmental body in India to supply programs for public consumption. Was it sustainable? Now, 35 years later, the university is serving more than 20 radio stations in the region;

2 a case from Tamil Nadu where support from Canada's International Development Research Centre increased the capacity of the TN University of Veterinary and Animal Sciences (TANUVAS) to incubate and support three Village Information Centres (VIC) and six additional information centres especially serving Self Help Women's Groups. All are community-driven and some are fully supported by their surrounding communities. The university continues to play a partnership role through some training and advisory initiatives and supply of content. (This was one of several case studies featured in a UNICT Task Force publication prepared for the Geneva phase of the WSIS [Colle and Roman, 2004])

Moving Forward

What might be done to promote greater involvement of African universities in ICTD and ICT4D institution-building initiatives? Based on our research and observing ICT and development initiatives around the world, we have proposed an initiative to build the ICT4D capacity in a *regional group* of African universities.

The intent is to demonstrate the potential of universities as partners in such ICT-related development activities as community telecenters, and to persuade important policymakers to factor universities into their ICT policies. The components of the initiative, expressed as outputs, include:

- a consortium of networked east/southern Africa agricultural/technology departments/ universities to collaborate with a North American university consortium in ICT-for-development programs;
- creation of a university-based center of excellence (ICT Resource Centre) in east/southern Africa for supporting the university consortium's ICT activities including practical training, production of educational and training materials, collaborative research, and exchange of information, knowledge and experience;
- a model curriculum and learning materials for ICT-for-rural development academic and training programs, adapted to the learning culture of the participating universities;
- a cadre of trained ICT for rural development "champions" on the staffs of the participating universities, accomplished through collaboration with US universities;
- an explicit policy and program at each participating university for recruiting students and in-service training candidates into ICT-for-rural development courses and workshops;
- a plan of action for establishing communication linkages among ICT policymakers in government, faculty in universities, scientists in research institutes, agricultural enterprises, farmer groups and rural communities especially to promote development issues such as the Millennium Development Goals.

Summary and Challenge

Telecenters (also known by other names such as Rural Knowledge Centers) are important local institutions that can provide education, training and information for people not served by conventional educational institutions. Universities can help these institutions become more demand-driven, thus contributing to their sustainability.

In the process of supporting multi-purpose telecenters, universities can educate students about the potential of ICT4D and train them to apply ICTs to development issues in their communities, and ultimately to support local and national policies that build ICT resources into health, education, government, and economic programs.

In a very practical way, initiatives that build the ICTD and ICT4D capacities of universities will influence the future character of higher education and help them become, and *be perceived as*, more relevant to the people of their countries.

There are two main challenges to potential donor agencies. The first is to sponsor a *rapid* appraisal to clarify and document *why* universities are on the sidelines regarding ICT4D and gain a general picture of what it will take to bring about institutional change regarding ICT4D. The second is to support efforts that *demonstrate* models of universities becoming involved in the ICT4D. At the time of writing, initiatives regarding universities, incubation of telecenters and ICT4D are being framed in China, Vietnam, India and various parts of Africa, but they require a strong push in terms of core funding. The core funding can leverage other resources such as refurbished computers from the World Computer Exchange as well as funding and services from other agencies and the private sector. For example, a project in India seems on the threshold of obtaining support from a private bank's "social responsibility program". A project in Vietnam has been designed and awaits funding from an Asian foundation and a private sector agency in Taiwan. Various individuals in the World Bank have endorsed similar projects for Africa, with actual funding not yet identified.

An endorsement of the university-ICT4D-telecenter concept by an agency such as the UNICT Task Force—reinforced with funds for planning and/or core activities—would give visibility to the idea and motivate others to examine the logic of this approach.

Notes

1 Prepared for the conference "Building the ICT Capacity of African Universities to Promote Development" organized by the Institute for African Development, Cornell University, 19–20 November 2004 at Ithaca, New York.
2 The project is reported in UNESCO, 2004.
3 New Partnership for African Development
4 We note the substantial number of students who have studied in distance learning courses throughout the world. The five largest programs are based in developing countries. See World Bank, 2000: 31.

References

Colle, Royal and Raul Roman. "University-Based Telecenters,"*Connected for Development: Information Kiosks and Sustainability*, in ed. Akhtar Badshah, Sarbuland Khan and Maria Garrido, UN ICT Task Force Series 4: http://www.unicttaskforce.org/perl/documents.pl?id=1361 (May 2004).

da Costa, Peter. "African Content on the Web," in *Rowing Upstream, Pioneers of the Information Age in Africa, Project for Information Access and Connectivity*, ed. L. Levey and S. Young: http://www.piac.org/rowing_upstream/ (2000).

UNESCO. "Women and ICTs—Mediating Social Change". Video (2004).

World Bank, Task Force on Higher Education and Society. *Higher Education in Developing Countries, Peril and Promise* (Washington: The World Bank, 2000).

Chapter Ten

Meeting the Information Challenge: Exploring Partnership Models with Africa

Stephen E. Little*

Introduction

Many regions occupy a marginal position within the new globalizing economy. Neither developed nor developing countries are homogeneous and conditions may vary as widely within them as between them. Within the most developed core countries there are marginal regions with declining industries that are falling behind better-connected areas favoured by the investment needed to develop and acquire new technologies and industries. At these margins, the development of the necessary capacities and capabilities is problematic and the bypassed or excluded areas gain little benefit from the new relationship of global production and consumption.

Many African countries face a task made even harder by a colonial past as contributors of raw materials, whether from primary and extractive industry, or through migration of labour. Infrastructure, both for physical transport (Headrick, 1981) and for science and technology, has been developed around the needs of the external consumers of locally-produced resources, rather than for coherent and balanced internal development. Such legacies limit the capacity to absorb or develop the capabilities necessary to negotiate a national space within an emerging global order. This international order is increasingly dependent upon information and communication technologies (ICTs) and the term 'digital divide' has come to encapsulate the imbalance of infrastructure and capability between the developed and less developed regions. However, the divide is equally one of knowledge and power. Science and technological capabilities lie at the centre of the 'knowledge divide' described by Chataway et al. (2003).

At independence, the African universities represented a key development resource to the new national governments. However, in common with universities on other continents, they have seen a reduction in direct government resources and a less central role in government policy. With 11–13 per cent of the global population, Africa spends around 1 percent of the global education budget (Mutula, 2003). As the nature of the knowledge and capability divide separating Africa from development pathways becomes clearer, the need to re-establish a sustainable key developmental role for the universities of the continent becomes obvious.

---

* Head, Centre for Innovation, Knowledge and Enterprise, Open University Business School.

This chapter examines how, in the face of severely limited resources, the strategic use of available information and communication technologies can assist in the development of African capabilities by facilitating partnerships for this key resource within and beyond the continent.

Beyond Colonial Models: New Technical Opportunities

The infrastructure of global communication is a diverse and heterogeneous assembly of technologies, and the adoption of particular sub-sets of technologies and practices allows the development of distinctly African forms.

Across the African continent, there is considerable variation in infrastructure conditions. In some areas, for example in urban South Africa, patterns of access to and use of mobile communications are close to those found in the most developed regions. The use of mobile phones by sole traders within the Johannesburg conurbation cited by the *Economist* (2005), for example, is little different from that in Los Angeles, London or Sydney.

Elsewhere on the continent, however, the community use of broadcast radio or of mobile telephony reflects a need to leverage limited resources. Patterns are closer to those seen in South Asia, as exemplified by Grameen Phone (see www.grammenphone.com). Individual cell phones may offer a whole community connectivity to absent members while providing a livelihood for one or more families within that community. The village scribe is being superseded by the villager relaying SMS messages for payment (Gough and Grezo, 2005). A single radio may travel around a community with or without its nominal owner, providing information and entertainment for an extended family (Spitulnik, 2000).

Clearly, Africa's technical trajectory for information and communication technologies has been and continues to be different from that of the West and of more developed areas. In the latter, digital technologies have been introduced over well-established and well-developed analogue infrastructures. In contrast, in many parts of Africa digital technologies represent a leapfrogging over under- or undeveloped analogue resources directly to wireless and satellite communications. In the Kalahari, for example, the deployment of Cybertracker, a solar powered digital data collection device developed at the University of Cape Town, by non-literate San people in order to capture information on local environmental conditions and to communicate instantaneously beyond their physical location provides a demonstration of such 'leap-frogging' (Little, Holmes and Grieco, 2001).

Difference in technology trajectories within Africa has allowed the development of distinctive characteristics which offer new possibilities. The selective adoption of ICTs, while a response to lack of resources, has created pathways around the limitations of post-colonial infrastructures. The connections created under colonialism generally retain the characteristics of an agenda of connection between resources and export routes rather than internal linkage to facilitate endogenous development. Railways, roads and land-line phones were originally mapped around the needs of the former colonial centres. However, the newer communication technologies allow a break with this model, just as a new generation of African airlines is breaking with the colonially-determined hub and spoke model which took Africans through a sequence of European capitals in order to reach their neighbours.

Nevertheless, much infrastructure investment is still driven by external criteria similar to those described by Headrick (1981) in his description of railway development in Africa. The key twenty-first century communication technologies are in some danger of mirroring the uneven development of the key nineteenth-century transport technology, with the extreme case of the internationalized enclave of the Free Trade Zone mimicking the trading fort of the nineteenth century (Little, 2004).

In overcoming the burden of colonial legacy infrastructure the ability of smaller and marginal actors to influence a dominant 'techno-economic paradigm' (Dosi, 1986) becomes central. One perspective is represented by the 1970s 'intermediate technology' movement where technologies which had been superseded in the most developed areas were shown to be of value elsewhere. In Africa the key issue is the distinction between fixed-line communications dependent upon a fixed power grid and wireless technologies capable of utilizing ambient energy, whether wind, solar or human/animal. Realignment of the new standard technical configurations to suit African conditions may involve the selection of components from nineteenth, twentieth or twenty-first century repertoires, as with the blended technology of the wind-up radio. The moped may be as appropriate a tool to bridge the gap between Internet access point and end user as a standard wireless router with modified antenna.[1]

The divide between technology-rich and technology-poor environments is also less relevant when collective skilling through partnership can be achieved largely through the communication links provided by intelligent and selective use of ICTs. The key issue for the development of understanding and capability is the connectivity and the virtual adjacency which connectivity delivers. However, the collective management of such adjacencies is critical if partnerships facilitated by the new forms of Internet connectivity are not to replicate older models of dominance. The next section examines the balance between partnership and autonomy necessary to avoid the replication of earlier unequal relationships.

Autonomy versus Partnership

The scale and scope of the key technologies which underpin the global economy make the pursuit of a fully independent technological path problematic for all but the most developed economies. Even then, the imperative for interoperability within the global system makes full autonomy undesirable.

Indeed, in the global economy autonomous technical development becomes the ground for suspicion. Within the continent of Africa, the history of technical autonomy in the Republic of South Africa reflects the response to sanctions under apartheid. In the post-apartheid era the institutional centres of skills and capability created in pursuit of strategic technological autonomy are re-aligning with their more collaborative and networked equivalents in other countries. Historically, the Southern African Development Community (SADC at http://www.sadc.int/) represented the response of nine neighbouring majority ruled states to coordinate development projects intended to lessen economic dependence on apartheid South Africa. It now aims to improve connectivity between all the countries of southern Africa

Partnerships offer the prospect of hybrid forms learning from experience at both ends of the relationship. British Commonwealth governments share experience with open distance learning through the Commonwealth of Learning (COL) http://www.col.org which aims to support publicly funded institutions in developing Commonwealth countries in the provision of affordable education to larger numbers of citizens.

The African Centre for Technology Studies (ACTS http://www.acts.or.ke/index.html) is an African intergovernmental initiative to generate scientific and technical capacity and policy relevant to African countries. Partners and networks include academic and research institutions inside and outside of Africa, national governments, UN bodies and NGOs.

The supporting role which can be delivered from the better resourced centre reverses the accepted logic of outsourcing and off-shoring. The value of such relationships resides in local and relevant content which is supported by the technology transferred into the target region. In 'normal' off-shoring relationships the technology is used to deliver lower value activities to relatively low cost locations, here it facilitates access to the locally produced high value element. The globalization of communication has opened new pathways to partnership for Africa, but as in all other locations, the need for interoperability reduces the ground for autonomy.

States of the Art—Mapping Technology in Africa

The visible and exemplary use of key available technologies is a source of inspiration for end-users and policy developers alike. The available resources and use patterns of information and information technology have been mapped at a number of points.[2] Ploghoft (1995) describes the initial deployment of ICTs in support of information exchange between African universities. Levey and Young (2002) provide a chronology of the adoption of ICTs across Africa from the 1980s onwards. A recent Vodafone report focuses on the economic impact of access to mobile telephony and the patterns of use presently evident in Africa (Vodafone, 2005)

Hafkin (2002) identifies three components of the ICT resource deficit in Africa: firstly the lack of capacity, with African universities offering only very limited

Internet connectivity to students via their main libraries and secondly the deterrent cost which accompanies even this limited level of technical support and finally the problem of content which is both relevant and under local control. For Hafkin the point of connectivity is to become a producer of content and not simply a consumer. Myers (2000) attributes much of the effectiveness of regional radio broadcasting in Francophone Africa to the critical role of locally appropriate content. All of the limitations identified by Hafkin have an added gender dimension, with female students often dissuaded from engagement with the technology and the underpinning skill development.

Given that levels of connectivity for many African universities are a fraction of those available to individual households in Europe and the USA (Holmes, 2004), many externally funded support initiatives focus on only one of these dimensions—the quality of access. Such technologically driven approaches have been taken with earlier generations of promising technology. In the 1980s the Centre Mondial Informatique et Ressources Humaines in Paris promoted the use of state-of-the-art computing technology in Saharan and sub-Saharan Africa (Roper, 1983). The current incarnation is the $100 laptop project which aims to deliver an affordable and viable computer to the most remote locations. Other specialized devices include the Indian Simputer, a robust low-cost hand-held solar-powered device suitable for non-literate users, which incorporates commercial smart card technology to provide cheap and secure storage of individual data separate from the device likely to be shared among a number of different users. While such devices can incorporate wireless networking technology, they require some form of Internet node with which to connect, and this can require a very different order of investment.

The emergence of satellite-based technologies which can provide high levels of connectivity at almost any point has underpinned initiatives such as the African Virtual University (AVU). VSAT (very small aperture terminal) satellite ground stations have been deployed with the intention of delivering high grade and reliable Internet and communication links, but the cost to end users means they are more likely to be of value in attracting foreign inward investors than in directly supporting indigenous capacities. In contrast, the SAT-3/WASC/SAFE fibre optic system was developed to link Africa with Europe and South and South East Asia.[3]

Telkom South Africa, was a key champion of this project, with support from a number of state-owned national carriers. The provision of a high quality link designed to service a significant proportion of African nations and to provide connection between them represents a significant break with the colonially inspired connections it replaced. However, pricing and access policies within individual African countries discourage the majority of potential users. Under-utilization means that the objective of retrieving some US$600 million repatriation annually to telecommunications companies based outside Africa is not being achieved (*Daily Champion*, 2006). In the six years since the SAT-3 fibre optic cable was commissioned, costs have reduced significantly. However, the connectivity problem then shifts from linkage to the high quality nodes to linkage to points at which the connectivity is needed by end-users. The UK Open University commissioned the South African Institute for Distance Education (SAIDE) to undertake a desktop study focusing on South Africa, Tanzania, Kenya and Nigeria to inform its Teacher Education in Sub-Saharan Africa (TESSA) project consortium of the current (2005) and potential future (2005–2010) access of primary teachers to online resources. The study found that radio, followed by television, remains the most accessible media on the Africa continent. For example, in 2003, in Sub-Saharan Africa on average there were 198 radios per 1,000 people statistics indicated that 250 in 1,000 people had a radio while 69 in 1,000 had a television set. Both South Africa (336) and Tanzania (406) exceeded the average density of radios while South Africa (177) and Nigeria (103) exceeded the average density of television.

The study also found that mobile phone penetration at 6.2 per cent in Africa as a whole was double the 3 per cent for fixed lines the end of 2003. In Nigeria, the number of mobile subscribers was expected to grow by 75 per cent between 2003 and 2004, while close to 60 per cent of the population in Kenya had cellular signal coverage. A study conducted by Vodafone in Tanzania found that 97 per cent of the people surveyed could access a mobile phone. In South Africa, 36 per cent of the population were mobile subscribers in 2003 and there were reportedly 19 million mobile users in 2004. For both academics and the wider user community the initial connection and its support is critical to the exploitation of the wider connectivity, whatever its quality. The success of the mobile phone reflects the simplicity of its use and its general robustness.

Overall Internet penetration in Africa was around 1.5 per cent. While 7.4 per cent of the population in South Africa has access to the Internet, only 0.7 per cent has access to the Internet in Tanzania. 3.3 per 1,000 people had access to a personal computer in Tanzania in 2001, with 72.6 per 1,000 people in South Africa having access to personal computers and 57 per cent of students and staff in higher education being Internet users in 2002.[4] These disparities reflected limited infrastructure, lack of competent personnel, high cost of hardware, software and connectivity, lack of awareness of appropriate use of technology in education and apathy towards use of technology in education among academics.

Partnership Within and Without Africa

Partnership arrangements can range from bilateral cooperation with geographically close neighbours to participation in wide-reaching networks of mentoring and collaborating institutions. Regional partnerships can support the development of regional approaches and solutions, wider partnerships can deliver capabilities not available locally. Both the Association of African Universities and the African Virtual University reflect the complementary relationship between these strategies.

The Association of African Universities (AAU) represents a strong regional partnership for sharing experience. It was established in 1967 by 34 universities as the apex organization and principal forum for consultation, exchange of information and cooperation among universities in Africa with the following objectives:

- to promote interchange, contact and cooperation among university institutions in Africa;
- to collect, classify and disseminate information on higher education and research, particularly in Africa;
- to promote cooperation among African Institutions in curriculum development, and in the determination of equivalence of degrees;
- to encourage increased contracts between its members and the international academic world;
- to study and make known the educational and related needs of African university institutions and, as far as practicable, to coordinate the means whereby those needs may be met;
- to encourage the development and wider use of African languages;
- to organize, encourage and support seminars and conferences between African university teachers, administrators and others dealing with problems of higher education in Africa (http://www.aau.org/).

The African Virtual University (AVU) developed initially with World Bank support as a means of delivering quality learning material from outside Africa. Juma (2001) describes the initial pilot development of the AVU from Kenyan perspective. She points out that between 1970 and 1991 Kenyan tertiary education developed from a single university with a student population of 2,786 to a system of five public universities with a combined student population of 40,000 with consequences for capacity utilization, quality, instructional materials, facilities, and access to university education.

Mutula (2003) points out that the Kenyan government also encourages a significant number of students to pursue university education overseas. Currently around 12,000 students study in India, the USA, Britain, and Europe. Bilateral relationships have been established between Kenyan and European universities, for example that between Moi University and Delft University of Technology in the Netherlands focuses on the development of Kenyan management and IT infrastructure capabilities. In this context the initial development of the AVU was aimed at the electronic delivery of high quality materials, particularly in science and technology, sourced from institutions outside Africa to provide additional capacity across Africa.

Juma (2001) describes how the AVU pilot programmes were conducted in three phases: a prototype pilot phase, from 1997–98 followed by undergraduate degree programmes from universities worldwide, and finally the offering of science and technology curricula by one or more partner institutions in sub-Saharan Africa. She lists 27 institutions across Africa that had started AVU courses during the 1998–99 academic year. Seminars were organized for the business community, sometimes transmitted via video-conference live from the Virginia Technological Institute in the United States, in addition to those facilitated by the Economic Development Institute of the World Bank.

Juma describes the AVU's initial achievements in terms of the provision of educational resources, introduction of new courses, capacity building, income generation, increases in enrolment, and the digital library. She acknowledges the task facing university lecturers in developing proficiency in new virtual teaching strategies, in the face of variable infrastructure quality and equally variable national communication policies. The use of external accreditation was seen as a mean to reduce the outward drain of the most qualified students to overseas institutions while the use of centres across the continent allowed cross-country student collaboration in addition to access to professors outside Africa. After a successful pilot phase, AVU has shifted from the role of free-standing institution to a support and capacity building resource for established institutions. It has changed from a World Bank project to an independent inter-governmental organization based in Nairobi, Kenya and supporting some 57 Learning Centers in 27 African countries and acts as a broker between institutions within Africa with identified needs and institutions elsewhere with relevant skills and programmes.

The AVU identifies its current context as follows:

> The African Virtual University (AVU) is an innovative educational organization established to serve the countries of Africa. The objective of the AVU is to build capacity and support economic development by leveraging the power of modern telecommunications technology to provide world-class quality education and training programs to students and professionals in Africa
>
> *Rationale for the AVU*
>
> Africa is an enormous continent with 53 countries and a population of over 700 million people, over fifty per cent of whom are under 20 years of age. There is a high demand for quality education at tertiary level on the continent. This demand is driven by the following five main factors:
>
> - a large percentage of high school leavers ready for university education are unable to enrol in university due to limited resources
> - overstretched government budgets owing to competing imperatives
> - an expensive and overly subscribed private education sector at tertiary level
> - a large labour force that directly requires the upgrading of skills and
> - the growing isolation of Africa from the Global Knowledge Society. (http://www.avu.org/about.asp)

Both AAU and AVU demonstrate partnerships which increase the capabilities and capacities of African institutions and individual through forms of interconnectivity.

However, a third and less formal set of connections between the more and less developed spheres also exists. The African diaspora is an additional resource which can monitor and mentor from outside and provide an alternative channel of communication and capability. Alongside the strategic view provided by a top-down approach, the grassroots experience of external technical and economic environments can assist the development of appropriate tactical engagements with the enabling technologies.

Autonomy and Connectivity: the Diasporic Dimension

The capacities of developing nations have long been limited by the loss of skilled and economically active individuals to locations offering greater opportunity and rewards. Across Africa the migration of professionals is a continuing concern, with an estimated 60,000 professionals (doctors, scientists, engineers, etc.) leaving between 1985 and 1990. Both India and China have seen similar outflows of talent and capability in the past. Recently, however, movement of scientists and engineers between these Asian locations and technologically advanced countries has not been simply one way. A growing range of diasporic communities have assimilated the key technologies and this has a skills transfer role in raising both awareness and capability levels within the home community.In recent years the concept of 'brain drain'; implying a one-way, definitive and permanent migration of skilled labours has been replaced by an understanding of 'brain circulation' in the context of a global knowledge-based economy.

While the monetary contribution of overseas workers to economic development and poverty reduction in their home countries through financial remittances is well understood, the remittance of intellectual capacity and capability is less widely acknowledged. Saxenian (2002) describes the critical role played by US-based Indian scientists and engineers to the stunning growth of India's software industry which has created 400,000 new jobs and led economic growth in regions such as Bangalore. In their examination of the Ghanaian diaspora Henry and Mohan (2003) suggest that the links to home may promote cultural stasis as much as they provide cultural stimulation. However, the constant communication provided by ICTs enables a closer alignment and synergy between the home and overseas communities than previously. Both connectivity and physical movement between locations are needed for active engagement in a global discourse

The Digital Diaspora Network—Africa represents an attempt to mobilize the technological, entrepreneurial, and professional expertise and resources of the African Diaspora.[5] Experiential learning by members of a diaspora, bridging the territories of potential partners provides a key safeguard to ensure that formerly dependent relationships can become truly interdependent.

Closing the Digital Divide—a Multimedia Technical Menu

The AVU was premised on the use of the most advance ICTs available in order to deliver a distance learning product of the highest technical quality. However, Wolff (2002) suggests that the initial choice of satellite-based broadcast television, while perhaps reasonable in 1997, has become relatively expensive and inflexible as the cost and availability of alternatives has improved. The subsequent shift from a free-standing university to a technology broker and facilitator to some degree is an acknowledgement of this. In order to benefit from these changes African institutions are faced with a range of critical choices in both technology and its configuration and use. The AVU is assessing technologies such as wireless and cellular mobile systems and their convergence with the Internet.

Selecting from a Range of Technologies

A study of current African conditions Commissioned by the British Open University led to the identification of some key features of ICT access in African context.

- Mobile devices (notebook computers and handheld devices) have such low penetration into African schools that it would not be advisable to build content based on these as meaningful forms of access. However in South Africa in a profile of over 1000 primary school teachers less than 20 per cent claimed any access to the Internet.
- Broadband Internet access is not accessible in most schools across the continent at affordable rates. Thus very few schools even in bigger rollout projects such as Gauteng Online (in South Africa) have access to broadband Internet connections (SAIDC 2005: 60).

Three possible but linked sets of technical scenarios were developed:

- a single computer where the best option of distributing content is likely to be CD-ROM;
- a PC mini-cluster. As with option one, distribution of content through CD-ROM is likely to be the best option. However, option exists for data-casting as an alternative form of content distribution;
- a computer laboratory. This remains the dominant model for providing learners access to ICTs and digital content across Africa. Distribution of content is through the Internet. However, Internet access speed remains constrained as many of these projects have not been able to afford to roll out meaningful broadband connectivity. Again, in this scenario, option does exist for use of data-casting as an alternative form of content distribution (SAIDC, 2005: 65)

The use of SMS on mobile devices to alert teachers to available resources was considered a practical possibility for each of these scenarios.

Public and Private Sector Roles

The *Economist* magazine has recently entered the debate over whether the development of Internet-based digital services is as significant for African development as the diffusion of mobile telephony. In the same vein, a Vodaphone report demonstrates the association between the penetration of mobile telephony and economic development in a number of African countries. These newer technologies reside in the private sector and they effectively bypass the institutional rent-seeking around state monopoly based on the existing systems.

The high costs associated with monopolistic behaviour, whether by governments or state monopolies, are as great a barrier to development as their physical limitations. In Nigeria the countries second telecom operator announced plans to replicate the SAT-3 fibre optic cable with its own infrastructure having failed to negotiate satisfactory access, diverting resources which might otherwise have improved internal connectivity. However, governments can play a positive role in the extension of the newer technologies to the population beyond the existing wired world. The South African requirement of GSM network licensees to provide subsidised GSM payphones in low-income areas is one example of the policies that are possible, while Uganda has committed resources to the development of regional Internet access.[6]

Balancing the Load: High Capacity Links and the Final Kilometre

In some respects the development of high capacity Internet links mirrors the focus on high profile flagship projects in early post-independence development. The critical connectivity between end users and the nearest quality connection has been tackled by a variety of imaginative grassroots initiatives. The imaginative blending of technologies and the sharing of resources has significantly extended the reach of the Internet in Africa and elsewhere. The success of top down flagship projects ultimately depends upon bottom-up ingenuity which delivers cooperative use of limited resources and hybrid solutions. The successful reconciliation of top down and bottom up approaches depends on the effective use of selected technology through social learning across distributed communities.

Experiencing Partnerships with Africa

The African Virtual University represents a sustained attempt to link African and external resources though ICTs in order to build capacity for economic development.

The initial pilot tested the viability of a transnational African vehicle for the delivery of externally source high quality material to support African students and the revised structure links African and external resources around identified problems. The UK-based Open University is collaborating with AVU on one key programme to deliver open content to African institutions: TESSA—Teacher Education in Sub-Saharan Africa. This partnership represents the transfer of externally-developed distance learning skill into an African context, albeit following a number of separate partnerships with more limited objectives. It represents an opportunity for both ends of the relationship as the OU's delivery methods are shifting from broadcast model to interactive and Internet based modes.

The OU has both a history of collaborative activities and partnerships in Africa and an African Vice Chancellor. OU learning methods have their-origins in broadcast open access learning in a developed context. Despite the shift from broadcast to Internet supported interactive mode, both print and broadcast elements still have a place in delivery.

OU DEEP Programme

The DEEP programme (www.open.ac.uk/deep) represents an externally-driven partnership to deliver electronic support to education, initially funded by the UK Department for International Development (DFID). The title reflects the digital enhancement of education programmes. It is intended to address the demand for teachers in the context of the Millennium Development Goal of Universal Primary Education in the context of more than 40 million children of primary school age in sub-Saharan Africa without school places.

Originally funded by the UK Department for International Development (DFID), DEEP is a partnership between the Open University (UK) and several project partners:

- University of Fort Hare (UFH) and the Nelson Mandela Foundation's Unit of Rural Schooling and Development in Eastern Cape South Africa;
- Programme, Planning and Monitoring Unit (PPMU) in Egypt;
- Open University, Tanzania;
- Relief International-Schools-Online (RI-SOL), Bangladesh

In addition to its technical exploration, DEEP attempts to engage with the aspects of the digital divide beyond the technical infrastructure itself. These include economic and political, in terms of level of provision and the issue of ownership and control of the key infrastructure resources.

Most importantly it is an exploration of a social justice perspective on technology:

> We critique the belief, dominant in many policy circles that some forms of human development and progress are a luxury that only rich countries can afford.
>
> We know that human freedom requires contemporary knowledge and contemporary educational skills, denying the opportunities of these to any group is contrary to the basic conditions of such freedom. The question, we would argue, is not whether or not to use the new forms of communication but rather how and how quickly. (DEEP presentation 2002 available at http://www.open.ac.uk/deep/Public/web/why/why.html)

AVU, OU and TESSA

The key to the TESSA programme is the mobilization of a range of African and international knowledge, skills and expertise to research and develop contexts, processes and resources. TESSA addresses the issue of the provision of high quality resources and support systems to improve teacher education. TESSA is an "open content" programme, free at the point of use. Phase 1 of the TESSA programme is aimed at improving classroom practice in basic education with a particular focus on literacy, numeracy, science, life skills, social science and the arts. The TESSA programme is planned to support a wide range of courses and qualifications including accredited courses and in-service professional development programmes. It is anticipated that the most effective use of the TESSA resources will involve support systems provided by colleges, universities or local education district staff. TESSA will provide advice on the range of models of successful support available.

The consortium partners have a history of more than 10 years cooperation. Partners have also worked collaboratively with international organizations such as UNESCO and the World Bank and reference to this wider work (see www.tessaprogramme.org). Two modes have been identified: downloadable materials for direct use by training institutions and organizations fully online resources where adequate connectivity is available. TESSA members expect the second mode to become more significant over time.

> The TESSA programme is planned for the period 2005 to 2015. Phase 1, focussing on basic education, will take place between 2005 and 2008. The consortium's first tasks will be:
>
> - to research and develop the TESSA framework of modules and version these to at least nine national contexts (See TESSA Consortium Partners). Versions of the resources will be made in Arabic, English French, isiXhosa and Kiswahili. In South Africa TESSA will be located within the Nelson Mandela Foundation's Unit for Rural Schooling and Development (based at the University of Fort Hare) and will be used by teachers in the Foundation's rural schools network. In Tanzania TESSA will be used by the OU Tanzania to create a new Diploma in Primary Teacher Education;
> - to carry out a number of research enquiries that will provide a knowledge and analysis to inform the development of the programme (studies of future ICT patterns

in sub-Saharan Africa and a comparative study of teacher education curricula have been commissioned);
- to engage in a dialogue with teacher educators across the region with a view to parallel or subsequent take-up of the TESSA programme (www.tessaprogramme.org).

The projects described in this section focus on the development and support of the human infrastructure necessary for local capability development and for the identification of emerging opportunities at their point of potential application. They also demonstrate an understanding of the mutual benefit of interdependent relationships.

Conclusion: Creating and Locating Content and Resources for Africa

Africa needs to derive benefit from an increasing range of information and communication technologies with potential for application to African problems. There is ample evidence of ingenious use of mainstream technology to solve local deficiencies and problems. These often take advantage of the change in relative costs of the components of ICTs.

Where adequate connectivity exists, the central hosting of open education materials, linked through locally developed portals has been promoted by the Development Gateway project (http://www.developmentgateway.org/). Material is drawn from AVU and elsewhere. The eGranary Digital Library reverts to the mature but now relatively cheap technology of the computer hard drive to deliver digital resources to institutions lacking adequate Internet access. Material archived from the web is delivered on drives that can be mounted in servers for use where a local area network exists, but where Internet connectivity is limited or non-existent. The approach requires release of the intellectual property by its originators, but depends ultimately on a reliable incremental update approach which allows for a range of delivery mechanisms that ensure that materials maintain their currency.

Such radical reframing of mainstream technologies for non-standard circumstances can provide inspiration for potential users. In the West the particular ingenuity of a minority of users led to the emergence of the "road-warrior" concept of highly mobile working which then influenced the direction of mainstream development of mobile technologies, The development and demonstration of equivalent systems within African contexts could influence the direction of mainstream development to some degree, but more significantly, would articulate demands for access to resources created in other contexts.

The main issue, however, is the development of a distinctive voice and presence in the new medium. Radio and broadcasting offers an example of how an African identity can be voiced in an externally developed medium. The development of radio in Africa has followed the wider trajectory, beginning with, government controlled broadcasting, generally on AM, then moving to FM in the 1970s and 1980s for local or regional stations. However, a combination of regulatory liberalization and technical development has allowed a range of distinctive and vibrant radio broadcast cultures to develop across Africa. An African approach to digital satellite radio has allowed a large number of stations at an acceptable quality from the bandwith used elsewhere to deliver high fidelity sound (Mytton, 2000). Stations such as Joy FM in Accra, Ghana, have developed both a wide domestic and external audience through utilization of Internet broadcasting.[7]

The members of the African diaspora have a role to play in the selection of technology and development of culturally appropriate electronic forms for the Internet. For example, diasporic experience triggered the creation of CawdNet (http://www.cawd.info/home/about.html) by a Nigerian IT professional working in the UK concerned with effective strategies to link individuals and groups in 'bandwidth poor' rural Nigeria with their 'bandwidth rich' counterparts. The diaspora has already been enlisted to tackle the gender dimension of access to IT for development: http://www.wougnet.org/Events/UNIFEM/ddi_ug.html.

Partnership models will not become new models of dominance if this resource is harnessed. The diasporic perspective offers a form of metagovernance which can moderate the top down character of external input by vetting and filtering such content with a grass-roots African sensibility. African universities and the African diaspora have a potential for connectivity and development which has been greatly under-recognized and, indeed, under-recorded.

Africa suffers from the disadvantages of marginality within the global technical system and a legacy of externally-driven infrastructure. Developments in information and communication technologies now offer the chance to redress these, but the technologies require skills and capacities which are scarce. The technologies themselves can be used to leverage existing resources so that the necessary skills can be developed. However, if the current inequitable situation is not to be reproduced in a new global infrastructure, this process needs to take account of African priorities and requirements. The key to this is a balance between external partnership and internal collaboration. The African diaspora offers a means of moderating such relationships.

Notes

1 See, for example, the mix of physical and electronic connectivity developed by Wizzy Digital Courier in South Africa http://wizzy.org.za. See also Alan Levy's comments on the adaptability of standard WiFi equipment at http://www.bytesforall.org/9th/html/matching_wifi.htm.

2 A 1998 overview of African Internet-based resources is available at http://www3.sn.apc.org/africa/projects.htm.

3 See http://www.safe-sat3.co.za/Configuration/Configuration.asp for a map of these connections.

4 See www.tessaproject.org for the summary of the report and links to SAIDC.
5 See http://www.ddn-africa.org/join.html.
6 See http://allafrica.com/stories/200411221610.html.
7 See http://www.joy997fm.com.gh/. For a regional overview of the full range of African broadcast media see http://www.ellenhume.com/articles/missionaries9_africa1.html.

References

Chataway, J.C., F Gault, P. Quintas, P. and D.V. Wield. "Dealing with the Knowledge Divide". World Summit on the Information Society, United Nations and the International Telecommunications Union (November 2003).

Daily Champion. "SAT-3 And Affordable Bandwidth", *Daily Champion* (Lagos), 9 February: http://allafrica.com/stories/200602090062.html (2006).

Dosi, G. "Technology and Conditions of Macro-economic Development: Some Notes on Adjustment Mechanisms and Discontinuities in the Transformation of Capitalist Economies", in *Design, Innovation and Long cycles in Economic Development*, ed. C. Freeman (London: Frances Pinter, 1986).

The Economist. "Mobile Phones and Development", *The Economist*. 7 July 2005.

Gough, N. and C. Grezo. Introduction in *Africa: The Impact of Mobile Phones*, Vodafone Policy Paper Series No. 2. March 2005

Hafkin, N. "Gender Issues in ICT Policy in Developing Countries: An Overview". Prepared for UN Division for the Advancement of Women Expert Group Meeting on Information and Communication Technologies and Their Impact on and Use as an Instrument for the Advancement of Women. Seoul, Republic of Korea, 11-14 November 2002

Headrick, D.R. *The Tools of Empire: Technology and European Imperialism in the Nineteenth Century* (Oxford: Oxford University Press, 1981).

Henry, L. and G. Mohan. 'Making homes: The Ghanaian Diaspora, Institutions and Development', *Journal of International Development* 15:5 (2003): 611–22.

Holmes, C. "Conference Aims to Improve Info-Tech in Developing Nations", *Cornell Sun*: http://www.cornellsun.com/vnews/display.v/ART/2004/11/22/41a16cebdcd52 (22 November 2004).

IOM. *The Link between Migration and Development in the Least Developed Countries* (Geneva: International Organization for Migration, 2001).

Juma, M.N. *African Virtual University; The Case of Kenyatta University, Kenya* (Kenya: African Virtual University—Kenya tan University, Nairobi, 2001).

Levey, L. and S. Young (eds). *Rowing Upstream: Snapshots of Pioneers of the Information Age in Africa* (Johannesburg: Sharp Sharp Media, 2002): see also http://www.sn.apc.org/rowing_upstream.

Little, S.E. "Networks and Neighbourhoods: Household, Community and Sovereignty in the Global Economy", *Urban Studies* 37:10 (September 2000): 1813–26.

Little, S.E. *Design and Determination: The Role of Information Technology in Redressing Regional Inequities in the Development Process* (Aldershot: Ashgate Publishing, 2004).

Little, S.E., L. Holmes and M. Grieco. "Calling up Culture: Information Spaces and Information Flows as the Virtual Dynamics of Inclusion and Exclusion", *Information Technology and People*14:4 (2001): 353–67.

Myers, M. "Community Radio: Development: Issues and Examples from Francophone West Africa", in *African Broadcast Cultures: Radio in Transition*, ed. R. Fardon and G. Furniss (Oxford: James Currey, 2000).

Mytton, G. "From Saucepan to Dish: Radio and TV in Africa", in *African Broadcast Cultures: Radio in Transition*, ed. R. Fardon and G. Furniss (Oxford: James Currey, 2000).

Mutula, S.M. "Assessment of Africa's Telematics Policy and Regulatory Infrastructure: Potential for E-learning". NTSEU International Conference Changing Working Conditions in Higher Education, University of Natal, Durban, July 2003.

Ploghoft, M.E. (1995) "Electronic Information Exchange in African University Development", Fid Newsletter: http://www2.ncsu.edu/ncsu/aern/NEWLET.HTML (Summer 1995).

Roper, M. "French Flock to Centre", *New Scientist* 97:1344 (10 February 1983): 358–61.

SAIDC. *Online Access and Connectivity of Primary School Teachers in Sub-Saharan Africa: Desktop Research focusing on Nigeria, Kenya, Tanzania and South Africa* (Braamfontein: South African Institute for Distance Education, 2005).

Saxenian. "Trans-national Communities and the Evolution of Global Production Networks: The Case of Taiwan, China and India", *Industry and Innovation* Special issue on global production Networks (Fall 2002).

Spitulnik, D. (2000) "Documenting Radio Culture as Lived Experience: Reception Studies and the Mobile Machine in Zambia", in *African Broadcast Cultures: Radio in Transition*, ed. R. Fardon and G. Furniss (Oxford: James Currey, 2000): 144–63.

Vodafone (2005) *Africa: The Impact of Mobile Phones.* Vodafone Policy Paper Series No. 2: http://www.vodafone.com/assets/files/en/GPP%20SIM%20paper.pdf (March 2005).

Wolff, T. "The African Virtual University", *TechKnowLogica* (April-June 2002): 23–5.

World Bank. *World Development Report, 1998/99: Knowledge for Development* (Oxford: Oxford University Press, 1998).

Chapter Eleven

Sharing Information on the Best Practices in Sustainable Development in Kenya

Paul K.Mwanzilo*

Introduction

It is generally recognized that information is a prerequisite for development. On the other hand, information gaps (a.k.a. the "digital divide") impede good communication and coordination of activities between different stakeholders—information sharing is also a prerequisite for development.

A serious information gap exists between the different stakeholders in Sustainable Agriculture and Rural Development (SARD). These stakeholders include 'poor' farmers in the South, local development organizations supporting them, researchers and policy-makers dealing with rural development in general. Information on successful technologies and practices is important to rural communities for solving local agricultural problems. Currently such information is hard to obtain in the country under study, Kenya.

A lot of agricultural research is undertaken in Kenya but there is no system set up for accessing all the research outputs to facilitate sharing of the research outputs. This chapter aims at looking at the current situation in Kenya on the aforementioned subject. It also concludes with recommendations on the way forward in achieving the overall goal of sustainable poverty reduction as covered in the UN Millennium Development Goals and focuses on activities of stakeholders in the agricultural sector

Agricultural Research Information for Development

Agricultural research for development plays an important role in addressing global challenges. Today the demand for agricultural information is stronger than ever. The increased market integration that is experienced by most remote farming communities, commonly referred to as the "have nots", greatly increase the pace of change. This, in turn, has led to the eradication of proper control of both security and poverty alleviation. Events and developments far away from home have profound effects on the livelihoods of farmers

Agricultural research information is needed to:

---

* Cataloger/Classifier, Egerton Unversity Library.

- exploit opportunities in time like the many emerging markets of agricultural products;
- raise awareness of the potential negative impact on choices such as crude methods and ingredients that do not modify agricultural products any better. Extension officers need to inform farmers to abandon the old myths held by some who believe that application of fertilizers to their farms will lead to loss of fertility;
- provide information about the experiences of other farmers in order to implement better opportunities and sustainable methods like mango grafting. Improved farming practices would increase produce and hence the livelihood of the farmers in Kenya.

In many Third World countries, and especially the sub-Saharan countries, including Kenya, information resources at large have not been considered a priority for nation building and therefore are managed by crises. Agricultural research information is not systematically documented or stored and cannot be accessed by the right people at the right time. The current study therefore looks into the current situation of sharing agricultural research information in Kenya and how this will enhance sustainable development.

This study was conducted using past experience of the researcher, who has worked in two large public universities in Kenya (Kenyatta University 1984–1991 and Egerton an agricultural university 1992 to date). The methodology used included interviews and observations in the following institutions were sampled:

- universities;
- Ministry of Agriculture;
- research institutions;
- CGIAR institutions;
- government departments; and
- other institutions, which generate, control or distribute research information in Kenya.

Users and User Needs

The needs of users of the agricultural research outputs and those who are agents of sustainable development can be summarized as:

- *agribusiness*: require information on a markets, consumers, policies, legislation, production, etc.;
- *extension officers*: should get easy access to practical guides, good practices and expert networks;

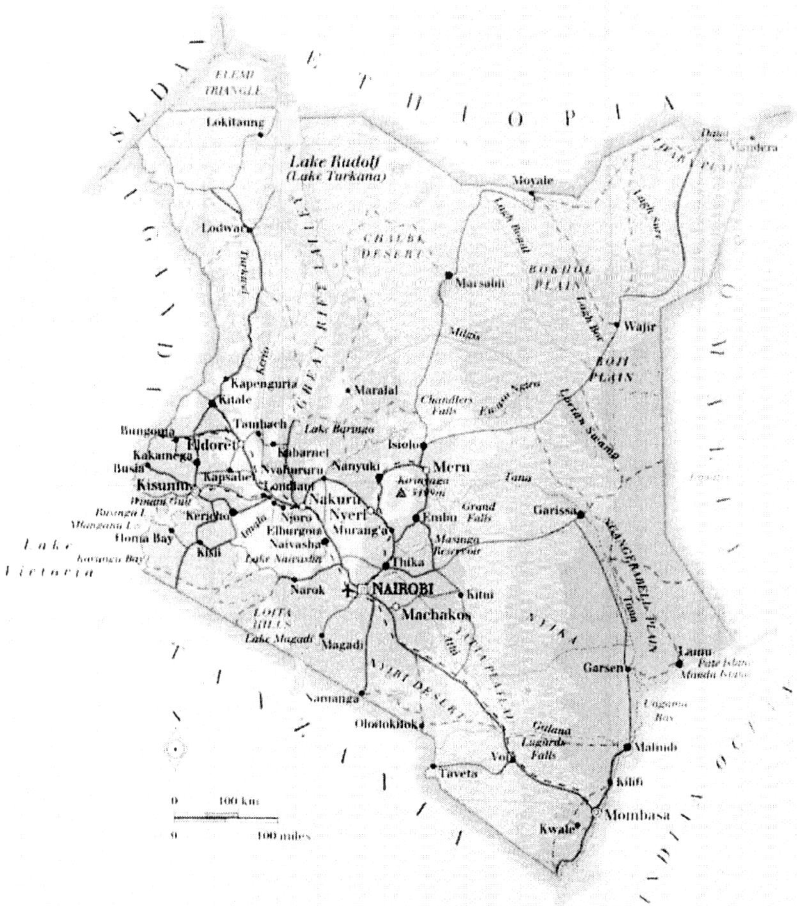

Figure Twenty-two Map of Kenya

- *farmers and farmer organizations*: should get access to good practices and specialists to solve local level problems;
- *policy-makers and donors*: should get access to state-of-the-art of projects, research outputs in technologies, options for investment, ongoing research and activities in order to enhance effectiveness;
- *researchers*: should have a solid base for research and be able to contact other researchers to enhance efficiency of research and form collaborative research ventures.

Agricultural Research Outputs Generation

In Kenya agricultural tesearch information (outputs) is generated by tesearch institutions, which include:

- the two CGIAR institutions based in Kenya:
  - CRAF—http://www.worldagroforestry.org—Agro forestry;
  - ILRI—http://www.ilri.cgiar.org—livestock;
- other agricultural research institutions such as:
  - ICIPE—http://www.icipe.org—insect research;
- Ministry of Agriculture departments, which include:
  - provincial and district level annual reports;
  - KARI—http://www.kari.org — Agriculture;
  - KEPHIS—http://www.kephis.org/—Plant inspectorate Service Seed Research;
- universities:
  - Egerton University—http://www.egerton.ac.ke;
  - University of Nairobi—http://www.uonbi.ac.ke/—College of Agriculture and Veterinary Services;
  - Jomo Kenyatta University of Agriculture and Technology—http://www.jkuat.ac.ke;
  - Moi University—http://www.mu.ac.ke/;
- Central Bureau of Statistics (CBS) (www.cbs.go.ke): a department of the Ministry of Planning and Economic Development established by an Act of Parliament, the Statistics Act Cap. 112 Laws of Kenya, to collect and analyse socio-economic data in the country. Once the data is analysed it is published in reports. CBS publishes between 1,500 and 5,000 copies of each report. These include agricultural reports (Mondo, 2005) as well as:
  - statistical abstract;
  - economic survey;
  - district development plans;
  - national development plan;
- United Nations Organizations:
  - FAO—http:// www.fao.com;
  - UNEP—http://www.unep.org/;
- agricultural NGOs:
  - Adra—Adventist Development Relief Agency;
  - Catholic Diocese of Nakuru—Rift Valley Province;
  - Danida;
  - farming systems of Kenya;
  - Sacred;

As we can readily see, there are many sources of agricultural research information to be coordinated and shared.

Agricultural Research Control

In Kenya the National Council for Science and Technology—NCST—controls research that is being done in the country. All researchers in Kenya are required to register with NCST through the Ministry of Education, Research Evaluation Unit. One applies to the Research Evaluation Unit with the proposal, which is passed on to NCST for evaluation. Once the research is complete one is required to deposit two copies of the findings with the department. One copy is then passed on to the Kenya National Science Information Documentation Center (KENSIDOC), NCST's documentation unit.

Agricultural Research Outputs

Apart from the institutions mentioned above which generate agricultural research there are others that receive the outputs as depositories. These are:

- Kenya Agricultural Documentation Center (KADOC), with an initial funding by FAO in the early 1980s, KADOC collects and documents all agricultural information generated in the country and those acquired from outside;
- Kenya National Scientific Documentation Center (KENSIDOC), the documentation center of the NCST where copies of the research materials surrendered by researchers are deposited for reference;
- the Kenya National Library Services (KNLS) (http://www.knls.or.ke/), the state-run library service. It doubles as national library and a legal depository of all copyright works in Kenya and World Bank materials. KNLS has branches all over the country. These include eight provincial, seven district and 17 community libraries. The impact of KNLS has been heavily felt. In agreement, Siringi (1999) states that KNLS has opened community libraries in Kenya to enable local people access information cheaply and easily in this 'time of information age. The community libraries are libraries where communities put up the building and KNLS provides reading materials and staff. However, INet is only at the headquarters in Nairobi.

Problems of Sharing Information Resources

Much has been written about the problems of provision of good and quality information services to clients in Third World countries and it is not necessary to repeat what has been said over time about such issues as lack of funds, poor infrastructure, etc.

Agricultural research information in Kenya is not systematically available in a central place where one can check for every output. This is because not all research is registered with the body that controls research activities in the country. It is an open secret that many NGOs never want their activities to be known and this includes any research activities undertaken. Thus even when they fund research they may not want the research outputs to be known locally but will submit the information to the funder. In this way agricultural research outputs leave the country with no copies available to local users. After depositing a copy of their research findings to the body where they are affiliated, other researchers have no obligation to take their research outputs to KADOC or elsewhere. KADOC on the other hand has no capacity either to monitor Agricultural Research activities in the country or to collect what has been generated immediately. They rely on research outputs being sent to them by institutions which generate research outputs.

Agricultural research in Africa is generally very dependent on financial support from donor agencies and international lending organizations such as the World Bank (Komen, 2000). This means that the researchers have more obligations to send their research output to the donor first. Very often such reports are not sent to any other institution thereafter. Findings have shown that these donors may post such material on the web. KADOC, for example, sends its materials to Agris where they are available as annual reports at http://www2.fao.org/BASIS/AGRIS/Web/Cat_ja/SDW?W%3DAN+PH+ANY+%2796*%27+AND+CI+PH+IS+%27KE%27+ORDER+BY+EVERY+CC/Ascend%26M%3D1%26K%3D%26R%3DY%26U%3D1

The above scenario creates a situation whereby research outputs are scattered in very many information centers both in Kenya and abroad—universities, research institutions, UN bodies, donors, KADOC library, websites in citations and sometimes in full texts.

Availability of Agricultural Research Output

Availability of repackaged information resources to the right people at the right time and place and repackaged for its users should be an information center's main objective. Agricultural research information for any locality should be essential to a particular group's livelihood. In Kenya there is a lot of agricultural research information (output) being generated from many institutions, as demonstrated above. Although KADOC has the responsibility of collecting and documenting agricultural research outputs and making them available to readers, it does not have the capacity to do so since the funding project by FAO ended in the 1980s. However, they send the materials to AGRIS where the outputs are summarized, digitized and put online. The materials can be accessed at http://www2.fao.org/BASIS/AGRIS/Web/Cat_ja/SDW?W%3DAN+PH+ANY+%2796*%27+AND+CI+PH+IS+%27KE%27+

ORDER+BY+EVERY+CC/Ascend%26M%3D1%26K%3D%26R%3DY%26U%3D1.

There are also quite a number of research outputs on Kenya being digitized and put on websites by several international Agricultural Research institutes such as CIAT (http://www.ciat.cgiar.org/) and CGIAR institutions.

The results of these information research outputs are not fully utilized because of poor information infrastructure, lack of information policy and poor professional associations.

Sharing Agricultural Information for Sustainable Development

In Kenya information sharing has always been on a 'gentleman's agreement' basis. Thus, whereas there is a lot of information being generated, there is no obligation on any of the information centers to share the same. Although they are funded from the same exchequer and offer similar courses, the state universities do not have an effective system for sharing information resources. The interlibrary loan system that they rely on extensively does not work well, at least partly because of laxity on the part of the library heads. For many years the poor road network has been blamed for lack of an efficient interlibrary loans system in Kenyan libraries. However, this is a poor excuse as it has been noted that there are frequent movements between universities and research institutions. With good arrangements these vehicles can be used to carry books on their way and aid in interlibrary loans for information resources sharing. The vehicles' missions to the institutions include:

- *procurement*: most procurement is done in Nairobi; many trips are made for procurement since the process is very long. There is a trip for procurement almost every two days;
- *meetings*: there are quite a number of meetings of committees of vice-chancellors, librarians, directors, permanent secretary, donors, etc. always held at different towns in Kenya by heads of departments. libraries;
- *airport pickups*: whenever a senior member of staff is leaving the country for official duty they are taken to the airport by institution vehicles and picked when they come back. On average this happens three times in a month;
- *library meetings*: yhere are also numerous meetings of heads of libraries, including the Kenya Library Association annual meeting held rotationally in a library in a major town. Then there are library training workshops, etc. held quite frequently. The vehicles these officers use can be used to facilitate interlibrary loans or document exchange and aid in resource sharing.

The vehicles undertaking these trips could deliver and pick up library materials for interlibrary loans, donations, exchange, etc, on their way. This is an issue which could be planned and implemented very quickly in the many librarians' meetings. At the moment, when a library user requests materials from another university where they are not a member, they are told to make their own private arrangements to go and use the materials in the other library. Many of the libraries in Kenya do not have an Online Public Access Catalogue for users to find out what materials are in other libraries nor is there a way users can request for materials to be searched for from other libraries. Many public funded libraries still do not have Internet access, so readers cannot search online from their libraries for materials. When the Internet is available it is not user friendly, as many institutions want to charge clients to use the facility and to make printouts.

The following are some of the many avenues of sharing information in Kenya for sustainable development.

- *The Central Bureau of Statistics* (CBS): the CBS distributes statistical information to:
  - academic and research institutions;
  - ambassadors in Kenya;
  - district information documentation centers;
  - district statistical offices;
  - donor community in Kenya;
  - exchange partners;
  - government ministries;
  - international statistical institutions where CBS is an affiliate;
  - Kenya's foreign missions.

  CBS has a mailing list of the recipient institutions though lacks funding for postage. Clients in Kenya arrange to pick their reports from the CBS offices in Nairobi but materials distributed abroad are sent through the Ministry of Foreign Affairs' diplomatic bags.

  CBS also disseminates its publications through current awareness by launching new publications at each of Kenya's eight provinces to which many institutions are invited, including the NGOs. Some of CBS's popular titles include:
  - *The Economic Survey*;
  - *The Statistical Abstract*;
  - The Sessional Papers explaining the government policy on different aspects like Agriculture, Education, etc.
- *District Information Documentation Centers*: in 1983 the Kenyan government decided that all projects would be planned at the district level for effectiveness and efficiency. Each district therefore has a documentation center where government publications can be accessed by planning staff during the planning of new projects. In fact this is a very good source of government publications deposited by the Central Bureau of Statistics, as seen earlier on. An interview with Danida

in Makueni district revealed that this is where they go to refer to government publications. The infrastructure varies depending on levels of funding. For instance, a few DIDCs have Internet facilities installed by donors funding projects in the district. Kitui and Kajiado are amongst the DIDC with iNet facilities.

- *Kenya Broadcasting Corporation* (http://www.kbc.co.ke/): the state-run radio station. It broadcasts sustainable development programs which include:
  - English service:
    - *Feed the Nation*;
    - *Our Environment*;
    - *Water for Life*;
  - Swahili service:
    - *Kwenu wakulima (To you farmers)*;
    - *Mazingira (Environment)*.
- *Newspapers*: the two leading newspapers *The Daily Nation* (http://www.nationmedia.com) and *East African Standard* (http://www.eastandard.net/) occasionally run very informative agriculture and environment feature articles. On weekdays the papers also show market prices of agricultural products in different parts of the country.
- *CGIAR institutions*: the two CGIAR institutions in Kenya mentioned earlier have a Memorandum of Understanding to share information within the CGIAR group in the world through a joint acquisition of periodicals using the INMAGIC software. They share information with other institutions in Kenya who are researching in agriculture. As mentioned earlier, they also serve many users from public institutions that are sent there by their institutions to obtain materials.
- *International Livestock Research Institute* (ILRI): ILRI transformed its library into an Infocenter. Tables Twenty-two and Twenty-three show statistics of sharing information resources with other libraries:

Table Twenty-two Interlibrary loans 2002

Borrowed by ILRI staff from other libraries	97
Loaned to other local libraries	167
Journal articles sent to other CGIAR centers	101
Journal articles received from other CGIAR centers	125
External users: External users registered	144

Sources: ILRI (http://www.ilri.cgiar.org/) website accessed in April 2005 and interview with Grace Kamau infocenter director.

Table Twenty-three Interlibrary loans 2003

Borrowed by ILRI staff from other libraries	32
Loaned to other local libraries	219
Journal articles sent to other CGIAR centers	47
Journal articles received from other CGIAR centers	64
External users: external users registered	34

Sources: ILRI (http://www.ilri.cgiar.org/) website accessed in April 2005 and interview with Grace Kamau infocenter director.

- *Kenet* (www.kenet.or.ke): a consortium of institutions of higher learning in Kenya for expanding Internet connectivity and sharing information. It serves students and all the members of the academic community countrywide. Kennet vision I is effected through the deployment of a cost-effective and sustainable infrastructure and through funding by USAID.
- *Kenya Agricultural Research Institute* (KARI): KARI has the following databases:
  - Africa MetPro 1.0;
  - AGRICOLA;
  - AGRIS;
  - CLIS;
  - CPC (Crop Protection Compendium);
  - EIARD-InforSys;
  - FAO on the Internet;
  - GARD;
  - KARD.
  - Land and Water Resources Information Systems
  - OVAD;
  - TEEAL;
  - TROPAG and RURAL;
  - World-renowned CAB.

  KARI distributes its materials to its 29 main centers, which have libraries and to another 12 subcenters which do not have libraries. The materials are distributed according to each center's agro-ecological zone.

  KARI shares information with universities and CGIAR institutions in Kenya which research on related subjects (Maina, 2005) .

  Table Twenty-four shows how many interlibrary loans have been made over the years.

- *The African Virtual Library Kenya Chapter* (AVL-K): AVL-K aims to enable academic and public universities to exchange information resources by creating

Table Twenty-four Interlibrary loans 2003—2005

Borrowed from	Universities	2
	Research institutions	15
Loaned to	Universities	0
	Research institutions	10

an environment where information will flow freely to rural communities via the iNet.

- *Kenya Libraries and Information Services Consortium* (KLISC): this is a consortium formed early this year with information sharing as one of its objectives among others. Membership to the consortium consists of universities, tertiary colleges, research institutions, and government information centers/ organizations (Were, 2005)
- *UNEP* (http://www.unep.org/): this is the United Nations environmental body and has its headquarters in Nairobi. Its library is open to the public to access environmental research outputs both local and international. According to Sommereyns (n.d.) the UNEP library is supposed to provide leadership and encourage partnership in caring for the environment by inspiring, informing and enabling nations and peoples to improve their quality of life without compromising that of future generations. The library operates gifts and interlibrary loans. The Internet at this facility was accessed by this researcher in undertaking this research on 22 April 2005.

Electronic Networks for Online Information Sharing

The new information environment creates demands for libraries to be more efficient in imparting readers with skills for access, evaluation and application of information rather than just providing the information itself. Information explosion has created vast resources available in various formats and localities. No library can effectively satisfy its users from the resources within its walls. We are living at a time where the worth of a library's is increasingly measured by the service it offers in terms of helping clients to access universal information, rather than by the collections it offers.

Khalid (2000: 57) has summarized the benefits of on-line information sharing in his observation that:

> Co-operation and networking in library and information systems provide a wider access to collection, improve public and technical services and enhance operations by sharing resources, reducing duplication and offering more cost-effective services.

Electronic networking will provide researchers and scholars around the country with better ways of exchanging and accessing information needed for development.

It is hoped that the emerging partnership in on-line information sharing in Kenya will enable the country to be well prepared to pursue the envisioned dream of industrialization by the year 2020.

Siringi (2000) reports that a librarian at the Kenya Agricultural and Research Institute reported in a Kenya Library Association conference that computer databases would now be used to market agricultural information.

In their knowledge studies of information technology for sustainable development Mansel and Wehn (1998) found that, in the last few years, there have been many initiatives at the highest levels of government and industry to promote the construction of a global information infrastructures to enable them participate in knowledge-based development and experience the predicted social and economic benefits.

LEISA, the biggest international magazine for the exchange for experiences on low external input, sustainable agriculture, focuses on the effects that the movement towards the dismantling of publicly-funded extension programs is having on the rural information landscape. The articles explain the role ICTs play in agricultural research information in developing countries. Also included is the importance of 'old technologies' such as newsletters and radio calling on the development community to use all available means to ensure that farmers have the information they need to continue to form sustainability

In Kenya the two electronic networks commonly used by public, international and private institutions are:

- PERI and TEEAL projects—PERI (http://www.inasp.info/peri/index.shtml): Kenya is a member of the Program for Enhancement of Research Information — coordinated by the International Availability of Scientific Publications— (INASP, http://www.inasp.info/rural/)—which has helped to create available journal articles online either in full text or citations to libraries in many Third World countries. Institutions in Kenya have formed a consortium whereby each contributes some fee to access all PERI databases such as AGORA, *African Journal Online* (*AJOL*), etc. There are 23 institutions in the project in Kenya, mainly from universities and research institutions.
- The Essential Electronic Agricultural Library (TEEAL) (http://teeal.cornell.edu/): TEEAL is a full-text and bibliographic CD-ROM library of over 140 of the world's most important scientific journals in library project in the field of agriculture. This project is coordinated by Mann Library, Cornell University and is available to some libraries in Third World countries.

  In Kenya it is available at Egerton University, University of Nairobi and the Kenya Agricultural Research Institute. Egerton University TEEAL project has expanded the use of TEEAL to many agriculture-based research stations by installing TEEAL in the institutions. They include:

  - Kericho Tea Research Center—Kericho;

- Kenya Sugar Research Foundation—Kisumu;
- KARI—Njoro plant breeding station.

Websites of Publications of Kenyan Agricultural Research Outputs

The key websites are:

- http://www.ciat.cgiar.org/africa/ciat_africa.htm;
- http://www.bananahill.net/Publications.html;
- http://www.ifpri.org/pubs/catalog.htm;
- http://www2.fao.org/BASIS/AGRIS/Web/Cat_ja/SDW?W%3DAN+PH+ANY+%2796*%27+AND+CI+PH+IS+%27KE%27+ORDER+BY+EVERY+CC/Ascend%26M%3D1%26K%3D%26R%3DY%26U%3D1;
- http://www.isnar.cgiar.org/publications/catalog/africa.htm#Kenya;
- http://www.foodnet.cgiar.org/market/market.htm.

The Digital Divide in Kenya

The government and stakeholders recognize the importance of integrating the use of ICTs in the development sectors of education, health, agriculture, small business and tourism to ensure effective service delivery and build knowledge in these areas. (Ministry of Information and Communications, 2004). The term "digital divide" is used to refer to such differing standards or imbalances between countries that are fully poised to reap the benefits of the information age and those that are not (Ifinedo, 2005)

In Kenya the best infrastructure is found in the urban centers. This is where there are libraries, documentation centers, universities, etc., plus Internet connections. This has become a preserve of the urban community where agriculture is not practiced, whereas in the rural areas where agriculture is practiced, farmers are without the Internet or the electricity to run a computer. This has greatly contributed to the digital divide.

By April 2004 there were 73 registered ISPs, 16 of which are active, approximately 1,030,000 users and over 1,000 cyber cafes and telephone bureaus. Telecom Kenya, the country's national postal service, has installed Internet cafes in every major post office in Kenya. This has greatly helped to minimize the digital divide, as one does not have to travel to district headquarters to get Internet services.

In order to keep up with the world trends in scientific innovation in agriculture and industry, the country has to have access to local and global information networks. In analysing the role of information technology in improving access and transfer of agriculture to the rural communities in Kenya, Kiplangat (1998: 303) comments:

> The key to increased agricultural production ultimately lies with the nation's ability to disseminate relevant information to the farming community to facilitate effective adoption of new production techniques, application of agricultural inputs, decision making on markets and prices, methods of conserving water, soil and vegetable resources.

Many libraries in Kenya, especially public-funded ones, still have not automated their services and operations nor do they have Internet access available to their users. This means that sharing information with many public institutions is not easy. However, the situation is now set to change with the liberalization of frequencies by the removal of the monopoly enjoyed by Jambonet of Telekom Kenya, which was the only firm allowed to operate and provide Internet services in Kenya up to June 2004.

To this effect Alare (2005) reports that by December 2004 the Communications Commission of Kenya (CCK, www.cck.go.ke) licensed two applicants—Kenya Data Networks (KDN) Limited and Jamii Telecoms –to operate Internet backbone and international gateway service provision in Kenya.

It will mean that access to the Internet will be cheaper and many will be able to afford to have it, including information centers. This, of course, will take sometime as the licence costs Kshs16m (US$210.300.00) and then there are the costs of other infrastructure. The firms will initially want to recover this investment, but within two to three years costs will go down.

Bridging the Digital Divide by Sharing Information in Kenya

This involves:

- community information centers;
- cooperative acquisitions;
- digitization;
- interlibrary loans;
- Internet;
- Online Public Access Catalogues.

Cooperative Acquisitions

The heads of libraries/documentation centers in Kenya should form Cooperative Acquisitions to acquire materials together. This is possible, as it has been achieved through donor-funded projects (World Bank project 1993–) (Ratansi Project, 2004) in the public universities. This will also enable the cooperating libraries to know what is available in each participant library and make it easy to share the information. It will also reduce duplication of the meagre public resources.

Online Public Access Catalogues

With the cost of the Internet coming down, as seen elsewhere in this chapter, heads of libraries should impress on their institutions to make available budgets for their library's automation and should eventually have their catalogues online for actual and potential access. The Kenet project was started with this aim. Heads of libraries should emulate Moi University in Eldoret where the Kenet project, through funding by USAID, has automated their library operations and processes. They can also making proposals to donors who, in many cases, are willing to fund automation of library services in public institutions in Third World country libraries. If Kenya were more comprehensively online it would enhance sharing of information through means such as the Illinet (http://www.cyberdriveillinois.com/library/illinet.html).

Interlibrary Loans

Heads of libraries/documentation centers should liaise with the transport departments so that materials can be sent to the other libraries whenever there are trips. The Internet—the costs of which will decrease over time, as argued earlier in the chapter—should be used to search for publications in the institutions with OPAC such as ILRI and emails then used to ask for materials.

The excuse of unreliability of the transport or postal services does not arise, since whenever there is need to travel one always travels. Arrangements can be made. When one wants to send parcels and luggage unaccompanied, it is always possible to use the postal services or the many courier services which operate everywhere in the country.

Courier Services

There are quite a number of courier services offered in Kenya. Depending on how much one wants to spend, parcels and luggage can be delivered to the office or in the nearest town where the courier has offices.

Many public passenger companies also offer delivery of parcels and letters at very fair rates. With good arrangements, sharing of information can take place using these services.

Digitization

Digitizing agricultural research outputs and putting them on the World Wide Web can be a very effective way of information sharing. Putting the materials on the Web will mean that they will be available anywhere any time for all to use provided that one is connected to the Internet. It is not very hard to put the materials on the WWW as all word processing is done by computer and saved in soft copies. Once the research is complete, the output can be send to an agricultural online database. The newly formed Kenya Libraries and Information Services Consortium should be able to come up with a way of doing this. Agricultural donors can be approached by libraries attached to agricultural institutions to do this. KARI, which has so many agricultural databases, should find a way of putting them online, as they would form a very good database for resource sharing.

As seen elsewhere in this chapter, the cost of the Internet is bound to decrease so with time many institutions should be able to offer it to their users and also use it to share information. The government of Kenya recognizes the need to ease online communication, which is why the draft ICT Policy points out that:

> Internet Node and Backbone Operators will be encouraged to establish Internet access nodes at all districts and local exchange areas. Special consideration will be granted to universities, research institutions, *community telecenters* and other public institutions to have direct access to the Internet backbone. The Government will encourage the rollout of wideband access technologies such as DSL and low-cost wireless access technologies for Internet access.

Besides, this is the direction the world has taken.

Attitude

The attitude of the management of institutions has been identified as negative towards information centers in the institutions. Heads of the institutions allocate very little funding to libraries and documentation centers. Library staff are poorly paid, so most of the time staff are not concentrating on work but keep on looking for greener pastures, especially in international institutions, or engaging in private business activities.

Community Information Centers (CBS)

This is a system by which everyone in the community collects information about a wide variety of subjects in the local area and organizes it into a database. This database can therefore be used whenever one needs information about something in a given locality. All research in agriculture in every district can be collected and put in a database, for instance, by the district Agricultural Officer, so that whenever anyone wants to do research in the district they can start from the CBS database.

Community information service is definitely one of the best solutions towards a sustainable future. As Wanyoike (1998) summarizes the functions of a CBS to a community: "They supply information that is directly concerned with issues affecting that particular community." There is an initiative in Kenya to start a community information service through collaboration with the University of California, Los Angeles.

Conclusions

There are quite a lot of agricultural research outputs in Kenya. The information carried in these outputs should be passed on to the users of information such as extension officers, so that they can pass the knowledge on to farmers. This would considerably assist sustainable development so that many farmers in Kenya can be raised out of subsistence farming to commercial farming. As argued elsewhere in this chapter, there are also a lot of materials digitized and available free. The newly-formed Kenya Libraries and Information Services Consortium (KLISC) should be able to link all information/documentation/libraries and come up with a practical way of sharing the resources available at the moment. When the researcher was gathering information on this chapter, in every institution visited everyone agreed that the key to having a good system of sharing the masses of information available in the country is not lack of funds or infrastructure but the lack of commitment and policy together with a negative attitude. Agricultural research should be controlled so that all research outputs are deposited centrally where they then can be digitized and put into an online database for all to use. There should be links to all the URLs of agricultural research output databases so that all the research outputs can be accessed.

References

Alari, Alare. "Uunet Denied Internet Licence", *East African Standard*: www.eastandard.net/, 3 January 2005.

Ifinedo, Princely. "Using ICT", *International Journal of Education and Development* 1:1 (2005).

Khalid, H.M. "Cooperative and Networking in Library and Information Systems of Advanced Countries: a Framework for Countries with Less Developed Systems", *Library Review* 49 (2000): 57–63.

Kiplangat, Joseph. "An Analysis of the Opportunities of Information Technology in Improving Access, Transfer and use of Agricultural Information in the Rural Areas of Kenya." *Information for Sustainable Development in the 21st Century: Proceedings of the 13th Standing Conference of Eastern Central and Southern Africa Librarians 27th to 31st July* (Nairobi: KLA, 1998): 303–24.

Komen, J., J. Mignouna and H. Webber. *Biotechnology in African Agricultural Research: Opportunities for Donor Organizations* (ISNAR, 2000).

Mansel, Robin and Uta Wehn. "Knowledge societies: IT for Sustainable Development", *United Nations Commission for Science and Technology* (1998): 1.

Ministry of Information and Communications. *National Information and Communications Technology (ICT) Policy* (draft under discussion) (2004)

Siringi, Samuel. *Daily Nation*, 14 June 1999.

Siringi, Samuel. *Daily Nation*, 4 December, 2000.

Sommereyns, Raymond, Chairperson of the Steering Committee for the Modernization and Integrated Management of UN Libraries Director, Outreach Division Department of Public Information United Nations.

Wanyoike, John Waiganjo. "The Camel Comes of Age: Academic and public libraries' partnership in sharing information through information technology", in *Kenya—the Role of African Virtual Library Project*. Internet, April 2005

Interviews

Mr Mondo, Librarian, on the role of CBS in distribution of government statistical reports, April 2005.

Mr Patrick Maina, KARI Headquarters, Nairobi Library, on the role of KARI in information sharing, April 2005.

Samuel G.O. Okech, Technical Officer/Telecom Licencing and VAS Communications Commission of Kenya, Nairobi, on the impact of removal of monopoly enjoyed by Jambonet in provision of April 2005.

CHAPTER TWELVE

ICTs IN AFRICAN EDUCATION: THE DOT-EDU PROJECT

William W. Wright Jr*

Introduction: ICT as a Tool for Strengthening Education and Learning Systems

dot-EDU, a five-year project funded by the US Agency for International Development (USAID), uses information and communication technology to strengthen education and learning systems in developing counties. Implemented by the Education Development Center (EDC), dot-EDU works closely with two other USAID grantees that deal with other aspects of ICTs for development. These are dot-ORG, implemented by the Academy for Educational Development (AED), which focuses on increasing access to ICT and dot-GOV, implemented by Internews, which focuses on telecom policy. The three cooperative agreements (or grants) work together on what is being called the DOT-COM Alliance.

Each of the "dots" has a number of partners. dot-EDU works with over 25 resource partners (universities, NGOs and private sector partners) that bring considerable strength and experience at using ICTs to improve education.

This USAID mechanism is demand-driven. That is, when USAID missions (in-country offices) want to set up ICT-and-education interventions, they contact the dot-EDU team and provide support from their mission budgets. For example, two of the early projects, started in 2002, came from requests from missions in Rwanda and in Mali. The former wanted to set up distance learning centers associated with a teacher college in Kigali; the latter wanted training for faculty, students, and administrators at the University of Bamako.

While USAID missions tend to work with primary education, a few of the 20 or so projects under dot-EDU (such as the two mentioned above) work with post-secondary education in Africa. In this chapter I will describe several projects in Africa but will give more detail about recent work at teacher colleges in Uganda and Namibia.

While dot-EDU puts an emphasis on bringing digital technologies to developing nations, several projects use radio. For example, the Sudan Radio Service broadcasts in nine Sudanese languages using Sudanese presenters. Zambia's Interactive Radio

---

* Previously Director, dot-EDU Project, Education Development Center (EDC): now Program Officer, Carr Foundation, with focus on Mozambique.

Instruction (IRI) project provides an alternative to formal schools for developing literacy and numeracy skills for out-of-school youth in remote communities as well as in urban centers. Children with limited resources attend learning centers with volunteer teachers trained by NGOs and compensated by communities. Radio programs offer classes for grades 1–5, and tests show that up to 22,000 children have learned basic skills in addition to children being taught in formal school classes.

dot-EDU: A Project Profile

dot-EDU started in September 2001 and ends in September 2006 (with some associate awards extending beyond that time). The following are the dot-EDU associate awards in Africa (funded primarily by USAID missions):

Table Twenty-five dot-EDU associate awards, Africa

Country	Start date	Description
Mali	July 2002	University to university linkage
Rwanda	July 2002	Internet at the Kigali Institute of education and distance learning centers throughout the country
DR Congo	September 2002	ICTs for education in community learning centers
Namibia	February 2003	Work with teacher colleges and a second project that works with SchoolNet/Namibia to set up laboratories in secondary schools
Zambia	February 2003	Interactive Radio Instruction (IRI) for out-of-school youth
Sudan	March 2003	Sudan Radio Service
Uganda	October 2003	Support laboratories in primary teacher colleges and develop a plan to sustain them when the project ends Oct 2005
Sudan	June 2004	Interactive Radio Instruction (IRI)

While the above projects are supported by USAID missions, dot-EDU also has a number of pilot projects that are being implemented by the Washington-based "leader" award. For example, we worked with MIT's Africa Internet Technology Initiative (MIT—AITI) to send MIT students to Ghana and Ethiopia. They instructed teachers and students in cutting-edge web-related technologies and programming languages. Other core-funded activities worked with SchoolNet Africa (ICTs in African Schools conference), the Harvard Berkman Center (survey of ICT and education), and with a World Bank project in Uganda (ICTs and HIV/AIDS Education). A pilot in the planning stage now will experiment with thin-client devices in a lab that can work in places where the electrical system is not stable.

Two dot-EDU associate awards that work with teacher colleges are being supported by USAID missions in Namibia and in Uganda. The Connect-ED project in Uganda is building on an activity set up under a previous USAID mechanism called LearnLink. Connect ED II, is bringing connectivity to eight primary teacher colleges (PTCs) and looking at ways to sustain the laboratories. The plan for sustainability ranges from policy changes (getting the ministry to allow PTCs to charge fees to students) to business plans that garner support from the community.

This project will also put curricula online and help tutors at the PTCs understand new project-based learning strategies. This dot-EDU project in Uganda and one of the projects in Namibia are both experimenting with online professional development. An online course being offered by Harvard University's Graduate School of Education is being introduced at both sites.

Associate Awards under dot-EDU

As we enter the fourth year of dot-EDU, USAID missions or bureaux have supported 20 associate awards in 18 countries around the globe (see Table Twenty-six).

Associate Awards in Africa

The following sections offer summaries of the associate awards in Africa which are being supported by USAID missions or bureaus under the dot-EDU mechanism. Some of these projects involve work in post-secondary education.

Mali (1 July 2002 to 30 September 2003)

dot-EDU established a university-to-university linkages program between the new University of Bamako and dot-EDU core partners Howard University and Michigan State University. USAID/Mali has supported the University of Bamako since its inception, and part of this support has involved establishing computer centers and wireless networks in the university's colleges. dot-EDU was engaged to assist the University of Bamako in learning how best to apply these digital resources to strengthen the institution and learning systems at the university. Howard University and Michigan State University trained faculty and students, and dot-EDU supported the training of system administrators and network managers through local training providers.

Rwanda (3 July 2002 to 2 July 2004)

The primary focus of the activity was to provide an integrated ICT (information and

Table Twenty-five dot-EDU associate awards, worldwide

Country	Start date	Description
Guatemala	June 2002	Teacher training in Quiche to promote sustainability and enhance educational leadership
Mali	July 2002	University to University Linkage
Rwanda	July 2002	To support network connectivity, train staff and provide ICT equipment for the Kigali Institute of Education
Haiti	September 2002	Support of education through interactive radio instruction
India	September 2002	Technical Tools for teaching and training
DR Congo	September 2002	Community Learning and Resource Centers
Sudan Assessment	December 2002	Assess/design for Sudan independent radio station
Lebanon	January 2003	"YouthCaN Med" Technology and Environment in the Classroom
Namibia iNET	February 2003	Initiative for Namibian Education Technology (iNET)
Zambia	February 2003	Interactive Radio Instruction through public and private partnership
Sudan Radio Service	March 2003	Enhancing peace-building initiatives through local languages programs
Honduras	April 2003	Support of preschool program through Interactive Radio Instruction
Namibia GDA Schools	May 2003	Alliance to Promote Information and Communications Technologies in Namibian
Yemen	June 2003	Internet for Yemeni HS
Macedonia	August 2003	ICT for support of education reforms at primary and secondary levels
Uganda	October 2003	Support Primary Teachers Colleges through on-line education
Peru	January 2004	Technical E-learning activity to create a communication and collaborative learning network with Huarascan Project
Sudan IRI	June 2004	Using IRI technologies to provide learning opportunities for children and adults, and training of teachers in southern Sudan
Zambia	September 2004	Using ICT to reach marginalized and vulnerable populations
DR Congo II	October 2004	Basic education, especially for Girls improved in targeted areas

communication technologics) "onc stop shop" for all academic and administrative needs of the Kigali Institute of Education (KIE). This project supported the (KIE) main campus and six distance learning centers that are set up in secondary schools around Rwanda. The infrastructure, set up in an interactive Internet- and Web-engineering environment, effectively delivers integrated support for the Institute's educational activities while also improving existing data warehousing systems. Beyond developing infrastructure, the project addresses the issue of capacity building for administrators and educators at the Institute by providing improved network connectivity and extensive staff training. This project was implemented by dot-EDU partner World Links.

Sudan (12 March 2003 to 11 March 2005)

As part of an effort to increase the participation of southern Sudan, the Sudan Radio Service provides access to balanced and useful information through radio-based education and entertainment programs presented by local presenters in several local languages, including Dinka, Nuer, Juba-Arabic, Zande and English.

The project links the ongoing Machakos peace process with other peace-building initiatives that engender good governance. Through informative, educational and entertaining programming, the Sudan Radio Service equips listeners with the knowledge and tools to participate more fully in peace-making, reconciliation and national development. At the time of writing, SRS had been broadcasting for almost a year and aired weekly programmes on civic education, issues related to formal education in southern Sudan, health (particularly HIV/AIDS) and the news regarding the ongoing peace process. Feedback from listeners has been abundant, with the vast majority of comments being very positive. Listeners appreciate the daily updates on the peace process and enjoy the music and culture programmes. Furthermore, the journalistic quality of SRS programming has improved greatly, partly due to a subscription to the BBC Monitoring Service. These additional resources of access to media report on Sudan throughout the world have provided SRS with the ability able to ensure that news reports are accurate and balanced.

Namibia iNET (1 February 2003 to 31 July 2005)

The Initiative for Namibian Education Technology (iNET) follows on from USAID/ Namibia's previous support to the integration of information and communication technologies (ICT) within the Ministry of Basic Education, Sport and Culture (MBESC) through the development of physical, online and human resources at the Ministry, as well as through policy development in relation to ICT, education and training. Since its inception in February 2003, iNET has undertaken training activities to support teacher resource center staff, teacher training college faculty and regional education planners. More recently, the project has succeeded in working with the Ministry to provide connectivity and computer centers at all four teacher training colleges, upgrade technology and training resources at Ministry resource centers, assist the Ministry in publishing online significantly greater numbers of educational resources and provided all regional education planners with laptops. The project has also assisted the education ministries and their partners in making significant headway towards developing a new national ICT and education strategy and strategy implementation plan. At the time of writing, a final draft version is under review by both ministers of education.

Namibia GDA (22 May 2003 to 21 May 2006)

The roll out of wireless and off-grid school-based computer laboratories to 50 schools through the country will become the third of three ICT and education activities currently underway in Namibia. The other two are iNET and another GDA project implemented by a GDA alliance including the American Federation of Teachers and the Discovery Channel Global Education Fund. As such, this activity will be the second dot-EDU activity as well as the second education GDA activity in Namibia. This alliance will work with SchoolNet Namibia (a dot-EDU Resource Partner) as its primary implementing partner. Final negotiations on planning with the alliance partners and development of the project work plan will begin shortly. At the time of writing, the alliance had completed its final draft work plan for consideration by alliance partners. Similarly, AED/ and EDC/Washington staff have completed a short-term consultancy for programmatic strategy.

Uganda (1 October 2003 to 30 September 2005)

Connect-ED Phase II aims to build on the infrastructure established in Phase I with a central focus on sustainability and a long-term information and communication technologies (ICT) strategy for KyU and the colleges and the primary teacher colleges (PTCs)

Phase I of the Connect-ED activity, originally established in 1998 by USAID under the LearnLink Initiative, set up computer centres at Kyambogo University (KyU) and eight Primary Teacher's Colleges (PTC) throughout the country. The program has also created an online teacher training curriculum and a digital resource library based on the Ugandan core curriculum. Working in close collaboration with the Ministry of Education and Kyambogo University, activities include developing business plans and policy reform to financially sustain the PTC laboratories, using ICT to increase teachers' capacity to incorporate student-centered teaching practices in the classroom, developing a Web presence for KyU and each PTC, continuing to provide computer training, and completing the digitization of the online curriculum. A sustainability and Phase II kick-off workshop was held in April 2004 in Jinja. It brought together key stakeholders from the primary teacher colleges (PTCs), the MOES, Kyambogo University (KyU), and other entities that are crucial to the sustainability of the project. An outcome of the meeting was the development of Operational Guidelines for the Connect-ED laboratories, which feed into a larger ICT policy.

At the time of writing, five of eight PTCs have developed draft business plans to help sustain their college computer laboratories. Medium-term sustainability has also been enhanced by the award of a grant to cover Internet connectivity for one year made by the Uganda Communication Commission's Rural Development Fund. Other policy support assisted the project's lead counterpart organization, KyU, in developing its ICT policy and master plan, which was recently finalized and approved by the faculty senate. In terms of teacher training, at the time of writing 36 teacher educators and project staff are participating in an online course with the Harvard Graduate School of Education. This course, "Teaching to Standards with New Technologies," is intended to assist participants in understanding progressive pedagogy better, as well as gaining understanding in how to integrate technology better to enhance teaching and learning. Finally, the project is continuing to build capacity in the PTCs to create useful educational resources and it has successfully enhanced over 30 percent of the units in the online curriculum.

Zambia (7 February 2003 to 30 September 2004)

Zambia's Interactive Radio Instruction (IRI) project provides an alternative to formal schools for developing literacy and numeracy skills for out of school youth in remote communities as well as in urban centers. Children with limited resources attend learning centers with volunteer teachers trained by NGOs and compensated by communities.

Along with churches and NGOs, a major partner is the Educational Broadcasting Service (EBS) which is part of Zambia's Ministry of Education (MOE). EBS trains "mentors" to manage the daily instruction while children are taught basic math and language instruction. Each daily program also carries a short segment of life skills education (health, nutrition and basic hygiene) and addresses values that children would otherwise have received from their parents and teachers.

Radio programs offer classes for grades 1-5, and tests show that up to 22,000 children have learned basic skills as well as children being taught in formal school classes.

Zambia—Phase II (29 September 2004 to 30 September 2009)

The expansion of activities carried out under the first phase of the Zambia project will continue in developing, expanding and helping to institutionalize the MOE's use and application of communication technologies as cost-effective means of delivering quality education to out-of-school children, supplementing and reinforcing instruction in government and community schools, supporting teacher development efforts and providing information to mobilize communities to address special issues, such as HIV/AIDS prevention and mitigation, promotion of girls' education and free and equal access to basic education, school governance and support, and/or other issues identified by the MOE and its partners.

Democratic Republic of Congo—Phase II (4 October 2004 to 3 October 2006)

As a follow-on to the dot-EDU pilot activities in the Democratic Republic of Congo, EDC's support of USAID's Strategic Objective Basic Education, Especially Girls, Improved in Target Areas—provides an important opportunity to benefit from recent lessons learned and apply this experience to programming that will have greater reach and more ambitious objectives.

As such, EDC activities will be expanded to reach a greater number of educators, community members and students and aim to have longer-term impact in the communities targeted by the initiative. The project has set goals to improve basic education by improving the quality of teacher skills, increasing access to appropriate texts and other learning materials (including through the use of technology). It also aims to increase community participation in education as well focus on access, retention and achievement of students, particularly of girls.

dot-EDU's Work in Post-secondary Education in Africa

As stated earlier, USAID missions tend to fund projects that work with primary education. We have been involved with interventions in post-secondary institutions in Mali, Namibia, Rwanda and Uganda. While we have worked with two universities (in Mali and in Uganda), it should be made clear that most of the work in post-secondary education is with teacher training colleges.

Challenges and Lessons Learned

In two of the projects (Mali and Namibia) project directors have reported problems with timing and with Internet connectivity. In Mali, we were asked to provide training, but connectivity at the university (under a separate contract with another organization) was not complete. Because of USAID regulations, our training phase could not be extended. So dot-EDU partners were forced to carry out training in some cases when there was no connectivity. Also in Mali, dot-EDU was asked to provide training for WAN and LAN administrators. The ambitious schedule imposed by the project did not synchronize with the hiring schedule at the University of Bamako.

In Namibia, with the iNET project, equipment was not put in place at the four teacher training institutes in time for the dot-EDU activities to start. In this case the procurement was being carried out by the Ministry of Education (with some equipment being added by the dot-EDU project). But, unlike the situation with the Mali project, there is more flexibility with the USAID agreement and an extension will be allowed. There is also a problem with having "less-than-robust" bandwidth, but the limitations are due to the size of the "pipe" bringing Internet to the country.

The project in Rwanda involved bringing the Internet to the Kigali Institute of Education (KIE), a three-year-old teacher training college. A second part of the project involved setting up distance learning centres so that secondary school teachers could be given in-service training. A dot-EDU partner, World Links, was able to bring enormous benefits to this project since they had just received funds from the World Bank to set up laboratories in secondary schools. At the start of this project dot-EDU staff were concerned that there was too much emphasis on equipment and too little on training and professional development. Having World Links as a partner helped us to overcome some of those problems: as part of their cost-share agreement they were able to bring in more training and an introduction to new pedagogical approaches.

USAID/Uganda supports the Connect ED II project, which is setting up computer centres at Kyambogo University (KyU) and eight primary teacher's colleges (PTCs) throughout the country. USAID began supporting this project in 1998 as part of the LearnLink initiative (LearnLink was a USAID-funded ICT-and-development mechanism that preceded dot-EDU). Under the current activity they want to see the PTCs develop business plans as a way to sustain the laboratories. They also hope that dot-EDU can help implement policy changes that will help with sustainability. One challenge came when the President decided, after USAID support began, that students at the PTCs in Uganda should not have to pay fees of any kind. That, of course, made it difficult for the colleges to cover recurring costs.

Some at USAID/Uganda feel that the colleges should be able to bring in revenue from the community by charging fees for Internet access and training. While this may be a good idea in some places, many of the laboratories are in very remote settings. While we continue to pursue this approach to sustaining the laboratories, it is a challenge.

A policy change at the Ministry of Education and Sports (MoES) that might lead to sustainability represents a breakthrough. Realizing the value of an ICT-enabled college, the Ministry sent an official letter permitting the PTC principals to charge a small fee to students each term. Of course we would rather have the Ministry budget funds for the laboratories so that students did not have to pay. At one point central funding was approved, but, at the last minute, the budget was cut.

So, although it was not our first choice, the policy change allowing students to be charged fees does make sustainability possible. We continue to explore the idea of charging fees to those in the community who want to use the laboratories after hours. For example, NGOs might bring in teams for training while students are on vacation. And there are other forms of revenue. Support from a special rural access fund at the Uganda Communications Commission (UCC) will provide additional funds for connectivity for a year after the USAID funding ends. So a multifaceted approach, with several revenue streams, seems to be the best approach to sustaining these laboratories in Uganda.

Pilot Projects under dot-EDU

The projects described above (associate awards) are, for the most part, supported by USAID missions. The dot-EDU project also has limited Washington-based funds for setting up pilot projects. Many of these are collaborations with dot-EDU partner organization or with other groups involved with ICT and education in the developing world. Core-funded activities include the following:

Table Twenty-six dot-EDU core-funded activities worldwide (October 2005)

Location	Description	Start date
Uganda	IT and HIV/AIDS pilot with World Bank Institute	January 2002
Peru	IT and early childhood development with IBM	August 2002
Southeast Asia	IBM Change Toolkit	October 2003
Ghana/Ethiopia	MIT's Africa Internet Technology Initiative (MIT–AITI)	April 2003
Global	ICT Survey—Harvard Berkman Ctr	September 2002
Africa-wide	ICTs in African Schools	April 2003
South Africa	ILI Literacy project	April 2003
Laos	Low-cost technology to reach semi-literate Mekong girls	November 2003
Africa-wide	Sustaining school networks with Benton Foundation	February 2004
Guatemala	Transfer Enlace Quiche to an NGO	February 2004
Colombia	Exploring new virtual community tool	June 2004

Others pilot projects since implemented include those shown in Table Twenty-seven.

Table Twenty-seven Newly implemented dot-EDU activities

Location	Description	Start date
Colombia	Online Centers of Excellence with dot-EDU partner Concord Consortium	December 2004
Jamaica	Leasing model that works with Cable and Wireless	November 2004

Some of the pilots and core-funded activities under dot-EDU might have applications in post-secondary education in Africa. For example, a "Sustainability Toolkit" is being developed that will help decision-makers in any institution think about financial sustainability of technology for education. IBM's Change Toolkit. which we worked with in Southeast Asia, can be used in both African countries and in African universities.

In the upcoming pilot, which will use "thin-client" devices, we hope to explore a way to solve one of the problems that has emerged in some of the primary teacher colleges in Uganda. In remote parts of Uganda power fluctuations have been doing considerable damage to equipment. Using an uninterruptible power supply (UPS) is not enough. Some of our colleagues with an ISP in Kampala have suggested that we try 12-volt thin-client devices. A battery system will be put in place that is charged by the grid, but the laboratory will run off of the 12-volt system. By using thin-client devices and LCD panels we should be able to keep the "load" to a minimum and allow the system to run off of the 12-volt system.

Other DOT-COM Work in Africa

Our colleagues in the USAID-funded DOT-COM Alliance (dot-GOV and dot-ORG) have, in addition to dot-EDU, been part of activities that are helping to bring digital opportunities to African universities.[4] For more detail on these activities visit http://www.dot-com-alliance.org

Summary

In this chapter, we have provided the opportunity to enter dot-EDU, a five-year project funded by the US Agency for International Development (USAID), which uses information and communication technology to strengthen education and learning systems in developing counties. We have seen the vast range of projects and programs at work in this area and identified the successes and problems encountered in undertaking this development goal. The increasing importance of

ICT for developing countries requires detailed knowledge and detailed auditing of these experiences in developing appropriate paths for progress.

Notes

1 See http://www.dot-com-alliance.org.
2 See www.sudanradio.org.
3 For more details see http://dot-edu.org or at http://www.dot-com-alliance.org.
4 For more details see http://www.dot-com-alliance.org.

CHAPTER THIRTEEN

GENDER DIMENSIONS OF E-GOVERNMENT AND E-DEMOCRACY IN DEVELOPING COUNTRIES

Eva M. Rathgeber*

Many proponents of information communications technologies (ICTs) have emphasized their potential to enable governments to more efficiently and effectively serve people living outside urban areas and at the same time allow people to participate more actively in e-democracy. As more and more people become connected worldwide, ICT optimists anticipate that the technologies will overcome barriers of geography and distance, providing opportunities within national and across international boundaries for users to have instant access to relevant knowledge and information. Most industrialized countries and some developing countries already are providing many e-government services to their citizens, often with positive outcomes. For example, the digitalization of land registration processes in Andhra Pradesh, India has resulted in more transparent services. Computerized land registration counters help citizens to complete registration requirements within an hour instead of the several days necessary under the old system, and there is no role for middlemen, which formerly led to corruption.

There are some potentially negative factors that accompany the growth of e-government and e-democracy, including a loss of personal privacy and security of information. For many people, especially women and girls, the global computer culture does not provide a welcoming structure for participation. This paper explores the relevance of ICTs in helping women, especially those in developing countries, to participate more actively and effectively in democratic processes and in government. It reviews some early evidence about the participation of women in e-government and e-democracy and identifies some of the obstacles that must be overcome to make e-government and e-democracy more inclusive. E-governance, as used here, refers to the electronic provision of services by different levels of government. E-democracy refers to the use of ICTs to enable citizens to participate in open fora that allow them to express their views and opinions.

A brief overview of research on e-government and e-democracy indicates that gender has not been considered to be an important variable for discussion. Most researchers overlook the fact that women and men everywhere have a different pattern of interaction with computers and the Internet. In many industrialized countries, female level of use of the Internet is comparable to that of males, but they use it mostly for practical purposes, i.e. to find information or to shop. Women

* Joint Chair of Women's Studies, University of Ottawa/Carleton University.

and girls are less likely to spend time surfing and playing computer games. In many developing countries women are much less likely than men to use the Internet because they do not have access, they do not have skills or they do not have time and/or interest. Therefore, the notion that ICTs can be a vehicle for making government services and public participation more widespread is flawed by the fact that many people simply do not use ICTs. From this perspective, the move towards digitization of government services and involvement of civil society in Internet discussion groups may be further marginalizing women. This does not seem to be recognized as a problem by most e-government sites. The onus is on women to become interested in ICTs, rather than on governments to ensure that they are not excluded.

While it is undeniable that information communications technologies are having a global impact on government, commerce, networking etc., the greatest benefits may accrue to transnational corporations that have been quick to utilize ICTs to create and reach new markets and to streamline and achieve savings in corporate communications. As will be discussed below, the ICT industry is investing substantially in helping developing countries to build up both infrastructure and technical expertise to enable them to improve their telecommunications services and to create core groups of skilled ICT users. While in some cases women are being targeted by the private sector, to improve their ICT skills, some have argued that this is part of a larger business strategy aimed at producing skilled information labour.

The Missing Gender Variable in Research on E-Governance and E-Democracy

At a broad level, e-government can achieve a number of obviously valuable benefits. It can bring government services closer to citizens through personal computers, kiosks and telephones; it can reduce the opportunity for corruption at point of service; it can streamline government services across departments; it can increase and capture revenue more efficiently and it can help to increase government transparency and accountability (Schware and Deane, 2003). It also reduces government costs in transferring information. At the 4th International Conference for Women in Beijing in 1995, two of the strategic objectives adopted were to take measures to ensure women's equal access to and full participation in power structures and decision making, and to increase women's capacity to participate in decision-making and leadership. Given this commitment, during the past decade, as public information has become more commonly available on the Internet, efforts should have been made to ensure that women are fully included. There is little evidence that this has occurred. A brief overview of some relevant literature suggests a number of attendant problems.

Access to the Internet

It is important to begin by putting the potential for the spread of e-government into perspective. According to the UN's Human Development database, in the high income OECD countries, 450.5 of every 1,000 residents have access to the Internet. In the developing countries, access drops to 40.9 per 1,000 residents and in the least developed countries it drops to 2.8 per 1,000 residents. Given these vast disparities, it is unlikely that e-government and e-democracy will be a realistic option for large numbers of people in the developing world for some years to come. Inexpensive and reliable connectivity is crucial, for e-government to be a realistic alternative. In many developing countries the cost of Internet access is still prohibitively expensive. Since late 2001, Asians have become the largest Internet user group in absolute numbers, but the most populous countries in the region (China, India and Indonesia) have relatively low Internet user densities (Gunawardene and Wattegama, 2003). Africa has the lowest Internet use density, especially outside the urban areas.

Some countries have made concerted efforts to achieve universal access. For example, Brazil has set up a Fund for Universal Access to Telecommunications that draws resources from privatization of the national operator and mandatory contributions from all telecommunications operators. The Fund is used to ensure that all public schools will have computers and access to the Internet by 2006. Other access points are being installed in public buildings and the Brazilian government is starting to make many of its services available on-line (Schware and Deane, 2003). Intensive efforts also are underway to train government employees in the use of open source software. Special efforts will have to be made to ensure that women employees also receive training. A UNDP evaluation found that a government ICT upgrade program in Vietnam reinforced gender disparities since not a single woman was among the civil servants selected for intensive training (UNDP Evaluation Office, 2004).

Sex-disaggregated Data

Despite many calls for systematic data collection (Hafkin and Taggart, 2001; Rathgeber, 2000), there continues to be a lack of reliable sex-disaggregated data on the use of ICTs, especially in developing countries. There are data for the industrialized countries, often compiled by marketing research companies, and Sørensen (2002) notes that, while men are still more active users of home computers, the Internet and mobile phones in Europe, the difference in level of use is declining rapidly. Middle-aged and elderly women are the least likely to use ICTs. Young women and girls are active users, but this has not led to the enrolment of higher numbers of women in computer science programs at universities (which in turn means that the computer science culture has continued to be very male-oriented). There are some scattered data for the use of the Internet in developing countries, but no single consistent source of information. A 2001 study of 560 users in Sri Lanka found that among the respondents, 71 per cent were male and 17 per cent female (others did not indicate their sex). Only 8 per cent of the users were aged above 56 years, more than one third of the users had completed at least a basic degree and a further 13 per cent were still engaged in full time studies (Gunawardene and Wattegama, 2003). Women also tend to be less knowledgeable than their male counterparts about computers. A Malaysian study of male and female university students found that males had greater computer literacy but even more importantly they perceived themselves as having higher programming skills and better ability in computer repair and maintenance (Zin et al., 2000). A Ugandan study of Internet Café users in Kampala found that the typical user was a 25-year-old single male with no children and with a minimum of secondary school completion. Eighty per cent of the users were aged under 30 and less than 4 per cent were older than 40. Sixty per cent of the users said they also had other sources of access to the Internet, which suggests that Internet Café users are not among the most disadvantaged sector of the population.

Fragmented services

Even in some developing countries, interactive e-government sites are becoming common. For example, in India citizens can access passport applications, registration procedures, school examination results, trade guidelines, telemedicine, customs information and land records among other services. In the developing world, e-government projects tend to be based in single departments or ministries and to be supported by donor funds. Even in cases where civil servants have access to computers, they do not necessarily have the skills to use them effectively. Early experience shows that effective e-governance initiatives must be part of an overall strategic plan. A fragmented approach can duplicate services, leading to unnecessary costs and even to the reinforcement of existing inequalities in access to information and/or services (Odendaal, 2003).

Low Priority

Despite these efforts, e-government is not necessarily a priority for Internet users in developing countries. A UNDP survey in the Asia/Pacific region in early 2005 found that the priority issues were: virus attacks, online fraud/cyber-crime, and spam; illegal content; privacy and data protection online; and availability, cost and reliability of the Internet (UNDP/APDIP, 2005). Overall, there was a strong sense of optimism about the potential of the Internet to contribute positively to the region. Although UNDP has emphasized the importance of collecting gender disaggregated statistics, this survey did not identify respondents by sex so there is no way of knowing how many, if any of the 1,200+ respondents were female and, if so, whether their opinions differed from those of their male counterparts. Unless gender issues are specifically integrated into ICT projects, they tend to be ignored and the male experience is accepted as the norm (Hafkin, 2002).

Need for Gender Analysis

Access to and use of the Internet does not equate with e-democracy or with the civic empowerment of women. For real empowerment through e-democracy, local people must have the opportunity for input and feedback on government policies and this feedback must be integrated into the policymaking process. Many factors can effect the participation of girls and women. For example, a study in Tanzania found that women were almost completely absent from on-going e-democracy initiatives (Planmo, n.d.). At an East African Community and UNECA-sponsored meeting on e-government held in Tanzania in late 2004, participants identified the priority e-government areas for the region as being customs, e-parliament, e-health, e-banking, e-procurement, e-commerce and information on meteorology. A strategic plan was developed but it had no emphasis on providing special training for women or for including gender analysis in the conceptualization of e-government services. Again, it is unlikely that services will be tailored to meet the needs of women or that women will become active users, unless efforts are made at the design stage to integrate gender analysis.

Many telecommunications regulatory agencies both in the North and in the South have given insufficient attention to ensuring that gender analysis is part of their policies. Recognizing this lack, the International Telecommunications Union (ITU) issued "gender aware" guidelines in 2001. The wide ranging guidelines urged for the involvement of women and gender analysis in all aspects, including human resource development, training and licensing activities, but there is no way of gauging the extent to which the guidelines have actually been implemented. Many regulatory agencies have focussed on universal access and rural communications services, but few have analysed the basic issues of availability, accessibility and affordability from a gender perspective.

North American World View

The international development community generally assumes that it is in the public interest to promote communication among people all over the world. It is widely accepted that it is to everyone's mutual advantage for as much knowledge and information as possible to be circulated and shared. However, the majority of the information that is available through the Internet is Western in origin and in conceptualization. It promotes a Eurocentric/American perspective. There have been important critiques of the capacity of ICTs to accelerate development processes. Some analysts argue that the faith of the international development industry in information communications technologies reinforces the earlier allegations by modernization theorists more than 30 years ago that knowledge, and specifically European organization of knowledge, was the central force of development (Mwesige, 2004; Schech, 2002). Increasingly, economic development is being linked with the existence of a strong ICT capacity. Thompson argues that the World Bank promotion of ICTs is aimed at ensuring that developing countries become part of global networks built on a "North American" world view (Thompson, 2004). Because most Internet hosts are concentrated in industrialized countries, the tendency is towards the sharing of information from the North in the languages of the North. This limits the sharing of information and perspectives of researchers, policymakers and general public in the South (Mansell, 2002).

Local Languages and Local Content

A pressing problem with the worldwide web, is the lack of content in local languages. Although some local languages are now being transcribed onto the Internet, there are often problems with standardization and attendant problems related to the use of sounds and characters that cannot easily be recognized by the computer. However, it will be necessary for governments to offer services in national languages, if e-government is to become the norm.

Local content is another critical issues. Most of the proprietory software that has been commercially developed is not available in local languages and cannot be adapted for local use. The use of open source software provides a solution to this problem as it can be translated into local languages and adapted to include local content (UNDP, 2004). The government of Brazil has set an example, by publishing guidelines for the use of open source software in government and signing a letter of intent with IBM to boost the use of open source software.

The Gender Focus in Public/Private Partnerships

Much emphasis has been put on public/private partnerships to provide the necessary expertise and capital to ensure that developing countries can build up the required infrastructure and technical competence in telecommunications. Many ICT companies have been working with the international development bureaucracy to achieve these aims. Their investments have been substantial and it is fair to assume that these investments have been made with future markets in mind. Indeed, e-government offers many possibilities for participation of the private sector in the delivery of services.

Interestingly, many of the public/private partnerships have been characterized by special attention to the participation of women. Transnational corporations have recognized the potential of women as ICT workers since at least the early 1990s. Over the past 15 years, offshore call and data processing centres set up in countries like India, Malaysia or Barbados have employed thousands of educated women

In 2003, through its "Unlimited Potential" program, Microsoft Corporation committed $1 billion in cash, software, curriculum and technology assistance to digital global divide-related activities. Microsoft has partnered with UNDP to provide technology-enabled training in community education centers and they are also supporting UNDP's Southern Africa Capacity Initiative to explore innovative opportunities to use technology to build capacity, facilitate e-government initiatives, and improve the delivery of basic services in countries most adversely affected by the HIV/AIDS pandemic. In Egypt, Microsoft's Future Generation Foundation (FGF) project trains young female university graduates with IT skills and Microsoft .net certification. In another project, they are providing IT skills training to unemployed women graduates to create new job opportunities in the SME industry. One advantage of ICT-related work is that it can often be done from the home and can therefore be combined with family responsibilities, providing technical training to young girls who may have restrictions on their ability to work outside the home.

In the Baltic countries, Microsoft is supporting a UNDP initiative aimed at building the capacity of Lithuanian women's NGOs to network and use the Internet. The company is providing software for the training facilities of five women's NGOs. The aim is to encourage women to use information technologies and strengthen women's NGOs to allow them to provide information and services to local communities more effectively. Ultimately the three-year project will train around 800 women, and lead to an increase in the number of women's NGOs using information technologies.

Cisco Systems also has given attention to the training of women, through its Cisco Academy network. In May 2001, the International Telecommunication Union (ITU) launched the Internet Training Centers Initiative for Developing Countries (ITCI-DC) to provide students and professionals in developing countries access to affordable and relevant technology training. Cisco Systems became a pioneer partner and began working with ITU to offer the Cisco Networking Academy at all Internet Training Centers. All Training Centres must have detailed plans for the facilitation of female participation and must pursue a minimum of 30 per cent female enrolment. Some gender-focused and women-only centers have also been established. Overall, the Initiative actively encourages the participation of female students and the training of female instructors. The program also receives support from local and national governments.

In Uganda, a Cisco Network Academy has been established in the Gender Studies Department at Makerere University in Kampala. Most Cisco academies have been hosted by Computer Science or Engineering departments in which female enrolment in usually low. In establishing an academy with a Department of Gender Studies,

Cisco is aiming to involve women who do not necessarily have a background in science and engineering. This strategy has been effective in improving female enrolment and providing access to IT learning where it otherwise would not have existed. It also provides a certain political "legitimacy" to the CISCO program as being gender sensitive.

Although these examples have been selectively drawn, they do highlight the special attention being given to the training of women by the private sector. This is consistent with earlier outsourcing of electronics work to developing countries and the tendency to employ young relatively educated women who were seen as hard working, uncomplaining and reliable employees. Since all these programs are focussed primarily on the acquisition of technical skills rather than on the analysis of the global computer culture and the social relevance of these skills, it is doubtful that many of the women who receive this training will become actively involved in ensuring that the computer culture becomes more accessible to other, less educated women.

ICTS and the Political Empowerment of Women

In developing countries, the primary users of computer-based ICTs are members of the elite, who have both the necessary skills and financial resources. This is not true of cellular phones, which have been adopted widely by men and women of every social class in countries where they are available at a reasonable price. The widespread use of cellular phones suggests that poor people, men and women, will use communications technology if it is affordable and has immediate relevance to their lives. Indeed, poor women have even become ICT entrepreneurs when the opportunity presented itself, as in Bangladesh's Grameen Bank's Village Telephone project where poor women have been assisted to purchase cellular phones and then sell phone calls to local people. Similarly, in Senegal, many women have become proprietors of small teleshops that offer telephone services to local customers.

The involvement of women as consumers, especially of computer-based technologies, has been much slower. This has created an important barrier to the delivery of e-government services to them. Similarly, women are less likely to become involved with e-democracy initiatives. Their political participation is substantially lower than that of men almost everywhere in the world. In the least developed countries, women's lower levels of education provide an additional obstacle as they are often illiterate and communicate only in their own indigenous language. Since there is little material available on the Internet in local languages, this makes it even less likely that women will use the Internet.

Many factors mitigate against the participation of women in politics. Aidah Opoku Mensah has identified some for the African context, but they hold true in many other developing regions: political parties rarely support female candidates; women have difficulty obtaining campaign funding; few women have political-campaign skills; women do not vote for women; women are taught to avoid confrontation; women in public are expected to follow, rather than lead; and women and men are heirs to customs, traditions, and legal systems that discriminate against women (Opoku-Mensah, 2000). Opoku-Mensah argues that the established media outlets in Africa are often owned by government and offer little opportunity for open discussion and exchange of opinion. They have tended to reinforce the prejudice against the participation of women in politics, giving less coverage or biased coverage to women candidates. The Internet provides an opportunity for a more equal playing field for women, allowing them to express opinions and take positions that are critical of the prevailing status quo.

In most developing countries, people gain access to computers through offices or through public access points such as Internet cafes, public kiosks or telecenters. Multipurpose telecenters have become common in many rural areas, offering not only Internet access but also a wide range of other services including fax, telephone, television/video, libraries and, often, computer training. Most telecenters charge small user fees but this creates an additional barrier for poor women, who usually have less disposable income than men and frequently do not have decision-making rights over use of family income. The Uganda Internet café study found that even in the urban area, men were more frequent users (Mwesinge, 2004).

There are also initiatives underway that use the Internet to help less educated women become more politically aware and active. For example, a project in western Kenya used ICTs to provide literate and semi-literate women with civic education materials. The focus was on teaching women about gender and equity issues; legal issues pertaining to women; voter education; human rights (women's rights); responsible citizenship; and reproductive health. Materials were prepared in Nairobi, sent to telecenters in the rural areas and downloaded for discussion with local women's groups. Women's group leaders were trained in computer skills and they in turn were intended to teach these skills to village women. Learning computer skills also enabled the women to communicate with other women's groups, exchanging ideas and learning about the activities of other NGOs (Khasiani, 2000).

E-networking has become a central component of the international women's movement. Over the past two decades there has developed loose concensus around many women's issues. This has resulted from active networking and sharing of experiences and expertise among women located in different geographical areas. Initially this international women's movement was fostered by participation in international and regional conferences, with follow-up correspondence. Today the Internet, e-mail, mailing lists, on-line conferences and websites are perhaps the most important tools used by women's groups. Of course not all women's groups have access to the Internet, but enough do globally, for it to have become a primary source of interaction. Global civil society is using the Internet for purposes of collaboration, publishing, mobilization, and observation (Surman and Reilly, 2003) and women's groups increasingly are represented within this category. For example, during the years leading up to the World Summit on the Information

Society (WSIS), an active Gender Caucus, composed mostly of female members from around the world, strategized regularly to ensure that gender issues were part of the preparation process. Other women's groups have collaborated similarly around different issues.

However, those individuals who are able to express their ideas clearly and concisely are at an advantage and knowledge of English (or another major world language) is an important requirement. Research has confirmed that power relationships that have long existed among non governmental organizations, continue to be replicated with the shift to the use of ICTs. A study of electronic networking among NGOs in the Gulf of California showed that the largest NGOs were the most active in electronic networks and set the agenda for discussion. Their staff was more likely to have had training and some exposure to issues. Other NGOs were marginalized and an elite group was created (Rodriguez, 2005). In general, developing country NGOs tend to be less likely to take advantage of the Internet than international NGOs (Souter, 1999). This is unsurprising since their staff are less likely to have the necessary skills but also because the cost of connectivity is usually much higher.

Conclusion

The first important point that emerges from this overview is that there has been little analysis of the relationship between gender and e-government or gender and e-democracy. Although many governments are moving ahead with the development of e-government services, there has been little attention to the different needs and styles of men and women. It is not clear that ICTs have served to politically empower women and there is a real danger that they are being channeled into the category of ICT workers but not managers, deicision-makers, hardware designers or framers of policy. There has been a tendency for the technology itself to assume an importance that overshadows the uses for which it was intended. ICTs were developed as tools to help people communicate more cost effectively and efficiently and if they fail to do so then they cannot be considered successful. However because they have been developed and championed by the private sector, the driving motivation is often to sell the technology rather than to focus on ensuring that the technology fulfills the tasks for which it was developed. This is reinforced by the constant upgrading of hardware and the hard sell by the computer industry to encourage us to buy new equipment. Women tend to be less susceptible to this.

To ensure that girls and women become full participants in e-government and e-democracy, a strong enabling environment must be put into place. This must cover all aspects of policy, training and accessibility. Gender analysis must be undertaken at the design stage of e-government programs because the directions in which the services will move will definitely be effected by the inclusion of gender concerns.

However the inclusion of women and girls in e-government is likely to occur only if at least some of the following factors are in place:

- a strong commitment by national government to ensuring that e-government services are designed in such a way as to be available to all citizens;
- telecommunications policy frameworks that ensure that the needs of girls and women are part of the national structure;
- ICT training for girls and women;
- affordable connectivity and safe, convenient centers where women can use computers (telecenters, post offices, community centers, etc.);
- clearly designed content in local languages; and
- feedback mechanisms that allow women and girls to have input into e-government

This is not an exhaustive list but simply reflects some of the issues that should be considered by national governments as they begin to design e-government services. It is evident that unless gender analysis is given careful attention, women and girls are less likely to benefit from such services.

References

Gunawardene, Nalaka and Canuka Wattegama. "Sri Lanka," in *Digital Review of Asia/Pacific 2003/2004* (Penang, Malaysia: Southbound, 2003): http://www.digital-review.org.

Hafkin, Nancy J. "Are ICTs Gender Neutral? A Gender Analysis of Six Case Studies of Multi-donor Ict Projects." UN/INSTRAW Virtual Seminar Series on Gender and ICTs. Seminar One: *Are ICTS Gender Neutral*? 1–12 July 2002: http://www.un-instraw.org/en/docs/gender_and_ict/Hafkin.pdf.

Hafkin, Nancy and Nancy Taggart. *Gender, Information Technology and Developing Countries: An Analytic Study*. Academy for Educational Development (Washington: USAID, 2001).

Khasiani, Shanyisa Anota "Enhancing Women's Participation in Governance: The Case of Kakamega and Makueni Districts, Kenya", in *Gender and the Information Revolution in Africa*, ed. Eva M. Rathgeber and Edith Ofwona Adera (Ottawa: IDRC, 2000).

Mansell, Robin. "Constructing the Knowledge Base for Knowledge-driven Development", *Journal of Knowledge Management* 6:4 (2002): 317–29.

Mwesige, Peter G. "Cyber Elites: A Survey of Internet Café users in Uganda", *Telematics and Informatics* 21 (2004): 83–101.

Odendaal, Nancy. "Information and Communication Technology and Local Governance: Understanding the Difference between Cities in Developed and

Emerging Economies", *Computers, Environment and Urban Systems* 27 (2003): 585–607.

Planmo, Markus. "From Patron-Client to Client-Server. E-democracy in Tanzania?" MA thesis, Uppsala University, Sweden, n.d.

Opoku-Mensah, Aidah, "ICTs as Tools of Democratization: African Women Speak Out", in *Gender and the Information Revolution in Africa*, ed. Eva M. Rathgeber and Edith Ofwona Adera (Ottawa: IDRC, 2000).

Rathgeber, Eva M. "Women, Men, and ICTs in Africa: Why Gender is an Issue", in *Gender and the Information Revolution in Africa*, ed. Eva M. Rathgeber and Edith Ofwona Adera (Ottawa: IDRC, 2000).

Rodriguez, Gabriela Romo. "Information and Communications Technology and Non-governmental Organizations: Lessons Learnt from Networking in Mexico", *Electronic Journal of Information Systems in Developing Countries* 21, 3 (2005): 1–29.

Schech, Susanne. "Wired for Change: The Links between ICTs and Development Discourses", *Journal of International Development* 14 (2002): 13–23.

Schware, Robert and Arsala Deane, "Deploying E-government Programs: The Strategic Importance or 'I' before 'E'", *info* 5:4 (2003): 10–19.

Sørensen, Kurt H. "Love, Duty and the S-curve. An Overview of Some Recent Literature on Gender and ICT", Sigis IST–2000-26329: http://www.rcss.ed.ac.uk/sigis/public/D02/D02_part1.pdf (October 2002).

Souter, David. "The Role of Information and Communications Technologies in Democratic Development", *The Journal of Policy, Regulation and Strategy for Telecommunications, Information and Media* 1:5 (October 1999): 405–17.

Surman, Mark and Katherine Reilly. *Appropriating the Internet for Social Change. Towards the Strategic Use of Networked Technologies by Transnational Civil Society Organizations* (New York: Social Science Research Concil, 2003).

Thompson, Mark P.A. "ICTs, Power and Developmental Discourse: A Critical Analysis", *Electronic Journal of Information Systems in Developing Countries* 20:4 (2004): 1–26.

UNDP/APDIP. "Open Regional Dialogue on Internet Governance. Internet governance priorities for Asia-Pacific", Summary Analysis of a Regional Survey (Bangkok: UNDP, April 2005): http://www.genderit.org/upload/ad6d215b74e2a8613f0cf5416c9f3865/ORDIG.pdf

UNDP Evaluation Office. "UNDP Practice Area: Democratic governance. Synthesis of lessons Learned", *Essentials* 15: http://www.undp.org/eo/documents/essentials/En-egov-essential-No-15.pdf (April 2004).

Zin, Nor Azan Mat, Halimah Badioze Zaman, Harirulliza Modh Judi et al. "Gender Differences in Computer Literacy Level among Undergraduate Students in Universiti Kebangsaan Malaysia (UKM)". *Electronic Journal of Information Systems in Developing Countries* 1: http://new.ejisdc.org/ojs/viewissue.php?id=1#Research_Papers (2000)

Websites

Andhra Pradesh land registration: http://www1.worldbank.org/publicsector/egov/cardcs.htm.

Human Development Report Database: http://hdr.undp.org/statistics/data/.

International Telecommunications Union Gender Awareness Guidelines: http://www.ictdevlibrary.org/downloads/itu_gender_guidelines.

EPILOGUE

ECONOMIC FRAMEWORKS FOR IT DEVELOPMENT: AN EPILOGUE ON BRIDGING THE DIGITAL DIVIDE

Sheila Robinson*

Introduction: ICT, Creativity and Economic Frameworks

This chapter provides an epilogue which contextualizes the environment of the African university in terms of current debates on shaping content and harnessing creativity to reduce the impact and potency of the digital divide. In the context set by the conference *ICT and Creativity: Strategies for a Creative Information Society* held in Vienna on 3 June 2005 (http://www.wsa-conference.org/data/wsa_conference_final.pdf), and the quotations from the keynote speakers below, the challenge is to consider whether the new economic frameworks will support the delivery of quality content, sustainably, across a global whole market:

- *Re-imagining the future*—Koichiro Matsuura, Director General of UNESCO;
- *Creativity as an engine of productivity*—Carlos Magarinos, Director General of UNIDO;
- *Content is not FREE*—Dr Peter Bruck, President World Summit Awards.

The proposition set out in Figure Twenty-three is that, to be effective, any framework will have to support the creative process, enable collaboration between all the parties to a transaction—not just the developers—and add value to the global market. The UK Commission for Africa asked these same questions and proposed protection for less developed economies.[1] The questions that we are raising are:

- is a new economic realm necessary for the continued delivery of quality content, and are there specific challenges for IT corporations; and
- does scale and technology limit the opportunity for the development of content?

The existing models are being challenged on many levels: they do not provide models for global business; they do not integrate individual development; they fail to support the fragile infrastructure in emerging markets; they do not give us a model to bridge the digital divide. Can we conceive of better ones?

Future economic models need to address the following key concepts:

---

* Solvebrand Limited and Consultant to Bob Geldof on ICT and Africa.

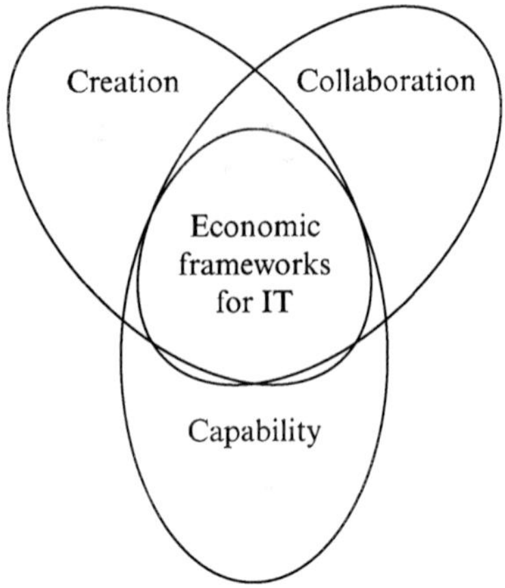

Figure Twenty-three Economic framework for ICT

- Who owns what?—how and when is it OK to add value?
- Who exploits or benefits?—what are the channels to market?—does this reduce the digital divide?—will emerging economies be supported?
- Are innovative business structures needed?
- What legal frameworks are required for sustainability in the long term?

Also, how will new frameworks be introduced? In the UK, for example, the public sector accounts for 40 per cent of GDP—that makes all public sector buying decisions hugely influential on the economy and technology trends. A public sector initiative to develop more sustainable economic approaches to IT development could lead the way. Companies themselves have influence too, the larger corporations have budgets as large as those of a small country and their spending can be more exactingly focused to serve a particular set of goals.[2] International groups are already reviewing options for new and more sustainable business approaches globally. The challenge may be seen as emerging from developing economies like those in Africa, where the mobile phone offers, communication, content and training as sophisticated as anything on a PC.[3] It may be that the key opportunities will develop from combined initiatives.

For the present debate we have to address two perspectives concurrently—microeconomics and the theory of the firm, and macroeconomics for the market.

In *The Modern Firm* (2004), John Roberts sets out a future perspective for effective company growth which provides a micro view. Here we summarize this perspective.

Company performance depends on:

- strategy;
- organization; and
- environment.

Each aspect can be used for development, but when, as now, there is great environmental change it is not useful to concentrate on sequential strategy and development of the organization.

To create a stable structure in times of great change, it is necessary to:

- fix the organization (i.e. set it and leave it alone);
- use the strategy and the malleable aspects of the organization (e.g. culture) to keep up with changes in technology and markets. Examples of this in action are Nokia and BP in the 1990s.

Basically, the focus for development is external not internal, maintaining adaptability to the market and to competitive changes provides the impetus for future performance. The key to success is to be proactive not simply reactive. Working to release a culture which is responsive and close to its environment and integrated into the potential capability of the whole organization to deliver globally requires transformational leadership too.

A corresponding macro view can be derived from John Hagel and John Seely Brown's book, *The Only Sustainable Edge* (2005). Although this sets out a model for all organizations—private, public and non-governmental organizations (NGOs), they focus on enterprise because they see that as the most effective way to deliver the change model. They argue that: "Only business executives can ensure the scalability of new approaches" (2005: 1).

The key, they argue, is the creation of a more dynamic, non-zero sum game by:

- dynamic specialization—work at the edge, be flexible;
- connectivity—embrace the business network, up and downstream;
- leveraged capability building—where the most value can be added, repeatedly.

This is possible if one works:

- at the edge where one firm interacts with another;
- the boundaries of mature markets, where they overlap, collide or converge;
- geographic edges (e.g. India and China currently);
- the edge between generations (as the younger generation learn, consume, collaborate; the baby boomers retire/switch careers).

The Edge is seen as the primary source of real, long term innovation. In the relationship "Edge—Core—Edge", it is the "edge" which provides the relationship to new markets and to emerging markets.

In their view, executives grow increasingly near sighted and apply near term tactics, when what they need is to anticipate and shape broad patterns of evolution. *Those who aggressively reshape their businesses to exploit the opportunities of global business and technology architecture will create significant value.*

Note that this will be based on technical innovation and a relentless shift in public policy to both reduce costs and increase value. Historically, an enterprise would simply have focused on its core competencies and the development of partnerships to increase its market competitiveness. To become truly effective a business will have to be excellent at delivering its core business, have a powerful ability to build long-term constructive relationships which add value and release budget, plus developing continuing, step change levels of innovation.

For an *innovation driven* strategy, it is necessary to:

- reconceive sources of strategic advantage;
- master new mechanisms to build advantage;
- sdopt new approaches for developing strategy.

For Hagel and Seely Brown (2005): "The competitive edge depends on a firm's capacity to *rapidly* deepen its distinctive capabilities, and to accelerate learning across enterprise boundaries". This process has to become dynamic so that a "larger pie" is created, and we avoid the risk of everyone simply competing again (and moving back to the traditional zero-sum game).

Innovation must involve the creation of "capabilities"—areas of greater specialization and learning. From that it follows from that "accelerated capability building is the most powerful source of strategic advantage in a global economy characterised by intensifying competition" (Hagel and Seely Brown, 2005)?

Organizational Paths and Steps

To return to the beginning of the Hagel and Seely Brown view, we encounter three key elements:

- dynamic specialization—focus on world-class capability building;
- connectivity—get the other specialist companies to join your party;
- leveraged capability building—then push out the boundaries with those other specialist companies, so everyone gains.

If we then turn to the view originally expressed by Ronald Coase—"Firms exist to economise on market transactions" (1937), i.e. the reasons that we have firms is that they are more efficient—and integrate that into the Hagel and Seely Brown view, we get a shift from "efficiency to capability building and systemic innovation". This is delivered through:

- process outsourcing and offshoring (with a view to accessing world-class capability *not* just savings);
- loose coupling of extended business processes (work the network, but for dynamic specialization, focus on specialism and capability and eliminate anything else);
- productive friction—work with widely diverse teams to create solutions to the impossible.

Challenges should be created intentionally, which pre-supposes a robust and supported culture where "mistakes" are simply learning experiences. Emerging from this approach, and searching for organizational paths for change and development, we need to focus on the practicalities of participation:

- *Performance fabrics*: "knitting it all together" with:
  - shared meaning;
  - reciprocal trust;
  - IT architecture and software;

  so that companies and other organizations can collaborate better across enterprise boundaries. The aim is external integration not just internal excellence.
- *Waves*:
  - *specialization*: shift the focus from "savings" to specialization and collaboration;
  - *connectivity*: coordinate the process across a broad range of enterprises;
  - *capability*: leverage capability building across large networks of businesses;
  - develop a balanced approach to strategy;
  - evaluate in your own organization how long has been or will be spent on the above. Where is the emphasis and best use of resources?
- *Edge diagnostic*:
  - identify the five most innovative business partners;
  - the customers who are the most innovative in their use of the products/services;
  - the large emerging economies with the most significant source of growth for your industry—which competitors use equivalent technology: are they more innovative than you? For example, O_2 has been more commercially innovative in the UK market over the last five years and was first of the mobile phone companies to move into profit.

The approach above has been provided in detail to enable a tangible review of the ideas relevant to organizational strategy in the education sector as well as enterprise in a context where there are now very many overlaps.

Practical Perspectives on Content Provision

Another less theoretical perspective on present global markets with particular relevance to content providers comes from a recent Gartner presentation (http://www.gartner.com/), which follows.

Recipe for Failure—Ignore Societal Trends

There is a need to pay attention to societal trends, not to do so is a recipe for failure and disaster. Particular issues which require attention are:

- *Cocooning*
  Some individuals are building everything around the home: *they* decide how and when they want to be contacted. It is market pull not market push, and requires a completely different marketing approach.
- *"Worst nightmare stakeholder"*
  People are using blogs to intimidate companies. It is becoming increasingly necessary for organizations to understand and learn the power of the media. The external environment is different and the response that is effective is one of openness and integrity.
- *Voluntary simplicity*
  No luxury, no pretence, no corporate world: what will motivate employees now? People are moving away from the expense account life to live to a set of principles. This offers corporations an internal challenge in developing future business if they can address it successfully they will have a workforce prepared to deliver long-term innovative, sustainable growth.
- *Information environmentalism*
  A movement aimed at getting rid of information overload and its effect on people's lives. There is evidence of backlash as people aim to draw personal boundaries around work. This impacts on organizations internally and externally, as new definitions of work are required.

There is strong evidence in European communication technology consumer markets of the move towards creating meaning and being. Research and market growth from the mobile phone companies on the use of SMS where we develop our own expression (Finland alone accounted for 4.2 bn text messages in 2004) and from the BBC on how we customize our use of the Internet (most people download radio links to run on their PC as soon as they have broadband access) amply demonstrate the change. Within Africa, Kenyans used SMS to change the outcomes of their last presidential elections. One hundred and sixty characters could provide one of the most significant message spaces that the world can share.

The Advent of the Individual Revolution

An interesting case in respect of the creation of meaning and being through communication technology is to be found in the concept of the "the Individual Revolution" promoted by Richard Duvall and now embodied in Zopa (http://www.rsa.org.uk/events/speakerCloseUp.asp?speakerID=1164). Zopa enables individuals to borrow from and lend to one another outside of the conventional banking structure:

> People who have spare money give it to a bank. Banks then do whatever they like with it. Some of it they lend to people who need to borrow. Some of it they give to their shareholders. Some of it they gamble on the price of tin, or the dollar going down, or whether there'll be floods in Asia. Banks make lots of money from all this, a fraction of which they give back to their customers.
>
> Zopa though lets people who have spare money to lend it directly to people, like them, who want to borrow it. No bank in the middle, no huge overheads, no unethical investments.
>
> To minimise any risk, the money each lender puts in is spread amongst at least 50 borrowers (and likewise each borrower gets their money from a number of different lenders).
>
> Zopa is, therefore, for people who want to be a part of something new. Who want to join a community of like-minded individuals and lend to them and borrow from them in a trusting but secure way. (http://www.zopa.com/ZopaWeb/public/how/idea.shtml)

A parallel "banking" innovation can be found in Africa: "Sambaza"[4] is a trend emerging from East Africa. It is literally the purchase of a mobile phone top-up card and then the passing on of part of the value of that card to another member of the family, or using the credit to pay for goods by "texting" the amount due. Currency is suddenly electronic and in the hands of the people, not of the institutions. This is a wonderful and strong trend to self empowerment. Africa is leading this for itself, and it is an innovation originating there.

As the advent of Zopa and "Sambaza" demonstrates, we are changing—suddenly, radically and permanently. The consumer revolution of the last 50 years is giving way to the Individual Revolution of the next 20. People who used to define themselves by what they consume—by the brands they wear, the cars they drive and the consumer electronics they own—now define themselves by their self-expression—who they are, how they lead their lives and what they care about.

Technology is enabling the change. We are at the start of the age of domesticating and humanizing information technology. The Internet, personal computer, mobile phone, gaming console and iPod are putting the individual in control—helping people to do things that once only professionals were able to do.

Our challenge is to develop effective economic frameworks in the light of these radical environmental (i.e. market) changes.

Lagging Legal and Social Structures

Inevitably, our legal and social structures lag behind our personal and technical innovations. It is relevant to refer to the research in the *Rise and Fall of the Freedom of Contract* by P.S. Atiyah, which was published in 1979, to reflect on the decline of the rights of the individual after 1870 and the move towards the increasing impact of Administrative Law because of the increase in public sector delivery of goods and services. Over the past 100 years we witnessed a move from contract to administration, from private to public law and public sector purchasing budgets are a direct consequence of that shift. It may now be that, as individuals are again claiming freedom of choice, there is a need for different legal structures which enable new economic development and protect those individual choices from both corporate and public control. Our lawyers may have to be as aware of the demands of the political economy as their British forebears were in the 1830s. Before we can look to the legislators however we have to develop the workable commercial frameworks that we seek to have enshrined.

New economic frameworks have also to be looked at in the context of the size and effective influence of corporations, many of whom are more powerful than small countries. There is a growing reflection of their global impact and the increasing need for more sustainable strategies. The Hagel and Seely Brown (2005) approach illustrates where major organizations[5] are likely to seek international competitive advantage, and to make markets both local and global , moving away from their historical national emphasis. It may be that there is a requirement for legislation which addresses both the maintenance of incentives for growth and protection of the individual creators, consumers and emerging economies to ensure they also have the right to trade. This would be based on the development of structures which offer self actualization and sustainable economic models on a world scale. The UK Commission for Africa report raises this issue and builds in incentives for both good governance and more balanced outcomes from trade. It is essential that it is policed if it is to result in effective change in support of the developing economies.

It is also evident from the Hagel and Seely Brown (2005) work that simple step function change is not going to deliver the growth that we need to create a truly global economy. To achieve that we have envisage the future that we want to achieve and work backwards to today. There will be a gap that we have to find a way to bridge if we are going to deliver something new and sustainable.

But we are human beings: social animals who crave community and meaning. These theories are remote from people, they create value for large-scale organizations but not individuals—we need a combination of strategies which integrate large-scale intent with local need. Imagining our own economic future will involve scaling it for individuals as well as corporations.

It is people who give names to airliners and trains (The Flying Scot still runs and although it is electric now and not diesel, it still resonates with the promise of a swift journey to a climate perceived by its Victorian exponents as "healthier" than the city, a quick transition to another lifestyle and the Blue Train of South Africa carried its own many signals and connotations). "We" create these meanings and embody them in romantic names, e.g. military aircraft and tanks named after girlfriends. Probably the most important consideration for us is that we need to create relationships to these objects. They are remote until we integrate them into our lives and into the stories that we weave around ourselves. As we name them, so they have a place in our individual myths and legends and we are able to work with them with some degree of effectiveness. This is the source of the value that we identify for ourselves. It is the reason that we will currently pay 3 or 4 euros (or the equivalent in another currency) for a few bars of a tune to use as a ring tone and refuse to pay for a CD. One gives us personal meaning, a defined identity in the world, the other relaxation—it is the meaning and identity that we are prepared to pay for.

To move to workable economic frameworks we have first to understand how we learn to choose our own stories and recognize our own ability to direct the choices that we make. The evidence of "self-actualization" in the market research will become an even more powerful driving force as people use it to consciously empower themselves and their environment. It is who we choose to "be" what we as individuals value and recognize, which will have the greatest impact on the next wave of economic growth. It is our stories which are then integrated into technology to create "content". To develop the new economics of sustainability requires further work, but it is critical to this work that we have the concept of the value of our own content and that we agree who can own the rights to the products that are produced.

Africa has produced "Time to Market (in Senegal, with a parallel initiative in Ghana), winner of one of the UN World Summit Awards in 2003, this project provides farmers with PDAs and access to a website where they can find the best market to sell their produce on the day its ready; this has provided a 20 per cent increase in local income. It works because it relates to existing "stories and behaviour patterns", there is no difficulty with the adoption of the technology, it is slotted seamlessly into business in Africa.[6]

To conclude, a comment from my business partner, David Cromar, seems very appropriate:

> This work is about the drive of culture changing individual, SME and corporate lifestyle, working and playing with IT content and technology.

> The plight and creative output for an average African is worlds apart from an Asian, European or American yet the G8 corporations e.g. Coca Cola, derive more profits from Africa than any other single continent. The Internet and mobile phone / hand held are the modern day tools we now use to create wealth. Digital Media content can be created, communicated and exploited in an instant—anytime—anywhere. The challenge is to create the IT framework and environment where the author has sufficient incentive and protection to choose to be innovative, collaborative and commercial.
>
> Just as the Industrial Revolution "colonised" our world in the 19th and mail order "furnished" North America in the 20th Century, IT is being challenged to feed, inform and create economic development in the Third World nations, which will sustain us, into the next Century.
>
> That challenge starts and finishes with the individual—can we be different—can we make a difference—can we create a different way in the World?

Please join with us in this debate, the solution is part of the answer to the digital divide and trade gap which currently exists. Local solutions by local people which link into global networks will provide a bridge: "edge" diagnostics are appropriate at every location. The report by the UK Commission for Africa identifies the accelerator effect that the introduction of technology, and in particular the use of the mobile phone, is already having on trade and communication in Africa. The phone may be the platform for economic change, certainly when all of Africa has access to communication we can expect a significant increase in trade, locally and internationally. Let us use this as an opportunity to build some real economic processes which support a global community of content producers and one in which African institutions, both private and public play their part.

Notes

1 UK Commission for Africa Report, Chapter 8—"More Trade and Fairer Trade".

2 In the extreme this can be for both short-term outcomes and aims that serve that single organization to the detriment of others and the environment. Legislation and current social structures have not yet developed effective checks against such an approach being pursued.

3 A video on hand held devices is being used to train people in healthcare, the initiative began in India and is being transferred to Africa.

4 Swahili for sharing

5 This perspective can apply equally to public sector groups and NGOs as well as corporations.

6 Making the technology simple to adopt, without need for training or training manuals is assisting the shift in developing economies.

References

Atiyah, P.S. *Rise and Fall of the Freedom of Contract* (Oxford: Oxford University Press, 1979).

Coase, R.H. "The Nature of the Firm", in *The Legacy of Ronald Coase in Economic Analysis: Volume I*, ed. S.G Medema (Vermont: Elgar, 1937).

Hagel III, J. and J. Seely Brown. *The Only Sustainable Edge: Why Business Strategy Depends on Productive Friction and Dynamic Specialization* (Harvard: Harvard Business School Press, 2005)

Roberts, John. *The Modern Firm: Organizational Design for Performance and Growth* (Oxford: Oxford University Press, 2004).

List of Contributors

Benjamin Kwasi Addom received a combined Bachelors Degree in General Agriculture and Diploma in Education from the University of Cape Coast, Ghana between 1993 and 1998. As a Ghanaian, he served his nation for one year through a mandatory National Service Program that applies to all students graduating from the country's higher education institutions and served as an Agricultural Extension Officer. He also taught agriculture in Secondary School (High School) in Ghana for few months before returning to the field. In the field, he worked with two different organizations between early 2000 to mid-2003 prior to his admission to Cornell University.

While at Cornell, he enrolled in Masters in International Agriculture and Rural Development (a professional program) for a year between 2003/2004. His interest in the use of the new information communication technologies (ICT) developed while in Cornell and was based on his experience of working between farmers and research station in Ghana. He conducted a survey on the e-readiness of seven universities in Ghana as part of his Masters research to assess how prepared the country's higher education institutions are in using ICTs for teaching, research and outreach/extension, with very interesting and promising results.

He is currently enrolled in a doctoral program in Syracuse University School of Information Studies, New York and exploring different ways by which these new technologies could be used to enhance access by all for the benefit of all.

Timothy Anderson is founder and president of World Computer Exchange and Executive Director of World Computer Exchange – Canada, which provides capacity building services, sister-schools, and thousands of donated computers each year to help the world's poorest youth bridge the global divides in information, technology, understanding, and opportunity. WCE's 450 volunteers have shipped 16,000 computers to connect 1,500 schools in 31 developing countries. He previously founded and managed: South Shore Charter School, Hull Environment and Services Corps, and Dovetail Consulting. He also co-founded: Boston Management Consortium, Boston GreenSpace Alliance; and managed: Boston Harbor Associates, Boston Zoological Society, and the New England Office of the National Alliance of Business. He served on the campaign staffs of Jimmy Carter and Senator Edward Kennedy and interned with US Majority Leader Thomas O'Neill. He was a consultant to the US Department of Education and the National Endowment for the Humanities. He has consulted with over 300 nonprofit and government organizations. In 2002, the President of the Republic of Georgia awarded him the Badge of Honour of Georgia. He is an honorary professor of the Tbilisi Orbeliani State Pedagogical University and an honorary citizen of Kutaisi, Georgia. He serves as Chair of the boards of VSA arts Massachusetts and the W. Seavey Joyce S.J. Community Service Award for Boston College. He is a juror for the Stockholm

Challenge. He is a member of the United Nations Information and Communications Technologies Task Force Working Group on Low Cost Access and Connectivity. He is on the Steering Committee of the e-Granary Digital Library of WiderNet at the University of Iowa. He was a member of the World Economic Forum's Global Digital Divide Initiative Task Force. He has been on 60 non-profit Boards of Directors. He earned a Master in Public Administration from Harvard's Kennedy School of Government in 2000 and his Bachelor of Arts from Boston College in 1973. He lives in Hull, Massachusetts USA with his wife and two sons.

Maria Beebe is the Director of Global Networks at the Center to Bridge the Digital Divide, Washington State University. She works as a program advisor to USAIDÕs Leland Initiative on the link between information and communication technologies (ICT) policy and sectoral applications, particularly on ICTs for education. She has provided leadership in the development of NetTel@Africa, a network for capacity building in ICT policy, regulation and applications. A key outcome of NetTel@Africa is the establishment of a collaborative Interdisciplinary Telecommunications Policy and Regulation Post-Graduate Diploma and Masters Program at several African institutions (Universities of Botswana, Dar Es Salaam, Zambia and Universities of Fort Hare, South Africa, Western Cape and Witswatersrand in South Africa). Moreover, NetTel@Africa includes an international peer to peer (regulator to regulator, academic to academic, and academic to regulator) component, a research component and community to community ICT applications program which exploits the synergies between telecommunications regulation and sectors, such as the education sector, as for example in setting universal service funds through eRates. She has provided overall direction in networking South African and American higher education institutions to exchange knowledge and form learning partnerships for sustainable development around the use of ICTs. Lessons learned from these experiences are highlighted in *AfricaDotEdu*, edited by Beebe, Koaukou, Oyeyinka and Rao.

Royal D. Colle is currently International Emeritus Professor. He has been a member of the Cornell University faculty for 36 years, 10 of which were as Chair of the Communication Department. He has lived and worked abroad in countries ranging from India and Indonesia to Western Samoa and Guatemala. He has served as a consultant for a variety of international agencies including the World Bank, FAO, the UN, UNFPA, UNESCO and USAID. His work has focused on the design of communication strategies and innovative uses of information technology for development. He continues to teach and work on projects such as telecenters and building the ICT4D capacities of universities.

Nancy J. Hafkin has been a pioneer of networking and development information and communications in Africa over the course of more than 20 years. She spearheaded the Pan-African Development Information System (PADIS) of the United Nations Economic Commission for Africa (UNECA), as Officer-in-Charge from 1987 until 1997. She later served as Team Leader for Promoting of Information Technology for Development, of the Development Information Services Division of ECA (UN) from 1997 until 2000, where she was Coordinator of the African Information Society Initiative (AISI), the African governments' mandate to use ICTs to accelerate socio-economic development in Africa. Nancy also served as a facilitator in establishing the Partnership for Information and Communication Technologies in Africa (PICTA), a coordinating body of donor and executing agency partners in support of the AISI. Nancy Hafkin has a long history of work on both gender and information technology for development issues. In 1976, she co-edited *Women in Africa: Studies in Social and Economic Change* (Stanford University Press). From 1976–1987 she worked as Chief of Research and Publications at the African Training and Research Centre for Women of the United Nations Economic Commission for Africa (Addis Ababa, Ethiopia). She also organized a number of major Africa-wide meetings on ICTs and development, including the Symposium on Access to Telematics in Africa (1995); Global Connectivity for Africa (1998) and African Development Forum '99: the Challenge to Africa of Globalization and the Information Age. She is now working as a consultant on gender and information technology. Nancy has a PhD in African history from Boston University.

Margaret Grieco holds her doctorate from the University of Oxford. She is the first Full Professor of Transport and Society, a post which she holds at Napier University, Scotland. She is salaried Visiting Full Professor at the Institute for African Development. She has previously held the positions of Professor of Sociology at the University of Ghana, Professor of Organisation and Development Management at the University of North London, Social Scientist in the Africa Region of the World Bank and Research Associate at the Transport Studies Unit, University of Oxford. She has published extensively on gender, transport and information communication technology most particularly with respect to Africa. She recently received an award from the Maria Goeppert Mayer foundation to provide three lecture courses on gender, transport and information communication technology within the engineering school the Technical University of Braunschweig.

Subramaniam Janakiram is Champion, Information and Communication Technology for Rural Development, Sustainable Agricultural Systems, Knowledge and Institutions, (SASKI) and E-Development thematic groups in World Bank. He led the design and implementation of rural information and knowledge systems in Russia which is considered as one of the successful Bank project activities in this area, and has been used as a case study in Cornell University. He has over 25 years of operational experience in design and implementation of rural development projects in transition, post conflict and developing economies in over 30 countries in Asia, Africa, Middle East and Latin America.

Stephen Little is Head of the Centre for Innovation, Knowledge and Enterprise within the Open University Business School (OUBS) and a co-director of the University's Centre for Innovation Knowledge and Development.

He has co-edited books and journal issues covering the influence of the Asian economies in the twenty-first century, intelligent urban development and meta-governance. *Design and Determination*, which examines the role of information technology in redressing regional inequities in the development process, was published by Ashgate in 2004.

He is researching new forms of mobility and regional development in the knowledge economy with colleagues from OUBS and other institutions in the UK. Europe and Asia and electronic governance with colleagues from government and non-governmental organisations in the UK and Africa.

Paul Mwanzilo, is Head of Cataloguing and Classification Unit, Egerton University Library, Kenya. He is currently involved in the Local Organisation of the forthcoming IAALD – Africa conference (http://www.asareca.org/iaald-africa/organisers_en.html). He has been a Mortenson Associate at the Mortenson Center for International Library Programs, University of Illinois Library at Urbana-Champaign and has also been an academic visitor at Vanderbilt University.

Muna B. Ndulo, Professor of Law, Director of the Institute for African Development, is an authority on African legal systems, human rights, constitutions, election monitoring, international development, and legal aspects of foreign investments in developing countries.

After receiving his LL.B. from University of Zambia, and LL.M. from Harvard Law School, he was Public Prosecutor for the Zambian Ministry of Legal Affairs. He was Dean of University of Zambia School of Law, and from 1986–1996 served the United Nations Commission for International Trade Law. From 1992 to 1994 he was Political Adviser to the UN Mission in South Africa. He joined Cornell Law School's faculty in 1996, and has continued to advise UN Missions in East Timor and Kosovo.

He teaches international organizations and human rights institutions; the legal aspects of foreign investment in developing countries; and the common law and African legal systems. He is also Director of Cornell University's Institute for African Development.

Mary Ochs is the Head of Collection Development and Preservation at the Albert R. Mann Library at Cornell University in Ithaca, New York. She is also Project Director for TEEAL (The Essential Electronic Agricultural Library) and a member of the coordinating team for AGORA (Access to Global Online Research in Agriculture). She has a Bachelor's degree from the College of Agriculture and Life Sciences at Cornell University and a Master's degree in Library Science from Syracuse University in Syracuse, New York.

Joseph Okpaku, a national of Nigeria, is the President and Chief Executive Officer of The Telecom Africa Corporation, a company dedicated to building a globally competitive indigenous African industrial capacity in information and telecommunications technologies. He also consults for governments and international organizations in the fields of development, governance, long-term strategic planning and futures studies.

He made his international debut as the founder, editor-in-chief and publisher of The Third Press, a New York-based book publishing company whose authors included Africa's leading writers, scholars and policy-makers.

He has devoted much of his professional life to the advocacy for, and design of, strategies for the development of Africa towards global competitiveness within the framework of her cultural priorities. He has become a leading thinker at the cutting edge of the development of information and telecommunications in Africa as strategic tools for furthering the continent's advancement. In this regard, he has crafted initiatives by Telecom Africa to build manufacturing, research and development, software and applications capacity in Africa through strategic partnerships and joint ventures with global and regional technology companies.

He holds a Bachelor of Science Degree in Civil Engineering from Northwestern University, a Master of Science Degree in Structural Engineering from Stanford University and Doctor of Philosophy Degree in Dramatic Literature and Theatre History, also from Stanford University.

Egondu Rosemary Onyejekwe, PhD, now works at Montgomery College and is President of Earthmap – Earthmap Foundation's Global Project is to map HIV prevalence and AIDS deaths both within the United States and across the globe, especially in African and other developing countries. She was previously Director of Emerging Technologies at Ohio State University. She is a Nigerian American, an engineer by profession and by most of her practice, but also holds a Masters degree in Health. Her interest is mainly in Telemedicine and telehealth where she views the biggest issues as being 'access', 'affordability', and 'sustainability'. She has served as President of the African Women Global Network (an electronic web-based network).

Eva Rathgeber is a specialist in gender and international development. She has published widely on gender, natural resource management, science and technology, and development and she has lived and carried out research in several African and European countries. She was trained at the University of British Columbia, McGill University and SUNY-Buffalo. She established and directed the International

Development Research Centre's (IDRC) highly visible Gender and Development Unit from 1986–1992. In 1992 she moved to Nairobi, Kenya, where she became the IDRC Regional Director for Eastern and Southern Africa, overseeing research activities in 22 countries in the region. In 2001, she moved to York University as a visiting professor of development studies. She joined Carleton University and the University of Ottawa as the Joint Chair in Women's Studies on 1 March 2002. Her most recent publications include *Gender and the Information Revolution in Africa* (2000) and *Turning Failure into Success: The Deconstruction of IDRC Development Discourse, 1970–2000* (2001).

Sheila Robinson is the Joint Managing Director of Solvebrand Limited. Solvebrand is a business development company which supports the growth of both private and public organisations through Consultancy, Training and Software. Currently developing an on-line business incubator, www.solvebrand.co.uk and partnered with a portal development company in the US. Solvebrand have partnered with a number of organisations to develop their businesses in the long term. Solvebrand has, amongst other projects, worked with: 4workingmagic to develop leadership through workshops and e-learning with an online community; the Commission for Africa/Culture and Participation Commissioner Sir Bob Geldof on the benefit of IT, mobile and new media in economic development in Africa; africawoman (www.africawoman.net), a charity creating online 'newspapers' written by African women journalists, founded by award winning journalist and broadcaster Lesley Riddoch, including events in Scotland in the run up to the G8; and Pax Warrior (www.paxwarrior.com), a Canadian educational documentary new media package aimed at teaching citizenship to students from age 16 up. Pax was profiled in the 2003 UN WSIS World Summit Awards.

Current reports include the economic impact of New Media regionally in the UK, and research on the impact of IT and mobile to developing economies around twice the impact as they have proven to have in the developed world. Research carried out on behalf of the UK's Commission for Africa has provided insight into the exponential economic growth possible through the expanding mobile channels used alongside traditional media.

William W. Wright Jr is Program Officer for the Carr Foundation, which is based in Cambridge, Massachusetts. The focus of his work now is a project in central Mozambique – the restoration of Gorongosa National Park (see http://www.gorongosa.net). His previous position was Senior Scientist at Education Development Center (EDC) where he directed a large USAID-funded, ICT-and-education project called dot-EDU. This initiative, with a budget of over $65 million, helped bring digital opportunities to developing nations. In the early 1980s, with support from Apple Computer, he started a network for rural teachers called BreadNet. This was one of the first projects to use computer-based communication networks in secondary education. In the 1990s Mr. Wright served as executive director of the Consortium for School Networking and, with others, worked to have the US Congress approve a mechanism (called the E-rate) that provided significant support for underserved schools and libraries.